Pictorial History
of the Sub-Machine Gun

Frontispiece.—British troops
clearing the Germans from houses
in Oosterbeek, Holland,
23 September 1944.

Pictorial History
of the
Sub-Machine Gun

Major F. W. A. HOBART (Retd.)

Charles Scribner's Sons
New York

Printed in Great Britain
Library of Congress Catalog Card Number 74-19683
ISBN 0-684-14186-8

Contents

Acknowledgements

I am grateful to so many people for their help in supplying facts and photographs for this book. The Quality Assurance Directorate (Weapons) of the Ministry of Defence very kindly allowed me to photograph the peerless collection of weapons in the Pattern Room at the Royal Small Arms Factory, Enfield, and once again I have received a tremendous amount of help from Mr Woodend in charge of the Pattern Room. He has done a vast amount to assist me and frequently given of his time and experience without stint.

I have to thank the Commandant of the Royal Military College of Science at Shrivenham for allowing me to photograph weapons held in the collection here.

Mr Thomas E. Cosgrove has given me much valuable information on the testing of SMGs in America and Mr Donald E. Thomas of the Military Armament Corporation, Atlanta, has gone to a great deal of trouble to supply information about Gordon Ingram's many weapons. Lt Col Hugh McWhinnie (USAR) of the Military Armament Corporation has also been very helpful.

Mr Mark Dinely, whose experience of small arms goes back to the early 1930s, has given me unique background information of conditions in the UK in this time.

I have to thank the firms of Erma, Heckler and Koch, Mauser and Walther in Germany who very readily supplied photographs, whilst in Italy S. Ugo Gussalli of Beretta gave invaluable assistance. Messrs Hochuli and Schad of SIG were very co-operative to me and produced both photographs and data which proved most helpful. Mr Ernest Vervier supplied the photographs of Belgian SMGs. Sterling Armament Co in UK have been most collaborative.

I have perused a great number of books on the subject and would wish to acknowledge that *The World's Sub-Machine Guns* by Thomas B. Nelson and Hans B. Lockhoven has been of the utmost assistance. I have also drawn guidance from:

Small Arms Committee Reports
Ordnance Board Proceedings
Aberdeen Proving Ground Reports
SMGs 1921 through 1945 by Mr W. H. Davis & Capt A. J. Gleason
The Gun that made the Twenties Roar by W. J. Helmer
International Armament by George B. Johnson and Hans Lockhoven
Small Arms of the World by J. E. & W. H. B. Smith
Articles published in France by Jean Huon – mainly in *Ciblies*.

To the many others, authors and correspondents, who have rendered assistance I give my grateful thanks.

The views expressed in this book are my own and do not reflect official opinion.

Foreword

BY
LIEUTENANT GENERAL SIR FRANK KING KCB MBE
General Officer Commanding-in-Chief, Northern Ireland

As a young officer I well remember the introduction of the first British Sub-Machine Gun – the Sten – to the British Army. It was heralded with especial ecstasy in many newly formed Battle Schools, by Senior Officers who extolled its ease of production, cheapness, simplicity and devastating fire power at short range. Indeed, there were many enthusiasts who described these advantages as decisive, and likely to change quickly the course of the war. This did not happen. The Germans possessed a similar weapon. And with its relatively short effective range the SMG became merely one of a family of arms required by Infantry to cover the requirements of their particular battle field.

Notwithstanding this it had, and indeed it has, a very effective military role to play and deserves a high place in the gradings of usefulness of weapons. Above all, it is perhaps most favoured by terrorists and insurgents, particularly when operating in urban or jungle environments where its undoubted excellence as a short range and powerful destroyer is accentuated by the ease with which it can be produced or procured, concealed, distributed and used. It has deservedly earned an important place in the history of small arms.

It may seem strange that the story of the Sub-Machine Gun should be related by a retired Gunner. Major Hobart saw through at an early age, the complex and at times almost ritualistic facade which obscures the relatively simple problems of field gunnery, and for many years now has devoted his considerable energy and enquiring mind to the more precise and intimate science that embraces Small Arms. There are few officers better suited or qualified for this task. He has produced a comprehensive, knowledgeable and authoritative history and his book must commend itself to every student of Infantry soldiers and of Small Arms design.

Introduction

The Sub-Machine Gun is a very young member of the family of weapons. It was first employed in the Italian Army in 1915 and achieved notoriety during the gang warfare in America in the 1920s. The British Army held it in low esteem before World War II and the disparaging comment 'a gangster type weapon' appeared frequently as a conclusion on the reports of the limited number of trials carried out between the wars. Yet in 1940 everything changed. The British Army could not get enough SMGs and we bought, at great expense, a near obsolescent model from the USA. The very original 'gangster gun' in fact – the Thompson SMG. When eventually we produced the Sten, literally in millions, we equipped not only our own forces and those of the Commonwealth, but also many contingents from other countries and resistance fighters in Europe and Asia. Similarly USA and Russian production was measured in quantities so large as to surpass that of all other types of weapon.

One of the characteristics of the Sub-Machine Gun is the tremendous fire power it puts in the hands of one man. A soldier armed with this weapon, and four loaded magazines, can fire as many shots in a minute as an infantry section of eight riflemen could produce in that time in World War II. This, coupled with the ease with which the weapon can be disassembled and concealed, has led to the SMG becoming a major weapon in the armouries of guerrilla groups, militant political factions and extremists generally. One has only to consider the Lydda airport massacre of 30 May 1972 when three Japanese fanatics killed 25 and wounded 76 innocent travellers in less than a minute, to realise just how much 'power' this gun has given to ruthless individuals.

In spite of the short time SMGs have been in existence their simplicity, cheapness and ease of manufacture have resulted in the production of a multitude of different models. In a book of this restricted size it is manifestly impossible to cover all SMGs, and the descriptive effort must be confined to those most frequently used. However I have tried to deal with British SMGs in rather more detail and I think that readers will find accounts of not only the well-known guns but some that have never been described before except in official documents.

To reduce the book to a minimum size, all the details of length, weight, cartridge, rate of fire and other physical parameters, have been put together in the tabulated data at the rear of the book.

The *Pictorial History of the Sub-Machine Gun* has been written for the newcomer to this field as well as for the expert. The glossary of terms and the chapter on the Characteristics of the SMG should make the subject clear to the reader entering new territory, whilst the development and detail of the weapons should provide material of interest to the enthusiast.

Glossary of Technical Terms

Barrel   Rifled tube which gives direction and spin to the bullet.

Barrel swaging   A process in which the rifling is produced in the barrel by placing the blank tube over a central bar – called a mandrel – in which the form of the rifling is raised in relief. Hammering the outside of the tube produces the rifling in the tube. This method is more accurate and cheaper in quantity production than the conventional drilling and then rifling using a cutter.

Bent   A notch cut in the bolt, or hammer, enabling it to be held by the sear in the ready to fire position.

Blowback operation   The system used in nearly all SMGs in which the cartridge case, blown back by the gas pressure, drives the bolt to the rear after firing. This gives the bolt the energy necessary to carry out the cycle of operations.

Body   That part of the weapon which contains the bolt and return spring. The barrel is located at the forward end. The buffer and end cap are at the rear end. The butt stock is attached behind the body. In the USA it is known as the receiver.

Bolt   The mass of metal which feeds the round from the magazine into the chamber and supports it during firing. It moves back after firing to produce extraction, ejection and subsequent feed of the next round.

Box magazine   The metal container holding a number of rounds which rest, one above the other, on a follower pressed towards the magazine lips by a spring. The structure of the magazine is generally called the body. The end closure is usually removable to allow extraction of the spring and follower. The cartridges emerge from the magazine lips.

Breech block   See Bolt.

Buffer   A spring – occasionally a hydraulic cylinder – placed at the rear of the body to absorb surplus energy as the bolt reaches the end of its rearward travel.

Butt stock   The wooden or metal shoulder piece of the weapon.

Cap   A centrally placed insert in the base of the cartridge case which contains a detonating compound which, when struck by the firing pin, produces a flash to ignite the propellant.

Chamber	The rear part of the barrel enlarged to hold the cartridge before firing. It has the same internal shape as the cartridge and must be sturdily constructed to contain the gas pressure on firing.
Change lever	The lever which controls the mode of fire – ie single shot or automatic. Sometimes called the Fire Selector Lever.
Closed breech firing	A system in which the round is ready in the chamber with the bolt fully closed when the trigger operates. It gives a short lock time but there is a risk of 'cook off'.
Cock (to)	The process of pulling back the bolt, or hammer, to the 'ready to fire' position and at the same time storing energy in the return spring or hammer spring.
Cocking handle	The projection from the bolt which the firer pulls back to cock the gun. In the USA it is called the retracting handle.
Compensator	A device at the muzzle to direct the emerging gases upward and so force the muzzle down.
Cook off	The ignition of the propellant charge due to heat conducted from the chamber walls.
Cycle of operations	The successive processes involved in the firing of the weapon ie feeding, chambering, firing, extraction, ejection, storing energy in the spring.
Disconnector	A device which disconnects the trigger from the sear after each round is fired. To fire a second round the trigger must first be released to allow the reconnection of trigger and sear.
Drum magazine	A circular magazine in which the rounds are loaded axially and spring driven to the lips.
Ejector	A projection in the bolt way which strikes the head of the cartridge case, after it is withdrawn from the chamber by the extractor, and throws the case out of the gun.
End cap	The rear end closure of the body. Often this is detachable to permit removal of the working parts.
Extractor	A spring loaded claw attached to the bolt head which springs over the rim or extractor groove at the head of the cartridge and withdraws the case from the chamber as the bolt moves to the rear.
Fire selector lever	See Change lever.
Flip rearsight	A double backsight which consists of two Vs or apertures mounted at right angles, either of which may be rotated into position to give two alternative range-settings.
Follower	The platform on which the rounds rest in the magazine.
Fore-end	The wooden furniture extending forward beyond the magazine housing.
Foresight	A blade or pillar placed above the muzzle. It may be laterally adjustable for zeroing. In some cases it may also be raised or lowered to provide vertical adjustment when zeroing.

Fullering	Longitudinal grooves pressed into the magazine body to increase strength and permit dirt to drop to the bottom of the magazine.
Grip safety	A safety device – additional to the safety catch – generally incorporated in the pistol grip – which must be squeezed before the gun can be fired. Fitted to prevent accidental discharge on dropping the gun.
Grooves	The series of helical spirals cut into the bore of the barrel.
Holding open device	An arrangement operated by the magazine to hold the breech block to the rear after the magazine is emptied. This enables the firer to see – or feel – the cause of the stoppage and makes re-loading quicker.
Lands	The raised portions between the grooves of the rifling. The jacket of the bullet is engraved by the lands to provide the spin required for stability and also to prevent the gases escaping past the bullet.
Line of sight	The straight line from the firer's eye to the target through the sights.
Lock time	The time interval between trigger operation and cap initiation. It is least with closed breech firing where only a hammer and/or firing pin move. It is greatest in an open breech firing system where the whole mass of the bolt has to move forward, feed and chamber a round before firing.
Muzzle brake	A device at the muzzle to deflect the gases sideways or – preferably – backwards, to reduce the recoil of the weapon.
Obturation	Rearward gas sealing. The arrangement adopted to prevent gases escaping over or through the breech closing system. In a SMG the parallel sided cartridge case will be pressed outwards by internal gas pressure and so will seal the chamber even whilst moving back.
Open breech firing	A system in which the bolt is held to the rear when the gun is in the 'ready to fire' position. The ammunition is in the magazine and the chamber is empty and open to allow cooling and thus 'cook off' is unlikely. A long lock time results with reduced single shot accuracy. The system is employed in nearly all SMGs.
Operating spring	See Return spring.
Pistol grip	The grip for the firing hand, placed immediately behind the trigger.
Propellant	The charge of chemical energy which, when burnt, produces a large volume of hot gas to force the bullet up the bore.
Rearsight	A 'V' or an aperture placed over the breech which, with the foresight, allows aligning the barrel. It may be raised or lowered to provide the correct tangent elevation for the selected range.
Receiver	See Body.
Retracting handle	See Cocking handle.

Return spring	The helical spring, generally behind the bolt, which is placed in compression as the bolt moves to the rear. The compression causes the spring to store energy which is used to drive the bolt forward again. In USA it is called the Operating spring.
Rifling	A series of helical grooves cut in the interior of the barrel to give the bullet the required spin needed for stability during its flight through the air.
Round	A complete cartridge comprising bullet, cartridge case, propellant and primer.
Safety catch	The catch which operates a mechanism preventing unintended firing of the weapon, by locking the trigger, disconnecting the trigger from the sear, locking the sear or locking the bolt.
Sear	A part of the trigger mechanism which engages in the bent of the bolt or hammer to hold that part stationary.
Sighting	The process of aligning foresight and rearsight to give the correct line and also applying the correct tangent elevation to ensure the trajectory of the bullet intersects the line of sight at the required range.
Sights	The foresight and rearsight allow aiming the weapon and so pointing the muzzle in the right direction. Elevation is obtained by raising the rearsight an amount appropriate to the required range.
Tangent elevation	The increase of elevation of the barrel above the direct line of sight to the target, to allow for the drop of the bullet due to gravity.
Zeroing	The process carried out by the firer to ensure that the mean point of impact of his shots coincides with the point of aim. It involves moving the adjustable elements of the sights for line and elevation.

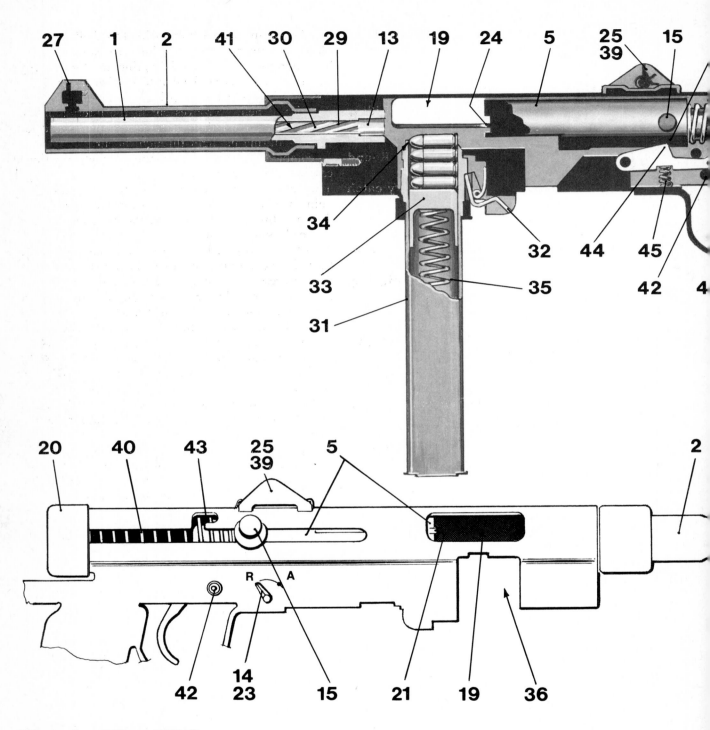

Fig. 1. The SMG

This is not a representation of a particular gun

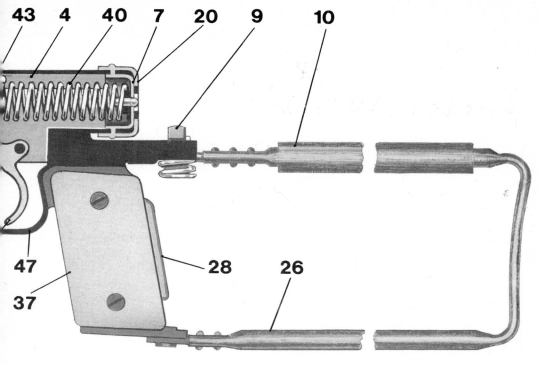

43 4 40 7 20 9 10

47

37 28 26

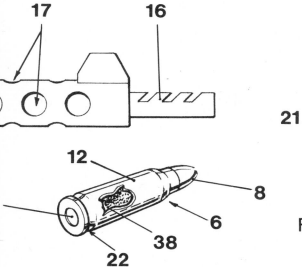

17 16

12

8

6

38

22

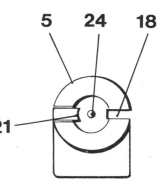

5 24 18

21

Front Face of Bolt
(not to scale)

1 Barrel
2 Barrel jacket
3 Bent
4 Body
5 Bolt
6 Bottle neck (cartridge)
7 Buffer
8 Bullet
9 Butt release catch
10 Butt stock
11 Cap (cartridge)
12 Cartridge case
13 Chamber
14 Change lever
15 Cocking handle
16 Compensator
17 Cooling slots
18 Ejector Way
19 Ejection opening
20 End cap
21 Extractor
22 Extraction groove (cartridge)
23 Fire selector lever
24 Firing pin
25 Flip rearsight
26 Folding butt
27 Foresight
28 Grip safety
29 Grooves
30 Lands
31 Magazine
32 Magazine catch
33 Magazine follower
34 Magazine lips
35 Magazine spring
36 Magazine well
37 Pistol grip
38 Propellant (cartridge)
39 Rearsight
40 Return spring
41 Rifling
42 Safety catch
43 Safety slot
44 Sear
45 Sear spring
46 Trigger
47 Trigger guard

Characteristics
of the
Sub-Machine Gun

The term 'sub-machine gun' is now well established, not only in military language but in every day use in newspapers, magazines and books. Where it is so employed there is often no definition of what is meant by the expression and it is used loosely to cover a variety of weapons ranging from automatic pistols through automatic rifles to light machine guns. This has been very noticeable in the radio and television reporting of the events occurring in Northern Ireland during 1971 and 1972 when this book was written.

A sub-machine gun fulfils certain clearly defined functions and has particular characteristics which place it in a category which is quite distinct from the great majority of other types of military weapon although, as one would expect, it merges into other species of weapon at either end of its range of examples. The following characteristics are common to all sub-machine guns.

It is a lightweight, one man weapon; ie it is not served by a crew, and it is fired by that one man from the shoulder. This does not eliminate the countless numbers of weapons that have a collapsible or telescopic shoulder stock which can be used to reduce the overall length and permit the weapon also to be fired from the hip in close quarter battle.

It fires a low powered cartridge designed originally to be fired from the pistol in service with the military forces of the country concerned. A low powered round must produce limited range and accuracy. The cartridge will invariably have a case which over the large part of its length will be parallel sided. The reason for this shape of cartridge will come later. It will be noted that this description covers the semi-bottlenecked cases such as the 7.63mm Mauser and the Russian 7.62mm 'P' type. Drawings of typical sub-machine gun cartridges are shown at the end of this chapter at Fig. II.

The trigger mechanism will be so arranged that once the trigger is operated and held back, the gun will continue firing automatically at its cyclic rate until either the ammunition supply is exhausted or the trigger is released. This 'cyclic rate' is the natural firing frequency of the gun and will in most cases be about 450–600 rounds a minute. Some earlier guns – for example the Finnish Suomi – fire at a rate of 1000 rounds a minute but although there are psychological advantages in this and the firer's morale may gain, there are distinct practical drawbacks from the loss of accuracy and control and probably an increase in ammunition supply problems. There will be more frequent need to change magazines and during this period the firer is helpless. The ability to produce automatic fire is essential. Weapons such as the Thompson 1927 model or the Smith and Wesson 1940 model which fired only single shots are best described – as in fact they were – as 'carbines' or 'light rifles'. Many sub-machine guns – SMGs hereafter – also incorporate a change lever which is a simple switch which, when operated, brings a disconnector into play and the mechanical train from the trigger via the sear to the bent is broken after a round is fired. To fire a second shot the trigger must be first be released then squeezed again. This mechanism, providing the ability to change from automatic fire to single shot fire or vice versa is known as a 'selector' and the weapon is said to produce 'selective fire'. Selective fire is an advantage tactically and also helps to save ammunition. For reasons that will be apparent later, a series of single aimed shots will give a greater chance of a hit than a burst firing the same number of rounds in very quick succession.

From the requirement to be able to fire automatically it follows that the weapon must have an ammunition capacity in excess of a single round. This will consist invariably of either a box shaped magazine or a circular drum. The advantages of the two types will be examined in due course.

The weapon must be cheap to produce and should be designed to require the minimum of machine tools in its manufacture. This need for cheapness demands simplicity of construction, the use of readily available metals, and a minimum of working parts.

The foregoing can be summarised to show the factors common to all SMGs:

    a.   A light weapon fired from the shoulder by one man.
    b.   The use of a low powered parallel sided cartridge.
    c.   Limited range, accuracy, and penetrating power.
    d.   Automatic fire – sometimes with the provision of an alternative single shot capability.
    e.   Simple and cheap to produce.

By far the great majority of SMGs have been designed to work on what is called the principle of 'blow back' operation. The term 'spent-case projection' is sometimes used. This method of operation will be described here for convenience. There is basically no difference in this method of operation first introduced in 1918 in the German MP 18.1 (Bergmann) to that employed in the SMGs of America, Britain or Israel today.

BLOW BACK OPERATION

There are three types of blow back operation used in SMG operation. These are: dead bolt firing, delayed blow back, and floating firing.

Dead Bolt Firing: In this system the bolt is stationary when the cap is struck. If the gun fires from the open bolt position the bolt energy is dissipated firstly in crushing up the case and then if this does not halt the bolt, by contact with the breech face. The full firing impulse is available at once to drive the unlocked bolt to the rear and so this must have substantial mass and a stiff return spring or the case will emerge from the chamber whilst the pressure is high and blow out. A separate hammer is generally employed to drive an internal firing pin forward. In the few cases where the SMG fires from a closed breech this system of dead bolt firing will invariably be employed. Dead bolt firing is not used in the majority of SMGs.

Delayed Blow back: This system avoids the heavy weight of the bolt found in dead bolt firing by having a device incorporated which holds up the bolt face until the pressure has dropped to a safe level. The best example is the Heckler and Koch MP5 **178*** which fires from the closed breech system using a hammer. This SMG uses a two part block with roller delay in the bolt head and is described in detail on page 138. Delayed blow back is also sometimes used with guns firing from the open breech position – for example the Villar Perosa SMG **180** and the Hungarian M39 **177**.

Floating Firing: This method is sometimes called 'Advanced Primer Ignition' or the 'Becker system' after the German who produced a 20mm cannon on this principle in 1917. It is the most common system applied to SMGs and was used for example in the Sten gun and the US M3 SMG. It is in fact used so frequently that it will now be described in some detail.

The cycle starts with the bolt or breech block, the two terms being synonymous – held to the rear by the sear engaged in the bent. The return or operating spring is fully compressed, trying to force the bolt forward. The ammunition is held in the magazine and the first round is forced into the path of the bolt by the compressed magazine spring. When the trigger is operated the sear is lowered and frees the bent; the bolt is forced forwards by the spring and accelerates towards the breech. It picks up the first round in the magazine, pushes it through the magazine lips and into the chamber. As the cartridge case lines up with the barrel the extractor on the face of the bolt springs over the extractor groove and at the same time the face of the bolt bears against the rear of the case.

As the case continues forward into the chamber there very soon comes a time when the friction force between chamber wall and cartridge case slows the case and as a result the firing pin – which is usually a fixture on the face of the bolt – imparts enough energy to the primer to detonate the cap.

When the propellant burns, the resulting high pressure is exerted in every direction. The bullet is forced into the rifling and up the bore; the cartridge case is forced radially outwards and backwards. Since the heavy bolt is still moving forward at the moment of firing its momentum has to be overcome before it can be driven back. This causes a delay which enables the bullet to leave the muzzle and the pressure to drop in the chamber. This drop in pressure frees the case from the chamber wall and the residual gas pressure is sufficient literally to blow the case back out of the chamber, pushing the bolt rearwards. The parallel sided case prevents any escape of gas over the cartridge and out into the breech. The expression 'spent case projection' which is sometimes used in lieu of 'blow back' should now be self explanatory. One feature of interest is that since the case is pushing the bolt there is no need for an extractor. In practice one is always fitted to hold the case to the bolt head and ensure correct positioning for ejection; it is also essential for the removal from the chamber of a misfired cartridge or a drill round. The impulse applied to the breech block drives it rearward against the resistance of the return – or operating – spring which is compressed and so stores energy. The ejector is generally a fixed projection which strikes the base of the empty case and pivots it around the extractor and out of the gun through an opening cut for that purpose in the body.

The spring and the rear cap of the body bring the bolt to rest. If the selector is set to 'single shot' the sear will have risen to hold the bolt to the rear until the trigger is operated again. If the selector is set to 'auto' the bolt will move forward again, driven by the spring, and the cycle will be repeated.

It will be seen that the process is essentially a simple one involving a longi-

* Figures in bold type refer to illustrations.

tudinal reciprocating movement of the bolt, an alternative compression and expansion of the return spring and a transverse movement of the ammunition. The breech block starts from the rear in what is termed the 'open breech' position. This is done to ensure that between bursts the chamber is empty, allowing air to circulate and cool it. If a live round were to be left in the chamber the heat from the chamber walls would cause speedy ignition of the propellant charge and this 'cook off' would cause the bullet to emerge with possible tragic consequences.

To enable the bullet to leave the muzzle quickly and the pressure to drop rapidly, the barrel must be short. There are few barrels that exceed 8–10in long. Some of the most successful have been as short as 4in. It will be seen that with such a barrel length the muzzle velocity will not be high and the accuracy and range will both be limited. The change of position of the centre of gravity as the bolt reciprocates, and the vibration set up as the bolt forward motion is abruptly checked, will also tend to produce inaccuracy. Thus the SMG is essentially a close quarter weapon with a maximum effective range of about 200m.

THE SMG CARTRIDGE

The choice of cartridge is largely a matter of national preference depending chiefly on the pistol cartridge available. The Americans use the .45in ACP (Automatic Colt Pistol) cartridge which has a bullet weighing 230 grains (there are 7,000 grains to the pound) and having a muzzle velocity of about 950 feet per second (ft/s). This is a heavy slow bullet which although very effective in stopping targets at close quarters is not very accurate and is limited to a maximum effective range of about 100m. The most popular cartridge is undoubtedly the 9mm Parabellum. This has a bullet weight of 115 grains fired at 1,250ft/s and is effective to 200m. The Soviets used the 7.62mm 'P' pistol cartridge which gave a muzzle velocity of 1,600ft/s but the light bullet of only 86 grains did not range well and in spite of the high muzzle velocity the maximum effective range was not in excess of 200m. This round is still used by all these countries such as North Viet Nam which have obsolescent – but very effective – Russian equipment. There are other sub-machine gun cartridges such as the 9mm Mauser and the Bergmann Bayard which for various reasons have not achieved wide popularity but are still very effective. In fact the 9mm Mauser is probably the best SMG round, firing a 126 grain bullet at 1,500ft/s. In short all SMGs fire a pistol type cartridge, parallel sided and of limited power.

ACCURACY

The sub-machine gun is not an accurate weapon at ranges over 200m even at single shot. At full automatic fire it is considerably less accurate. During the firing of a burst the muzzle climbs and generally moves over to the right. This causes the shots to go successively higher and if the target is not hit with the first round it is unlikely to be hit at all. The progressive rise of the muzzle is caused by the fact that the centre of gravity of the weapon does not lie in the bore. The design invariably places the centre of gravity below the barrel and so there is a couple produced which twists the weapon about the centre of gravity, forcing the muzzle up. When fired from the shoulder the butt is below the barrel and this also produces a turning moment. The first bullet goes where it is aimed and the muzzle is still rising when the second is fired. This goes high and also adds to the rate at which the muzzle lifts. Each successive round increases the angular acceleration of the muzzle and the bullets go higher and higher.

To prevent this various devices have been used. The most common is the compensator. This was initially – in the American Cutt's Compensator – a screw-on muzzle attachment with slots cut in the top through which expanding gases escaped upwards. The reaction forced the muzzle down. Subsequently other designers cut 4 or 5 slots directly in the top of the barrel at the muzzle. It is doubtful if such a system provides other than a marginal reduction in the rate at which the muzzle rises at automatic fire.

An alternative solution is to use a muzzle brake to reduce the recoil impulse which causes the turning moment. The muzzle brake has a series of slots at the muzzle which direct the emerging gases sideways and backwards. As a result the muzzle is forced forwards and so reduces the recoil. To be effective all the gas must be diverted through a large angle. The greater the amount of gas and the greater the angle, the more efficient the brake. But this produces a blast of muzzle gas straight back at the firer and so the angle is rarely more than 120 deg. A considerable proportion of the gas will follow the bullet and go straight forward. Tactically the muzzle brake is not favoured because the blast picks up dirt and small stones which obscure the firer's view and cause discomfort not only to him but also to nearby firers.   In some cases the compensator and muzzle brake are combined in one muzzle fitting. The Soviet wartime SMGs embodied such a combination.

SIGHTS

The SMG has a limited range and is frequently fired hurriedly so the sights are best made simple in design, easily used, and if necessary readily adjusted. The foresight is either a simple blade moving in a dovetail for lateral adjustment when zeroing or a pillar which is either eccentrically mounted for adjustment or sometimes screws up and down. The rear sight is either a broad V or a fairly coarse aperture. The flip sight which consists of two Vs or apertures cut in blades at right angles to each other, is often used. When one is up the other lies flat and change of elevation is affected by flipping over the blade. Optical sights are not required but the Singlepoint collimater has been used successfully on a SMG. In this sight the firer keeps both eyes open. A red or green spot is projected back into the firer's master eye and the correct aim is achieved when this spot is superimposed on the target picture. This enables very quick accurate shooting.

THE BOLT

The heart of the SMG is the bolt. This must be of simple design, cheap to manufacture and of inexpensive readily available steel. Over the years 3 types of SMG bolt have evolved.

The commonest, simplest and cheapest is a simple cylinder hollowed out at the rear end to take the return spring and machined on the front face to form a fixed firing pin. Feed horns, ejector ways and an extractor slot are formed on the cylinder. The second category is the two section bolt. The forward portion is generally cylindrical and of a diameter approximately twice that of the cartridge. This ensures a good feed of the round into the chamber. The rear half is of larger diameter and provides the necessary mass to hold up the cartridge until the pressure drops.

Lastly comes the recent development of the 'wrap round' bolt. In this design the fixed firing pin is not on the front face of the bolt but is located halfway back. The section forward of the firing pin is hollowed out to fit over the barrel with an ejection slot cut in the appropriate place. Thus after feeding the cartridge into the chamber, the bolt is wrapped round the barrel. The advantage of this configuration is that only part of the bolt lies behind the firing pin and so the overall length of the body can be reduced. Alternatively for a given length of weapon, the barrel can be made longer. Putting the mass of the bolt further forward reduces the shift of the centre of gravity as the bolt comes forward and so helps to improve the consistency of the weapon. This system used in the Uzi and the Steyr MPi69 SMG has been very successful.

There are a few SMGs that operate on the delayed blow back system. The Hungarian M39 carbine is an early example. Here there is a two part block. A lever is mounted on the forepart with one end bearing in a recess in the body and the other end bearing on the rear part of the block. As the cartridge pushes the forepart back, the rotation of the lever is resisted by the rear part and its return spring. As the rear part is much the more massive of the two parts, some short time elapses before the lever is rotated out of the body and the forepart of the block can be blown back. By this time the bullet is well on its way and the chamber pressure is greatly reduced. (See Fig. III on page 136.)

Before a SMG can be fired it must be cocked. To draw back the bolt a cocking handle is fitted. Since it is a permanent fixture it will reciprocate with the bolt, moving backwards and forwards in a slot cut in the body. This slot will often have a recess at each end in which the cocking handle can be housed as a safety measure. Often this is the only safety device on the gun and prevents accidental discharge. The position of the cocking handle varies and all possible positions have been tried. To accommodate both left and right handed firers the cocking handle was placed on top of the body in the Thompson SMG and a similar solution has been adopted in the latest MAC Ingram SMG. To prevent blocking the sight line a U notch must be cut in the cocking handle and this can be used as a battle sight in emergency.

Most men are right handed and so most cocking handles are located on the left of the gun. This enables the firer to retain his hold of the pistol grip whilst cocking the gun. However the bolt has been retracted by handles placed on the right and even underneath although the only example that comes readily to mind here is the Reising Model 50 SMG. The USA M3 .45 SMG had a cocking handle which was rotated to cock the gun and its successor the M3A1 has a slot in the breech block itself into which the firer inserts his finger to pull back the bolt. The Steyr MPi69 SMG has the sling attached to the bolt and cocking is accomplished by tightening the sling. However whatever method is adopted it is essential that it can be operated with cold, wet, or oily fingers without discomfort and with assurance that the cocking handle will not slip from the fingers and fire a round inadvertently. The very great majority of the SMGs have unlocked bolts. If the weapon is carried – as often it is – with the bolt forward, no round in the chamber, and the loaded magazine in place – it is not completely safe. The example most often quoted is the Mk 1 Sten. When this weapon was dropped, or jarred, the heavy bolt could set back and move over the rounds in the magazine. It would not go far enough back for the bent to engage the sear and when the return spring forced it forward again it would feed, chamber and fire a round. There were many casualties from this design fault particularly when a soldier jumped from a vehicle. The USA M3A1 SMG still has this fault. To prevent this failing the designer of a modern weapon incorporates some method of securing the bolt. The Russian wartime SMGs had a small catch on the cocking handle which engaged a slot cut in the body and so locked the bolt.

21

A similar principle was used in the later Stens where the cocking handle was rotated into a recess cut at either end of the cocking slot in the body. The American Ingram SMG has a cocking handle mounted on top of the body and this is rotated through 90deg to lock the bolt. Since the sight line is thus obscured as the U notch is now facing sideways, the firer is always aware when this safety is on. Undoubtedly the safest SMG is the Israeli Uzi which has a squeeze safety in the pistol grip. Until this is held firmly in, the gun can neither be cocked nor fired and the bolt cannot move.

THE MAGAZINE

Surprisingly that part of the SMG which is most difficult to design and is the most productive of stoppages, is the magazine. There are many facets to the problem. The spring strength must not be too great to allow easy loading. If it is too strong the bolt will not be able to pick up the first round and if it is too weak the last few rounds will not be held up for the bolt to feed, when the weak spring is fully extended. The spring must be so tempered that it can be stored under the compression of a full load of ammunition without failing. The body of the magazine must be strong and also allow grit and sand to pass down to the bottom without jamming the rounds. Fullering, or pressing grooves in the body, provides strength and a free passage to dirt. The lips must be strong to resist deformation. The fitting of the magazine to the gun is critical. The magazine must be firmly held in the gun body without either longitudinal or lateral movement; the securing catch must hold it absolutely firmly and yet allow instant release even after the wear associated with numerous insertions and removals of the magazine.

There are two kinds of magazine used in the SMG. These are box magazines and drum magazines. The box magazine is relatively simple, easy to attach to the gun and simple to remove. It rarely holds more than 30 rounds. Earlier magazines had two staggered columns of rounds which merged into one at the lips. It was necessary to have a magazine filler which was one more piece of equipment for the soldier to lose. The modern box magazine is designed in such a way that the rounds form two staggered columns and the bolt picks up the top round from each side in turn. In the most modern type – produced by Carl Gustav – the magazine is wedge shaped towards the front and so the top round is inclined inwards towards the axis of the bore and this makes the process of chambering much more efficient. In some guns the magazine housing pivots so that the loaded box can lie flat and parallel to the barrel until required. It can then be swung into position. This idea, like many others, originated with the SIG of Neuhausen, Switzerland.

The spring driven drum magazine has been used in many SMGs. Its great asset is the large number of rounds it can contain. The 1921 model Thompson SMG had a 100 round drum and the Russian used a 71 round capacity drum magazine on several of their guns.

The rounds are loaded axially within the drum and forced to the lips by spring tension. To load the rounds into the drum the cover must be removed, the rounds inserted into the spiral guides and the cover replaced. Tension is applied to the spring by hand. At best this is a cumbersome procedure and time consuming. At night, or in the haste of action, it can easily result in misplaced rounds which inevitably cause misfeeds and stoppages. When the magazine is loaded it is heavy and of such a size and shape that make it difficult to fit into pouches carried on the soldier's equipment. Drum magazines are rare in modern weapons.

The position of the magazine on the weapon has a significant effect both on handling and performance. A drum magazine can only be placed below the barrel transversely across the body but there are choices available to the designer who uses a box magazine. Since the centre of mass invariably lies below the barrel a turning moment causes the barrel to lift successively as each round is fired. A magazine mounted vertically above the gun raises the centre of gravity towards the bore and so helps to reduce the turning moment. This position assists the feeding since gravity helps the spring but it brings some disadvantages as well. The magazine increases the silhouette and also a man firing from his right shoulder and using his right eye has a blind zone to his left front where a target appearing suddenly may be unobserved. The sights have to be offset to give an unimpeded sight line. A magazine fitted below the gun lowers the centre of gravity and increases the barrel lift. The capacity of the magazine is limited, otherwise the bottom grounds when the firer is in the prone position or firing over cover. This reduces the ease with which the gun can be shifted from target to target. The spring has to lift the ammunition against gravity and with a spring weakened by being compressed over a long period, it may fail to feed the last rounds into the boltway. In spite of this the under-mounted magazine is very often used because it is very easy to position and remove and obviously will not readily catch on undergrowth. In modern designs such as the Uzi, the magazine often follows automatic pistol practice and is fitted into the pistol grip. This holds the magazine firmly and makes it easy to locate the magazine in the dark using the 'hand finds hand' procedure. The best alternative is a side loading magazine. This keeps the centre of gravity constant in the vertical plane as the magazine empties. There will be a reaction force tending to push the muzzle sideways as the rounds move across but this is not a significant cause of in-accuracy. The task of the spring is not augmented by the weight of ammunition. The left hand side mounted magazine allows easy changing and also provides a forward grip for the firer but it does tend to catch in undergrowth or personal equipment.

WEAPON CONFIGURATION

The SMG is designed to be fired from the shoulder, using the sights, but there are many occasions in which short length is desirable. Such situations arise from the restriction on movement imposed inside an Armoured Personnel Carrier, the need to swing the gun quickly in close quarter battle and the acceptance of 'hose-piping' when firing from the hip at targets appearing suddenly. To meet this requirement many SMGs have the built-in ability to reduce the overall length. This is obtained by telescoping the butt, folding it under or over the barrel, side folding it forward or in some cases detaching it from the gun altogether. There are innumerable methods but the successful design must have a release catch easily found in the dark, simple to operate without undue force yet unlikely to be operated accidentally by contact with personal equipment or undergrowth. Many early designs pinched the operator's fingers or trapped the unwary soldier's hand. Some swung over the barrel and fouled the ejection opening. Some moved the butt in stages and were difficult to operate quickly, and others made enough noise to betray the firer's position. The best modern butt designs allow the metal butt stock to swing or slide quickly, quietly and with positive locking to a position where it provides a rigid connection between the weapon and the firer.

In many countries it is considered necessary to have a bayonet for the SMG.

This means that there must be a muzzle fitment to allow easy attachment and removal of the bayonet. If a bayonet is intended to be used for its primary purpose consideration must be given not only to the strength of the barrel at the muzzle to withstand the stress imposed but also to the weapon furniture. The soldier's hand can easily be hurt if there is no secure grip, insulated from heat and with no projections or rough edges. When the bayonet is not in use it is often convenient if it can be housed at the muzzle, held in a socket with point and edge properly shielded.

SILENCING

The SMG lends itself well to the process of silencing. The noise from any weapon comes from the mach wave associated with the supersonic travel of the bullet and the expansion of the propellant gases to supersonic velocity as they emerge from the muzzle. To make a SMG silent both the bullet and the gases must be kept below the speed of sound in air. This critical velocity varies with air temperature. In a temperate climate at sea level this will be about 1050ft/s. In arctic zones this velocity drops. A rough guide is that one degree Celsius (°C) makes a difference of 2ft/s. In North West Europe the figure of 1,050ft/s is the limit which neither bullet nor gas must exceed. This leads immediately to tactical as well as technical problems. SMGs are generically short range weapons so any reduction in muzzle velocity must mean a still shorter effective range. It also means that a weapon which normally fires a supersonic bullet will have its sights designed and manufactured for the trajectory associated with that bullet, and the use of a low velocity will result in a trajectory which does not match the sights. The point of impact will be below the point of aim by an amount which increases non-linearly with range. The lighter the bullet the higher the velocity it requires to achieve a given range and so the effect of silencing is more noticeable, ballistically, on a calibre such as 9mm (.380in) than on .45 calibre. The 9mm Parabellum cartridge produces a muzzle velocity of 1,250ft/s to project a bullet of 115 grains whereas a .45 ACP cartridge develops 950ft/s with a bullet of 230 grains. It follows that .45 calibre SMGs are less effected by silencing than those of 9mm calibre.

It is also necessary to ensure that the propellant gases emerge to the atmosphere at subsonic velocity. Normally in a SMG the gases following the bullet up the bore will expand to a velocity rather more than twice that of the bullet. There are two ways of achieving this reduction in bullet and gas velocity. The first is to use a standard gun with subsonic ammunition. The second is to use standard ammunition in a subsonic gun.

Using a cartridge with a reduced propellant load automatically produces a subsonic bullet velocity. The gases can be led off at the muzzle into a screwed-on cylinder full of metal gauze in which they dissipate their energy and emerge at a low speed. This system works well but is not widely used because of the practical disadvantages of having two types of ammunition of the same calibre in the Infantry section. In spite of colour markings on ammunition boxes and cartridges there is a distinct possibility of loading the wrong round – particularly at night before a patrol sets out.

The second alternative method involves the production of a special gun. The barrel is drilled radially with a series of holes through the barrel wall and is enclosed within an expansion chamber. This is filled with wire gauze baffles and extends forward of the muzzle. The gases bled off in the barrel produce a reduced muzzle velocity since they never build up to the normal pressure. Their energy is lost in the gauze filling. Beyond the muzzle the bullet passes through a central hole in a series of baffles and finally emerges as it penetrates a rubber plug. The muzzle blast is dissipated in the baffles. Because of these baffles it is inadvisable to fire at full automatic since they can be shifted by successive pressure waves and after a while the bullet comes into contact with the baffles. This type of silencer reduces smoke emission by day and flash by night. The only noise from a well designed silenced SMG – such as the Sten Mk IIS – which can be heard more than 50ft away, is the clatter of the bolt reciprocating. The effect of the silencer on a 9mm SMG is to reduce the maximum effective range from 200m to about 150. Since the gun is used mainly at night this is not significant. The sights of course are calibrated for the actual muzzle velocity produced. The silencer adds to the bulk, and the weight of the gun is generally increased by about 1lb. This increase in weight is smaller than might be expected but this is partly accounted for by the fact that the reduced pressure produces a reduced blow-back force to operate the firing cycle and so the breech block must be lightened and the return spring reduced in strength.

Overall the silenced SMG is a very effective weapon and during World War II it proved its value in the hands of Commandos, Special Forces and with thousands of Resistance Fighters in Europe to whom it was dropped.

TACTICAL EMPLOYMENT OF THE SMG

The German offensive in the spring of 1918 nearly broke the Allied line in two. At one time it looked as if the Channel ports were in danger again. After three years of static trench warfare the deadlock was broken. The Germans achieved this not by using artillery barrages lasting several days nor by employing tanks. They succeeded by using small bodies of men infiltrating into defended areas, not rigidly controlled from above, not carrying heavy weapons but having the advantages of surprise, movement and firepower. Several thousand Schmeisser designed MP 18.1 SMGs had been made in readiness for this offensive and they proved remarkably effective. Since this time the SMG has been the ideal weapon for guerrilla troops, infiltrators, Commandos and partisans. Its lightness, small bulk, simplicity and reliability have appealed to unorthodox troops in all the wars since 1918. It was used by jungle fighters in the Gran Chaco war of 1932–1935, irregular and partisan troops in the Spanish Civil War, and in Korea the Chinese employed vast numbers. The successive wars in South East Asia – Korea, Indo-China, Viet Nam and Borneo – have seen the SMG as the principal weapon employed.

Regular armies were slow to adopt the weapon. The British tested the Thompson in 1921 and again in 1928. The Small Arms Committee report in 1936 referred to the Suomi as the 'gangster weapon'. We also tested the Erma – designed by Volmer and designated by that name in 1932 – and were not impressed. Yet this same gun was the forerunner of the MP 38 and MP 40 which misnamed as the 'Schmeisser' were admired, feared and sought after by every British soldier in the series of losing battles fought until late 1942.

The Americans several times tested, but did not adopt, the Thompson between 1922 and 1938 and only the evidence of the effectiveness of such a weapon led to its adoption when America came into the war.

Is the SMG only a guerrilla weapon? The Russians did not think so. They manufactured at the very least 7 million SMGs and equipped entire Infantry Battalions of tank riders solely with these weapons.

How does the SMG fit into the pattern for the future? It seems unlikely that

25

7.63mm (.30) Mauser
TYPE: Rimless, bottleneck case
BULLET: 86 grs, jacketed
MUZZLE VELOCITY: 1410 ft/s
MUZZLE ENERGY: 375 ft-lbs

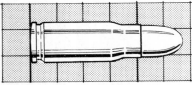

7.63 mm (.30) Mauser

7.65mm (.30) Luger
TYPE: Rimless, bottleneck case
BULLET: 93 grs, jacketed
MUZZLE VELOCITY: 1220 ft/s
MUZZLE ENERGY: 307 ft-lbs

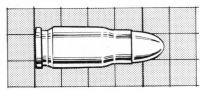

7.65 mm (.30) Luger

.38 A.C.P.
TYPE: Rimmed, straight case
BULLET: 130 grs, jacketed
MUZZLE VELOCITY: 1040 ft/s
MUZZLE ENERGY: 312 ft-lbs

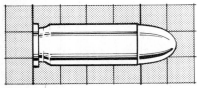

.38 A.C.P.

9mm Glisenti
TYPE: Rimless, straight case
BULLET: 124 grs, jacketed
MUZZLE VELOCITY: 985 ft/s
MUZZLE ENERGY: 267 ft-lbs

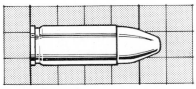

9 mm Glisenti

9mm Mauser
TYPE: Rimless, straight case
BULLET: 127 grs, jacketed
MUZZLE VELOCITY: 1360 ft/s
MUZZLE ENERGY: 520 ft-lbs

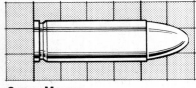

9 mm Mauser

.45 A.C.P.
TYPE: Rimless, straight case
BULLET: 230 grs, jacketed
MUZZLE VELOCITY: 920 ft/s
MUZZLE ENERGY: 425 ft-lbs

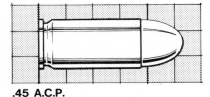

.45 A.C.P.

Fig II Examples of Sub-Machine Gun Cartridges (actual size)
(Muzzle velocities will vary from weapon to weapon according to the barrel length.)

there will be mass attacks by infantry in the future. Tactical nuclear weapons should destroy them in their forming up places. The vast number of tanks possessed by the Soviet bloc will give them local numerical superiority which will undoubtedly allow them to punch holes in the Allied defensive positions and motor on carrying large numbers of infantry in Armoured Personnel Carriers. But we hope that eventually their lines of communication will be cut, their petrol supplies stopped and the destruction of local supplies render them inert hulks to be destroyed by infantry weapons and anti-tank missiles. However if this looks like happening these infantry will debuss, and lightly armed, they will become bodies of well trained infiltrators capable of destroying vital installations, and armed with their equivalent of the SMG – the Avtomat Kalashnikov – capable of moving at speed on foot to objectives well defined beforehand. Operating as far as possible at night they could disrupt communications, destroy command posts and Headquarters, capture vital features

.32 A.C.P.
TYPE: Semi-rimmed, straight case
BULLET: 71 grs, jacketed
MUZZLE VELOCITY: 960 ft/s
MUZZLE ENERGY: 145 ft-lbs

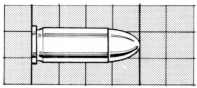

.32 A.C.P

.380 Auto
TYPE: Rimless, straight case
BULLET: 95 grs, jacketed
MUZZLE VELOCITY: 955 ft/s
MUZZLE ENERGY: 192 ft-lbs

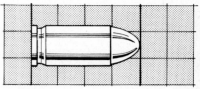

.380 Auto

9mm Parabellum
TYPE: Rimless, straight case
BULLET: 115 grs, jacketed
MUZZLE VELOCITY: 1250 ft/s
MUZZLE ENERGY: 400 ft-lbs

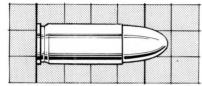

9 mm Parabellum

9mm Bergmann-Bayard
TYPE: Rimless, straight case
BULLET: 136 grs, jacketed
MUZZLE VELOCITY: 1115 ft/s
MUZZLE ENERGY: 375 ft-lbs

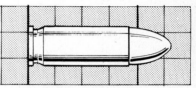

9 mm Bergmann-Bayard

.455 Mk II
TYPE: Rimmed, straight case
BULLET: 265 grs, lead
MUZZLE VELOCITY: 600 ft/s
MUZZLE ENERGY: 210 ft-lbs

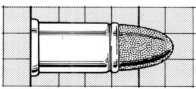

.455 Mk. II

7.62mm Tokarev (Type P)
TYPE: Rimless, bottleneck case
BULLET: 86 grs, jacketed
MUZZLE VELOCITY: 1,600 ft/s
MUZZLE ENERGY: 475 ft-lbs

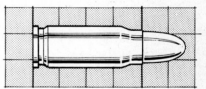

7.62 mm Tokarev (Type P)

and defend these for some considerable time whilst they awaited relief. Dislodging them after they had been allowed to dig themselves in would require more than the use of artillery – which itself would be involved in major battles on the flanks of the penetration, or the limited strike aircraft not committed to battle elsewhere. Infantry would be required in large numbers – able to match the firepower of the defenders. All this, I hope, points to the need for infantry firepower and amongst their weapons the SMG would take a prominent place. However if, as all sensible people hope, the European war never does come, there can be no doubt that there will be wars across the globe involving the armies of emergent states, older free Republics like India and Pakistan, and inevitably the politically conscious troops of the various countries in South America. All of these will use sub-machine guns and in spite of the introduction of the high velocity, lightweight .223 bullet it seems certain that the SMG will have its part to play in future warfare.

American Sub-Machine Guns

The credit for the first production SMG goes to Italy which had the Villar Perosa SMG **180** in service in 1915, but it seems that the versatile genius of Hiram S. Maxim produced a working SMG in the 1890s. This toggle-joint model of about .22 calibre was never developed and is now in the United States Marine Corps Museum at Quantico, Virginia. It is probable that Maxim had in mind a weapon with the characteristics of an automatic pistol and the increased accuracy obtainable with a shoulder stock. In this he anticipated the developments made some 20 years later with nearly all the military pistols. The Borchardt **1,** Mauser **2,** Luger **4,** Webley and Scott **6,** and Browning pistols **5** were all fitted with shoulder stocks – which frequently also functioned as holsters – to give a greater chance of a hit at extended ranges. None of them was truly successful although they were more effective than with the pistol fired unsupported from the hand.

The trench warfare of 1915–18, where ranges were often extremely short, showed the need for a weapon of small bulk, firing a pistol type cartridge and having a large magazine capacity to sustain a high volume of fire. The design and production resources of all the countries involved in World War I were fully stretched to produce conventional weapons and little thought could be given to unconventional arms. However in America one man of experience in weapon design and production did work on such a weapon.

THE PEDERSEN DEVICE

J. D. Pedersen was a weapon designer of great ability and experience. He had a considerable reputation from his inventions – largely taken up by the Remington Arms Co who were one of America's largest and oldest small arms producers. He designed the Remington pump action shot gun, their automatic pistol of unusual design in .45cal which had been recommended for adoption by the Navy Board, and the 'trombone' action rifle. In August 1917 Pedersen demonstrated a new weapon to senior officials of the War Department.

The gun consisted of a 1903 Springfield .300 rifle. The conventional bolt could be replaced by the 'device' which was of the same dimensions and inserted in exactly the same way as the bolt it replaced. This new bolt was a small, blow back operated, semi-automatic pistol with its barrel of the same size as the

.30–06 cartridge case. There was a 40 round magazine projecting upwards and to the right at 45deg **7**. The cartridge fired by this adapter was of .30cal and the bullet of 80 grains was discharged at 1300ft/s. The empty case was ejected through a slot on the left of the device and the rifle – known as the Springfield Mark 1 – had a corresponding port cut in the receiver. This in no way effected its functioning or accuracy in its primary role. The small barrel of the device had a fine rifling – larger in bore diameter than that of the rifle barrel, so the bullet gripped the grooves of the Springfield barrel without difficulty.

The device – with its metal scabbard – weighed 2lb and the loaded magazine weighed 1lb. The bolt of the Springfield rifle was placed in a pouch on the soldier's waist belt ready for replacement when required.

The .30 calibre small cartridge was about one-fifth of the size of the .30–06 rifle round. The muzzle energy of the bullet was about one-tenth that of the rifle bullet – some 260ft.lb – and it penetrated about 8in of wood at point blank range. It was considered lethal to a range of 500yd. Thus the soldier at the appropriate time could replace the rifle bolt with the Pedersen insert and fire off his 40 rounds as fast as he could operate the trigger. Each soldier would have ten loaded magazines. This could readily be seen as allowing a vast increase in fire power, either in defence – or in firing on the move during the assault.

The War Department sent an officer to France to show General Pershing the new weapon and 100,000 were ordered at once. This was later increased to 500,000. When the war ended in November 1918 65,000 had been completed. None were used in action. After the Armistice a review of the value of the device was made and it was then considered that the disadvantages which were considered to be (a) the possibility of loss of the rifle bolt, (b) the added load on the soldier and (c) the lack of morale effect at the target of the sound of the bullet passing overhead – outweighed the advantages and the existing 65,000 were destroyed in about 1923. During production in 1918 the Pedersen device was called the 'Automatic Pistol, Calibre .30, Model 1918' purely as a security measure.

THOMPSON SMGs

The Thompson SMG was the invention of John Taliaferro Thompson who spent most of his working life in the Ordnance Department of the United States Army. He was born in Newport, Kentucky, on 31 December 1860 and followed his father's career, after graduating from West Point in 1882, in being posted to the Second Artillery Regiment. He transferred to the Ordance Department in 1890 and was responsible for the supply of munitions in the Cuba campaign of 1898. Whilst at Tampa he played some part in helping to organise the Gatling gun detachment which gained fame at San Juan Hill under Lieutenant John H. Parker. After working on the development of the Springfield 1903 rifle and the .30–06 cartridge, he was appointed assistant to General Crozier, Chief of Ordnance, working on the design and development of small arms. The adoption of the Colt .45 M1911 SL pistol is ascribed to him. In November 1914 he retired from the Army and joined the Remington Arms Corporation as Chief Consulting Engineer. He laid out a new rifle factory at Eddystone, Pennsylvania, to produce rifles for the British Army and in 1916 he set up another at Bridgeport, Connecticut, to make the Moisin-Nagent for Russia.

When he left the Army in 1914 he planned to design and develop an automatic rifle. He rejected recoil operation as too heavy and gas operation as too complex. He was convinced that the 'blow back' system used for many .22 rifles could

1

1 The Borchardt SL pistol was produced in 1893. It was later fitted with the wooden stock and leather holster shown here.

2 The Mauser SL pistol is shown here inside its wooden holster which became a shoulder stock.

2

3 The Mauser 7.63mm SL pistol with long magazine and wooden shoulder stock holster.

4 Luger '08 9mm. 8in Artillery Model SL Pistol with 32 round snail magazine and wooden stock and leather holster. The Luger was developed from the Borchardt shown at Fig 1 above.

5 Browning FN 9mm Mk 2* SL pistol made by Inglis in Canada.

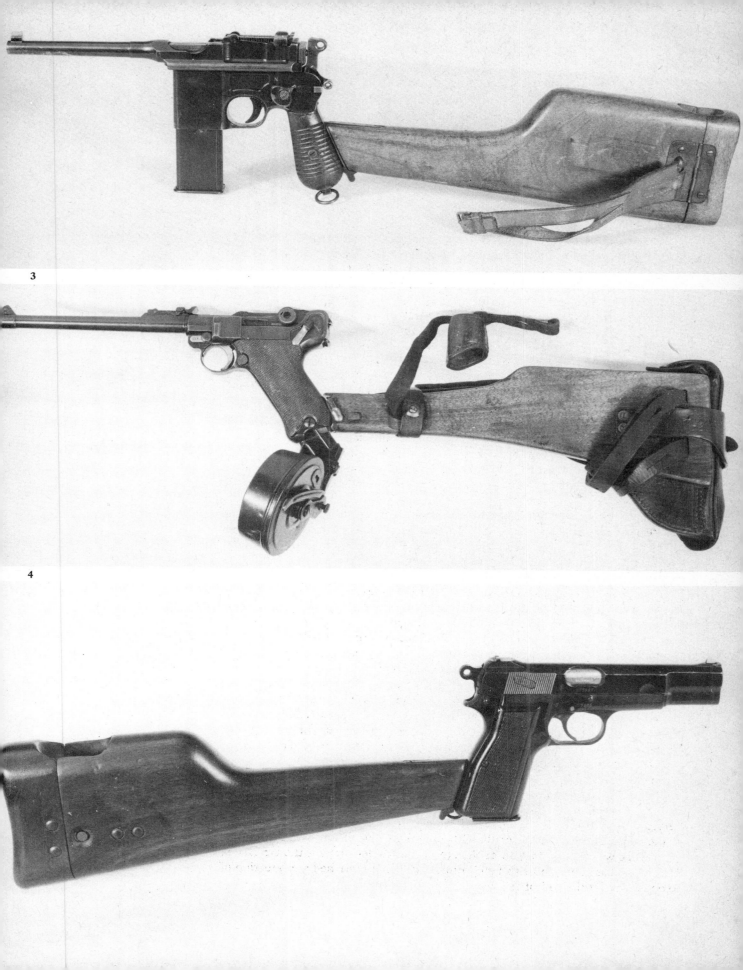

3

4

provide the answer. His rifle would require a high powered round so he had to find some method of providing a delay to the movement of the breech block whilst the pressure was high. In 1915 the answer seemed available. USA Patent 1,131,319 granted to Commander John Blish, USN (Retd), was for a breech delay system based on the inventor's experience that a screw breech gun mechanism which remained firmly closed at high pressures, would open under a reduced charge pressure. His patent employed a metal wedge, riding in inclined slots in the body, which jammed firmly at high pressures to hold up the breech block; when the pressure dropped, the wedge moved up its slots allowing the block to be blown back. It was in effect a friction device with only 2 parts – the wedge and the block, both of light weight. Thompson approached Blish and offered him shares in a company he would float, in exchange for the use of his patent. Blish accepted and Thompson set about floating his company. A friend of his son Marcullus' father-in-law, Thomas Fortune Ryan, agreed to put up the capital. The Auto-Ordnance Corporation was formed in August 1916 with 40,000 shares – 18,000 held by Ryan, 10,000 to Thompson and 1,500 to Blish.[1] Thompson chose as his Chief Engineer, Theodore H. Eickhoff, who from 1909–14 had worked with him in the Ordnance Department on pistol trials. Eickhoff designed a test rig which was made by Warner and Swasey in Cleveland in late 1916. When the USA entered Word War I in April 1917, Thompson was recalled to the Army as a Colonel and Eickhoff purchased some machine tools and carried on with the research. It was discovered that full powered rifle cartridges would only function if lubricated and the only un-lubricated round that would work with the Blish device was the .45 ACP cartridge used in the 1911 Colt pistol. This led to a change in the role of the weapon. It was no longer possible to regard it as an automatic rifle and Thompson saw it as a hand held machine gun that he said would be a 'Trench Broom' sweeping the enemy away. Eickhoff took on Oscar Payne to assist him and the first gun was made in October 1917. It was belt fed and incorporated a new design of the Blish system – known as the 'H' piece – which straddled the bolt and effectively held it up until the pressure dropped. The gun was called the 'Persuader' **8**. It failed on every trial after firing 6 or 7 shots, mainly because the Blish piece did not function adequately; the bolt came back too rapidly and the inertia of the belt feed system led to failures. An attempt was made to reshape the bolt without success and a 20 round box magazine, known as the Type XX, was then tried. This worked and the model incorporating it was known as the 'Annihilator' **9**. Further work was carried out on the mechanism to improve functioning and in the summer of 1918 it showed great promise. Thompson insisted on perfection and the first prototypes were ready for testing in November 1918. The war ended on 11 November 1918 and the Thompson had lost its main chance of rapid adoption by the USA Army. Speculation on what difference it would have made had it been ready a year earlier is pointless. Nevertheless the US Army clearly saw the need for a fast firing close quarter weapon and this was shown by the adoption of the Pedersen Device for the Springfield 1903 rifle.

Thompson was promoted to Brigadier-General in August 1918 and retired again in December. In the following March he was awarded the Distinguished Service Medal 'for exceptionally meritorious and conspicuous service as Chief of the Small Arms Division of the Office of the Chief of Ordnance . . .'. His main work was the production of the .300 Rifle Model 1917 for the US Army. This rifle – based on the British .303 Enfield P14 rifle – reached a production of 10,000 a day by the end of the war.

After his retirement the work continued on the .45 calibre gun – now called the Thompson Sub-Machine Gun. The Auto-Ordnance Corporation developed the 'Annihilator', I, II and III. The Annihilator I had belt feed, the II was magazine fed with a finned barrel and Annihilator III was further sub-divided into types D, E and F. The Model F was of some interest because it consisted of only 11 parts. During this early post-war development Payne incorporated the two oil soaked felt pads placed in the receiver to lubricate the bolt, and also developed the drum magazine. This had a six armed rotor which, powered by a clock spring, drove the cartridges round to the feed opening. The original magazine held 100 rounds and was called the type C 12. A later 50 round drum was known as the type L. The SMG was tested on 27 April 1920 by the Ordnance Department at Springfield Arsenal. There was only one stoppage in 2000 rounds and the report was good. In the summer of 1920 it was tested by the US Marines at Quantico, Virginia. Again the report was favourable.

Thompson was encouraged by these trials and approached Colt's Patent Firearms Corp with a view to their producing the gun. Colts did not wish to produce under contract but offered to buy the rights for $1,000,000. Ryan refused this offer and agreement was reached for Colt's to produce 15,000 firing mechanisms for $45 each. Auto-Ordnance produced all jigs, tools and gauges at a cost of $210,323. The Lyman Gun Sight Corporation provided sights for $69,063, the Remington Arms Coporation produced walnut stocks and grips for $65,456. The total cost to Auto-Ordnance (including $9,105 to Colt for spares) was $1,034,653 provided by Thomas Ryan against a mortgage on the Auto-Ordnance property.[1]

The gun produced by Colt was designated the Thompson Sub-Machine Gun Model 1921 12. It was an elegant weapon with a detachable butt, provision for single shot and automatic fire, sighted up to 600yd, and had the 100 round drum magazine. The cyclic rate of fire was 800 rounds per minute. The first production models were tested by the US Marines on 4 and 6 April 1921 at Quantico, both on the ground and in the air. On 8 April 1921 tests were carried out by the Army at Fort Benning, Georgia. The reports were favourable but no orders were forthcoming. Thompson toured Europe, visiting England, France, Spain, Rumania, Czecho-Slovakia and Belgium. This latter country showed great interest for a long while but nothing transpired. The Thompson received a lot of unfavourable publicity when it was revealed that 495 guns had been loaded on to the collier 'East Side', berthed at Hoboken on the Hudson River, for the Irish Republican Army; further notoriety came its way during the spate of gangster activity following the Volstead Act which on 16 January 1920 introduced prohibition into the States.

In 1923 a model with a 14in barrel, firing a higher powered Remington-Thompson .45 cartridge to give greater range, was introduced but failed to sell. In 1927 a semi-automatic version of the M1921 was introduced. This also was not purchased. In January 1927 the US Marines used the Model 1921 in Nicaragua with success in their jungle operations. As a result of their comments the Navy Model was introduced in 1928 with a lower rate of fire, a straight fore-end and the Cutts' Compensator. This was a device fitted to the muzzle, with slots cut in the top. The emergent gases forced the muzzle down. This device was invented by Colonel Richard M. Cutts (Retd) and his son Richard M. Cutts Jr both of whom were officers in the US Marines.

In 1924 the Belgium Army showed renewed interest in the Thompson but wanted it in 9mm Parabellum. Thompson got the English Birmingham Small

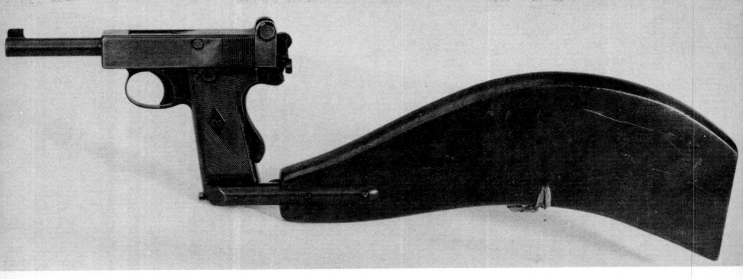

6 **6** Webley and Scott Pistol SL .455 Mk 1 No 2. This was issued with its wooden stock in April '15 for use in the trenches of World War I.

7 The 'Automatic Pistol, Calibre .30, Model 1918' was the official cover name for the Pedersen device which was a replacement bolt for the Springfield '03 Mk 1 rifle, allowing 40 .30 pistol cartridges to be fired at semi automatic as fast as the soldier could operate his trigger. The rifle was thus converted to a SMG.

7

8 The Thompson 'Persuader'. This was the first prototype and was 'tape' belt fed. It never fired more than 6 or 7 consecutive shots due to the 'Blish' piece failing to hold up the bolt long enough.

8

9 The 'Annihilator'. A 20 round box magazine – type XX – produced automatic fire. This like all the subsequent Model 1919 prototypes had no butt.

10 The first Thompson with a finned barrel and no barrel casing. This was No 2 of the 1919 models. The pistol grip assembly was immediately behind the magazine opening and the gun could take either box or drum magazines.

11 No 8 of the Model 1919 series. The pistol grip has been moved further back. Like all the Model 1919 guns the rate of fire was over 1000 rounds a minute.

12

14

13

15

Arms Co to work on this and in 1926 George Norman of BSA produced a design with no compensator and a plain barrel. The gun was only 32in long. The BSA model of 1929 was 36in long with a finned barrel and compensator. It was chambered for a number of European cartridges – 9mm Parabellum, 9mm Mauser, 7.63mm Mauser and 7.65mm Luger. It was tested in Belgium who expressed the request for 10,000 to be made under license by Fabrique Nationale d'Armes de Guerre at Herstal, Liege[2] but this came to nothing. By 1938 the total sales of the Thompson had reached only 10,300 – all from the original Colt production and the finances of the Auto-Ordnance Corporation were not good.

In 1938 the gun became a standard US Army issue[3] as the .45 M1928 A1 **15**. Although the European situation promised future orders, these could never be supplied without further funds. Thomas Fortune Ryan had died in 1928 and his nephew Walter Ryan wanted to sell out. To raise cash Thompson went to Russel Maguire, a Connecticut industrialist, but in so doing he lost control of the company.

In November 1939 – after World War II had started – both the French and British purchasing commissions placed orders. The French Government ordered two lots of 3,000 each and in February 1940 the British ordered 450 guns. By the end of 1940 the British order had risen to 107,500. By August 1941 318,900 guns had been ordered including 20,450 for the US Government.

General Thompson died on 21 June 1940 and so never saw the vast expansion of Auto-Ordnance, or his gun used by nearly all the Allies in the 1939–45 War.

Russel Maguire obtained a factory at Bridgeport, Connecticut, in August 1940 and purchased a lot of used machinery including one piece dating back to the Civil War.[3] In January 1941 he started making jigs and gauges. Many of these were later supplied to sub-contractors. The first gun came out in August 1941. The Savage Arms Co at Utica and the Bridgeport factory eventually produced 90,000 guns a month. When production ended in 1944 the number totalled 1,383,043.[3]

During the war various refinements were cut out to increase production. In November 1941 the 30 round box magazine became standard. In December 1941 the Lyman rear sight which consisted of fourteen separate components and took one hour to fabricate, was changed to a simple open sight protected by two wings. This was a single stamping pressed out in two minutes.

The Blish piece was eliminated with a saving of machinery time of over one hour. The Cutts' Compensator was omitted in 1942. The gun was standardised on 25 April 1942 as the SMG Cal .45 M1 **16**.

12 Model 1921. The first production gun. The weapon was produced by Colt's Patent Firearms Corp using Lyman sights and stocks from Remington. This particular gun was sold to the Irish Republican Army and used in the Irish Civil War in 1922–23.

13 General John Taliaferro Thompson at Bisley demonstrating the Model 1921, with 20 round box magazine, and butt detached. This model had a separate firing pin and hammer.

14 The Model 1928A had no compensator. The Model 1928AC had the Cutts's compensator. Both were offered with either a forward pistol grip or a horizontal, grooved foregrip.

15 The Thompson Model 1928A1 had a compensator and a modified ejector but otherwise was similar to the M1928.

16 The M1. This was a great simplification of the Thompson. The Blish H-piece was discarded with the Cutts' Compensator and the Lyman back sight. The 30 round box magazine became standard, and replaced the 20 round box magazine shown here.

When the hammer and firing pin were replaced by a fixed firing pin on the breech face, the gun was known as the SMG Cal .45 M1A1 and standardised as such on 27 October 1942 **17**.

In 1939 the Thompson M1928A1 cost $209. In 1944 the Thompson M1A1 cost $45 with spares.[3]

The Thompson SMG was obsolete before World War II started. The Germans, Swiss, Russians and Fins had all developed cheaper, simpler and equally effective weapons prior to 1939.

But when war came the only weapon of the SMG type available for manufacture in quantity in the USA was the Thompson. The way in which production grew is shown in this table.[1]

	M1928A1	M1	M1A1
1939	0	0	0
1940	3630	0	0
1941	213790	0	0
1942	344521	249420*	8552†
1943	570	36060*	526500†
1944	0	0	4091

* Produced by Auto Ordnance at Bridgeport.

† Produced by Savage at Utica.

Almost all the 1940 and 1941 production went to Europe and of these over 100,000 were lost to U boat sinkings in the Atlantic.

The 'Tommy' gun was the most famous of all SMGs and was employed in Europe, Africa, SE Asia and Russia. It was the first SMG to carry the fight back into Europe after Dunkirk, with the Commandos operating from Britain. It is still shown in the British Combined Operations badge.

HYDE SMGs

George Hyde came to the United States in 1926. He was born in Germany and during World War I had been employed on machine gun design. He worked as a gun-smith for the New York sporting goods firm of Griffin and Howe. He built 60 guns of his own design for the Lake Erie Co.[1]

His first sub-machine gun was his model 33. Only a few were produced and some minor improvements were incorporated in the model 35 **20**. The gun was blow back operated, firing from the open bolt position, using the .45 ACP cartridge. The barrel was finned and fitted with a screwed-on compensator. With a wooden pistol foregrip and a box magazine the forward part of the gun was somewhat similar to the later models of the 1921 Thompson. The receiver was tubular with a milled end closure cap from which protruded a cocking plunger. The weapon fired at single shot or full automatic with a change lever on the left of the body. Although the 20 round box magazine was standard, the capacity could be increased by having two or three boxes brazed together side by side. These were moved laterally across the gun as each in turn was expended. The model 35 was tested at Aberdeen Proving Ground[4] in October–November 1939. Its performance was better than the Thompson under adverse conditions; it was simpler in design, handled better and had less recoil. It had the disadvantage that the cocking handle located behind the receiver came back $\frac{1}{2}$in with the bolt towards the firer's eye and this, although not a practical hazard, was not popular with the firer. Other objections were to the muzzle flash and the weakly supported foregrip. A service test was not recommended.

17 The M1A1 had no separate hammer and firing pin but used a fixed firing pin on the breech face. Whereas the M1928A1 cost $209, the M1A1 cost $45.

18 An M1 fitted with an Enfield designed silencer for use by Commando troops. The Thompson was not difficult to silence because the muzzle velocity of some 950ft/s was subsonic.

19 Thompson SMG made by Viet-Cong. This was a home-made gun but the Chinese arsenals have also produced thousands of Thompsons. See **299** for the Egyptian-made Thompson SMG.

20 The Hyde .45 Model 35 was designed by George J. Hyde. It could take either a single 20 round box magazine or combination of two or three such boxes brazed together and sliding in turn across the gun. The cocking plunger behind the body came back ½in each time the gun fired and this upset the firer.

21 Hyde experimental SMG in .22LR. This was adapted from a rifle barrel and the action is straight blow back. It dates from the mid 30s but nothing is known of its purpose. It is now at the RSAF Enfield.

22 The Atmed .45 SMG was a modified Model 35. It was tested at Aberdeen Proving Ground and was the first gun to pass the mud test. It functioned erratically with many stoppages and was not developed.

23 The Hyde-Inland .45 SMG. This was accepted as the M2 but although production was started by Marlin Firearms Corp various manufacturing difficulties resulted in its cancellation.

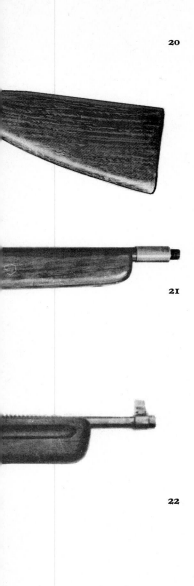

20

21

22

23

The next Hyde gun was produced for the Atmed Manufacturing Co of New York **22**. It bore a general external resemblance to the early Thompson Model M1 with a finned barrel, grooved wooden fore-end and no compensator. The box magazine held 20 .45 ACP rounds. It was tested at Aberdeen Proving Ground[5] in September 1942. It was the last gun to undergo the limited firing test of functioning, cyclic rate determination, accuracy at 1,000in and 300yd from a machine rest, velocity, dust and mud tests. About 750 rounds were fired.[3] During testing it functioned badly initially, with primers pierced by the fixed firing pin. The pin was shortened by 0.009in and the trouble disappeared. The sear spring was too weak and often instead of single shots it produced two or three. It functioned well in mud and dust – it was the first gun to pass the mud test. However it was not considered worth developing and only the first tool room batch was produced.

The Hyde-Inland was the next model **23**. The gun was developed by the Inland Division of General Motors Corporation. It was essentially a development of the Hyde Model 35. The cocking handle no longer moved towards the firer's eye as it had been re-located as a conventional pull back type on the right of the gun, moving in a slot cut in the body. The barrel finning and pistol fore-grip were removed. The stock enclosed the barrel and was extended well forward. The drop of the butt stock was reduced to give a more straight through action. The gun when tested at Aberdeen[6] from 2–15 April 1942 gave very promising results. Under the new programme it fired 6,080 rounds with only 20 malfunctions. It was considered more accurate than the Thompson in full auto-fire with a much reduced climb. Its slower cyclic rate of fire of 527rpm gave better control than that of the Thompson 1928 A1 at 610rpm and the Thompson M1 at 775rpm. At single shot it was not as good.

The gun was further improved and 5 models re-tested in June 1942. The tests revealed only fair performance after 500 rounds, but it was considered these faults – mainly failures to fire – could be corrected. It was decided that the magazine well should be deepened to take the Thompson magazine; a heavier return spring should be fitted to reduce the bolt impact on the buffer and give additional forward energy. The gun was approved as a required type and designated US Sub-machine Gun Calibre .45 M2 on 13 April 1942.[3]

Capacity for manufacture was available at the Marlin Firearms Corporation at New Haven, Connecticutt, which had been set up to produce the United Defence Model 42 **35** for the Dutch Government. On 10 June 1942 a letter purchase order for 164,450 M2 SMGs with spares was issued and formalised on 31 July 1942 when the weapons were scheduled at 13,500 a month.[3] The tentative price was $38.58. Initially it was intended that eight of the M2 components should be made by powder metallurgy to speed production and reduce costs. The Marlin Company could not find reliable sub-contractors for these parts and it was then discovered that dimensional tolerances could not be maintained and impact strength was low. After attempting to heat treat and machine these parts it was found necessary to make all of them, except the trigger, from bar stock. In April 1943 Springfield Armoury gave a production gun a 2,800 round test. 62 misfires, 44 misfeeds and several 'run away gun' resulted. After further tests Ordnance Engineers visited the plant and made numerous small changes.

Further test models were produced but in view of the poor results and the decision to produce the M3 SMG, it was decided on 18 June 1943[3] to declare the M2 obsolete.

In October 1942 work on a new SMG had been authorised. The requirement was for a gun of all metal construction, easily broken down, of cost and performance equal to the British Sten gun and capable of handling either the .45 or 9mm round with a minimum of changes for conversion. The designer of the weapon was George Hyde. He worked with Frederick Sampson – Chief Engineer of the Inland Division of General Motors Corporation.[3] The Project Officer was Colonel R. Studler. The first result was the Machine Pistol T15. This was modified by removing the single shot capacity and known as the Machine Pistol T20. Five prototype models were tested at the Aberdeen Proving Ground from the 18 to 24 November 1942.[7] During an endurance test of 5,000 .45 rounds there were only two malfunctions. Both were failures to feed caused by the magazine platform binding. The accuracy at full automatic was better than any weapon previously tested – due to the low cyclic rate of 400 rounds a minute. In mud and dust tests it was also superior to all models tried before. It was agreed by representatives from all the User Services that this was the best weapon of its kind in the field. It was decided that the sliding stock should be lengthened to make the distance from butt to trigger the same as in the rifle. The Infantry Board also wanted the magazine improved but this was not done. On 24 December 1942 the T20 Machine Pistol was officially adopted as a standard item of issue and given the nomenclature Sub-machine Gun Calibre .45 M3. The M1 and M2 were declared limited standard to be supplied only until such time as the M3 was available.[3]

The .45 cal M3 looks like its nickname – 'The Grease Gun' **24**. The body is cylindrical and the barrel projects forward from the centre and is secured by a knurled cap encircling the front of the receiver. The 30 round magazine is located in a housing below the forward end of the body and the metal pistol grip projects below the rear end. The stock is of tubular steel and is located by a catch above the pistol grip. The applied safety is a projection from the ejection slot cover. When the cover is closed and the bolt is forward, the projection enters a hole drilled in the bolt and prevents movement. When the bolt is retracted and the cover closed the projection comes in front of the bolt, forcing it back slightly off the sear and holding it back. Since the bent is now behind the sear, operating the trigger has no effect. Opening the cover allows the bolt to move forward onto the sear. If the cover is raised with the bolt forward, dropping the weapon can fire a round. Cocking the bolt is accomplished by rotating a handle located at the front end of the right hand side of the trigger casing. The cocking mechanism consists of nine component parts.

The gun can be converted to 9mm by substituting a barrel, replacement bolt, magazine adapter and a 30 round 9mm magazine of the Sten type. **27**.

It was decided that manufacture of the M3 should be undertaken by the Guide Lamp Division of General Motors Corporation located at Anderson, Indiana, which had produced car headlamps and had considerable experience of stampings. On 29 January 1943 the company was given a letter order for 300,000 guns at a contract price of $17.92 exclusive of the bolt. The bolt was to be produced by the Buffalo Arms Corporation. The price was later amended to $18.36 to include costs of changes and packaging. Initial production was forecast for May 1943 to be built up to 70,000 a month by September 1943. Right from the start this schedule proved to be over optimistic. This type of work was new, the tolerances had been established on the pilot guns which were made by different methods, and stresses set up in welding the semi-cylinders comprising the receiver, led to distortion. Instead of 20,000 guns in July 1943 only 900 were

24 The M3 .45 SMG. The 'Grease Gun' was designed to be cheap, simple to produce, able to fire either .45 ACP or 9mm Parabellum cartridges by substituting bolt, barrel and magazine, and with a performance equal to the British Sten.

25 The M3 with an American silencer.

Tube with wire mesh cylinder

Wire mesh washers (200 off)

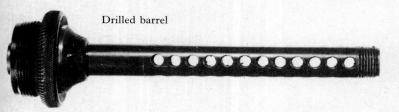
Drilled barrel

Forward tube

delivered; the schedule called for 60,000 in August 1943 but production did not reach 40,000 until December 1943. In February 1944 the requirement for the year 1944 was reduced from 458,362 to 333,319 and the monthly quota from 60,000 to 30,000 tapering off to 25,000 by the end of the year. Production was about 32,000 per month throughout 1944. It is noteworthy that the British method for cold swaging barrels on a mandrel, instead of the conventional rifling process, was used with great success.

During March 1944 the Office of Strategic Services (OSS) asked for 25,000 9mm conversions of the M3 for supply to the South Pacific area. This called for an intensive effort by the Guide Lamp Division, the Buffalo Arms Co and Rock Island Arsenal who completed the bolts. The last delivery of 500 guns was made in September 1944. These 9mm guns were not used in SE Asia but were dropped to the underground forces in Europe.

In January 1944 troops at Camp Bowie, Texas, training with the M3 reported that the rotating cocking lever and associated pawls were giving trouble. Similar reports came from troops in England. Experiments showed that the cocking device could be eliminated entirely and the gun cocked by inserting the fore-finger in a hole in the bolt. The ejection port and cover were lengthened. This idea started development of a modified gun known as the M3E1 and this was standardised on 11 October 1944 as the M3A1 **29**. Eliminating the retracting pawl made possible a simplified bolt design and it was no longer necessary to remove the trigger guard, stock and housing to remove the bolt; instead it could be accomplished by unscrewing the barrel assembly.

Five of the M3A1 SMGs were tested at Aberdeen Proving Ground and it was informally reported that the guns were the best pre-production guns ever tested there. In 27,500 rounds fired in 5 guns there were no malfunctions and very good sand and dust tests. On 19 April 1945 authority was given to replace all Thompson SMGs M1928A1, M1 and M1A1 with either M3 or M3A1 guns.

The M3 and M3A1 were produced as follows:

26 The M3 silencer. The barrel had 48 ¼in holes. A wire mesh cylinder fitted over the barrel. 200 wire mesh washers fitted in the forward tube.

27 The M3 in 9mm Parabellum with a magazine housing adaptor.

28 The M3 .45 SMG with a silencer designed at Enfield. This was more efficient than the American design but was never taken into service.

	M3	M3A1
1943	85130	—
1944	343372	—
1945	178192	15469
	606694	

At the start of the M3 programme it was expected that the cost of the M3 would be about $21.50 with spares. In October 1943 it cost $33.33, and in April 1945 the M3A1 was priced at $21.00 without spares. In June 1945 it had risen to $22 as the numbers decreased.

A further order for 70,000 M3A1 SMGs was placed with the Ithaca Gun Company, Ithaca, New York at the outset of the Korean War. 33,200 were completed and the contract was then cancelled.

OSS asked for a silencer for the M3. This was of conventional design with 48 holes drilled in the barrel. Two sleeves were fitted over the barrel; the sleeve nearest the breech was 7in long and $1\frac{1}{2}$in in diameter. It was full of wire mesh. The forward sleeve was 7in long by $1\frac{1}{8}$ and contained wire mesh baffles **25, 26**.

A silencer was also made by the Ordnance Factory at Enfield which was rather more effective **28** but was not adopted.

The M3 and M3A1 make George Hyde's best obituary. He died in 1964[8] having served the country of his adoption well.

THE REISING SMG

Eugene C. Reising of Worcester, Massachusetts, was a designer who produced a SMG in 1938. After some development work he applied for a patent on 28 June 1940. His gun was called the .45 Reising Model 50 and was manufactured by the Harrington and Richardson Arms Co in December 1941. Total production of this model and the Model 55 – which incorporated some modifications – was 10,000. The gun was tested by the Aberdeen Proving Ground[9] on three occasions. Minor improvements were incorporated after each test and the weapon was standardised for the US Marines, who took most of the production. Some were bought by the British Purchasing Commission and sent to Russia.[2]

The US Marines employed the Reising SMG in their operations on Guadalcanal. They frequently jammed and the Marines dumped large numbers of them in the Lunga river.[1] This delayed blow back gun **30** was unusual in that it fired, both at single shot and full automatic, from a closed bolt, using a cylindrical internal hammer which, when released by the sear, was driven forward by a spring to strike a floating firing pin in the bolt. There was a delay imposed on the bolt, which had to tilt out of engagement with a recess in the top of the body by the camming action of a downward inclined plane. This recess was the cause of jamming because when it was partly filled with sand the bolt could not rise and the trigger mechanism could not operate. The delay imposed by the bolt tilting and the hammer action resulted in a cyclic rate of 550rpm and a fair degree of control. The model 50 had a wooden butt and a stock extending forward under the finned barrel to the compensator. The model 55 had a folding wire stock, a rear pistol grip, and no compensator. Both models had a 20 round single column feed magazine below the body. A 12 round magazine was also available but never produced for service. The cocking arrangement was very unusual in that the firer had to insert a finger under the fore-end and pull back a rod which cocked the hammer **31**. In general the gun was excessively complicated and insufficient provision was made to protect the working parts

29 The M3A1 .45 SMG. This is cocked by the firer inserting a finger in the bolt recess. When the cover is closed the bolt is locked. The gun shown has the optional flash hider fitted.

30 Reising Model 50. This was a delayed blow back gun accepted by the US Marines. At Guadalcanal it jammed consistently and was thrown away in large numbers.

31 Reising Model 50 showing slot under fore-end by which it was manually cocked.

29

30

31

Finger cocking latch.

from the ingress of foreign matter. Military production ceased in 1945 but a few commercial orders were completed after this date 33.

THE UNITED DEFENCE SMGs

The United Defence Supply Corporation was formed to supply weapons to the Allied Nations in May 1941.[3] The first SMG it produced was designated the UD-1 34 and came out in late 1942. It was a blow back gun designed to take either the .45 ACP cartridge or the 9mm Parabellum and the only part which needed to be changed was the barrel. The gun had two barrels, therefore, of different calibres and the one not in use became the folding stock by screwing into a female fitting which was on the left of the body above the pistol grip. This fitting could be swung rearwards to enable the weapon to be fired from the shoulder or left as it was with the spare barrel under the body and perforated barrel casing. The 20 round magazine fitted horizontally into the body from the left and ejection was to the right. The arm could be fired at either single shot or full automatic, controlled by a selector switch on the right of the body. The safety held the bolt when the gun was cocked but with the bolt forward and the safety applied, any set back of the bolt resulted in a jam which could not quickly be cleared.

During limited tests at Aberdeen[2] the gun produced a cyclic rate of 1,150 rounds/minute and the barrel rose appreciably.

Although it withstood the dust test it failed to function in mud and further tests were abandoned. No more work was done on the gun.

The next gun was the UD Model produced in 1941 in prototype form. The production models were marked 'UD M 42' and this was the nomenclature adopted for the weapon. It was designed prior to World War II by Carl G. Swebilius of the High Standard Corporation of New Haven, Connecticut. The earliest tests were conducted in August 1940 at Aberdeen Proving Ground[10] with a .45 ACP model. The rate of fire was excessive and the 20 round magazine was considered to be too small. As a result it was modified and a double magazine produced. This did not move laterally through the gun but was turned over through 180deg for the second magazine to be inserted 35. The modified gun was tested at Aberdeen[11] in November 1941. It functioned well in the sand

32 Reising Model 55 .45 SMG. This differed from the Model 50 in having no compensator, a wire butt stock and a pistol grip.

32

and mud tests and was accurate but at this time the .45 Hyde-Inland (M2) although not yet tested at Aberdeen, was considered to show more promise and it was decided to do no further testing of the .45 High Standard Gun.

The United Defense Corp demonstrated the improved model to the Dutch and British Governments and the former expressed its intention to buy the weapon in 9mm calibre for the defence of the Dutch East Indies. Production capacity was set up at the Marlin Firearms Co at New Haven, Connecticut to supply 15,000 guns.[1]

The UD Model 42 was a blow back operated SMG using a reduced diameter bolt, firing from the open breech position with a separate spring-retracted firing pin. The hammer was contained within the bolt and was rotated against the firing pin when it contacted a fixed bridge in the receiver. The cocking handle was not connected directly to the bolt and did not reciprocate with it.

The magazine was either a conventional 20 round two position feed box or the double back-to-back 40 round pattern already mentioned. In general it was a well made gun – expensive to produce – which functioned considerably more reliably than some others made in much larger quantities.

THE SEDGLEY SMG
In 1940 R. F. Sedgley of Philadelphia, Pennsylvania, produced a 9mm SMG **36** which was demonstrated to the British Purchasing Commission. No detailed record of this remains except that it was considered to offer no advantage over the Thompson and insufficient capacity existed at the R. F. Sedgley Incorporated premises to produce in quantity.

The body of the gun and the slotted barrel jacket were made from a single steel tube. The wooden butt was of conventional shape and the weapon was half stocked. The 20 round box magazine was fitted under the gun and had a keyed section which fitted into a dovetailed guide rib at the front of the stock. The conventional hollow box magazine housing was not used. There was a selector lever on the left side of the body which rotated to provide single shot or full automatic. The cocking handle could be pushed in to hold the bolt in the cocked position but there was no safety arrangement when the bolt was forward.

As far as is known[2] the gun never got beyond the prototype stage.

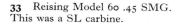

33 Reising Model 60 .45 SMG. This was a SL carbine.

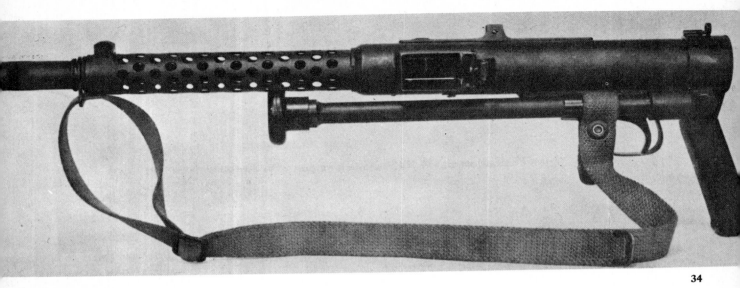

34

35

36

THE TURNER SMG

The Turner **37** was produced by Russel J. Turner of Butler, Pennsylvania. It started life as a contender in the light rifle competition of 1941 and was chambered for the .30 SRM1 cartridge. When it was rejected after tests at Aberdeen Proving Ground on 15 September 1941 it was re-submitted as a SMG. It was re-chambered for the .45 ACP cartridge. It had full and semi-automatic fire using an Allen screw wrench adjustment of the selector above the trigger assembly. The trigger mechanism was made like a lock with pins fastened to the receiver. It was a gas operated weapon with the piston acting on a bolt locking link. The magazine feed was from below using either 10 or 20 round magazines. It had a skeleton tubular butt stock with a leather covered butt plate. The $15\frac{1}{2}$in barrel had a perforated hand guard and a compensator. It was tested at the Aberdeen Proving Ground on 16 October 1942 and was rejected. It is probable that only one prototype was made.

THE WOODHULL SMG

The Woodhull **38** was produced by the F. W. Woodhull Corporation, Millington, New Jersey. It was submitted three times for the .30 SRM1 light rifle competition in 1941 without success. It was then converted to .45 ACP and re-submitted after modification, as a SMG. It had a blow back operation system based on the Winchester 1905 Cal .32 SL Rifle. The gun utilised a large number of Winchester parts including the receiver, bolt assembly, internal hammer firing system. Using .45 ACP it was found necessary to harden the bolt and also to harden and specially polish the chamber. It had a wooden butt and a wooden fore end under the barrel. The magazine held 10 rounds.

It was tested at the Aberdeen Proving Ground on 2 February 1942 and rejected. It is doubtful if more than one prototype was produced.

THE INGRAM SMGs

Gordon B. Ingram came back to the USA after World War II with a considerable practical knowledge of sub-machine guns. He believed that simplicity of design made for reliability and that automatic fire was the best method of producing a high chance of a hit in battle. He also had a good knowledge of the practical economics of weapon production and all his guns are extremely straightforward to produce using the minimum of expensive machining operations. To avoid confusion with the US, M1, M2, M3 and to allow for a possible US M4, his first model was called the Model 5.

Ingram Model 5: His first gun was the Ingram Model 5. Only one prototype was made and this is shown **39**. The magazine shown is the 12 round Reising. Production versions were intended to hold 25 rounds. The barrel housing was made of perforated seamless tubing and the trigger mechanism and firing mechanism consisted of only three moving parts – the trigger, sear and bolt. The rear end of the bolt was hollowed out to take the return spring which pressed directly onto a firing pin which passed through the bolt and permanently projected. The wooden butt was non-detachable but in spite of this the gun only weighed 6lb. The sole prototype of this gun appeared in 1946 and a sales brochure issued in that year by the Lightning Arms Co – describing it as the Lightning Model 5 – advertised its availability. 1946 was not a good year for weapons sales and plenty of war surplus stores from various countries made the launching of a new design difficult.

Ingram started work on a new gun in 1947 and worked steadily for two years before he was satisfied with its performance.

34 The UD1. This was designed to fire either .45 ACP or 9mm Parabellum. The barrel not in use formed the butt stock.

35 The UD42 9mm SMG. Early prototypes were in .45 ACP but all production models used the double magazine with a total capacity of 40 9mm cartridges.

36 The Sedgley 9mm SMG. This was produced in 1940 but did not offer enough advantages to warrant production.

37

38

39

The Ingram Model 6: In April 1949 the Police Ordnance Company was formed by Gordon Ingram, Jack Percell, John Cook and Thomas Bright. All of them had seen active service and they believed that a new SMG could find a market with the many US Police agencies. Gordon Ingram was both the Designer and Chief Engineer of the company and his Model 6 was demonstrated for the first time at Sacramento to the Californian Police Chiefs' Convention **40**.

The Model 6 appeared in the first 'Police Ordnance Company Manual 1948–9' where the company was shown to be operating in El Monte, California. The gun was offered in .45 ACP, .38 ACP (Super auto) and 9mm Parabellum. Although the descriptive writing said that the gun fired automatic only, a later version did feature a trigger mechanism which gave single shots when the trigger was pulled halfway back and full auto when fully back. This was achieved using a trigger mechanism with a bolt operated tripper. It is also stressed in this manual that the gun fires whilst the bolt is still moving forward ie – floating firing. Three types were offered. These were the 'police' model with a shaped pistol foregrip like the Thompson Model 1921 and cooling rings on the barrel, the 'guard' model with a forearm like the Thompson M1 but a smooth barrel, and a 'Military' model which differed from the others in having (a) heavy foresight protectors, (b) full stocking under the barrel, and (c) a 10 inch spike bayonet locking to the lower part of the muzzle cap with a spring catch. The rear sight was changed in later models by adding sight protectors and a windage adjuster.

The model 6 sold mainly in .45 ACP and apart from Police Forces in USA it was sold to Cuba for the Navy and to Peru for Army use. It was also produced in Peru. Production of the Ingram Model 6 was as follows:

9mm Parabellum – between 12 and 20 only.
.45 ACP   – 15,000 in USA.
                 – 8000 in Peru. (Ingram spent at least a year in Peru supervising the setting up of production).

The Ingram Model 7: This was externally indistinguishable from the Model 6 but fired from the closed breech position. This feature was incorporated since police use mainly required single shot fire, and closed bolt firing produces less lock time and greater accuracy. A two part bolt and a spring loaded firing pin were used. At full automatic the cyclic rate was increased from 600 to nearly 700 rounds a minute. The model 7 **41** was offered as a semi automatic weapon or with a selector lever giving either full auto or semi auto. It was available, as before, in Police, Guard and Military types in .45 ACP, .38 ACP and 9mm Parabellum. It appears few Model 7 were produced, and only one in .38 Super.

The Ingram Model 8: Gordon Ingram left the Police Ordnance Corporation in 1952. During this time he experimented with some improvements to the Model 6 and in 1953 he interested the Government of Thailand in the improved gun. In 1954 he went to Thailand to help in laying out a production line in Bangkok for the Model 8 which was designated as the weapon for the Thai police. The Model 8 differed from the Model 6 in that a cover was incorporated for the cocking handle slot in the body and for the ejection port. The safety arrangements were improved and the bolt could be locked either in the forward or cocked position. The gun could be stripped by pulling out a locking pin and sliding the butt group off the barrel. Two Thai models were made – corresponding to the Police and Military versions of the Model 6. The military version took a bayonet. Eventually only one of each model was produced.

The Ingram Model 9: This is very similar to the Model 8 but had a sliding

37 The Turner .45 SMG. This was a converted .30 carbine and never passed Aberdeen Proving Ground Tests.

38 The Woodhull .45 SMG. This was based on the Winchester 1905 Cal .32 SL Rifle and contained many Winchester parts. It was rejected when tested at Aberdeen.

39 The Ingram Model 5. Only one prototype was produced and this is believed to be the only existing photograph of it. It was made in 1946 which was not a good time to produce weapons with a vast surplus available.

spring steel butt of the type used in the M3 SMG. It was produced in 1959. Only one prototype was made.

The Ingram Models 10 and 11: In 1969 Ingram went to work for Sionics Inc – a company based in Atlanta, Georgia. They specialised in suppressors and achieved very good results in Viet Nam with their equipment fitted to 7.62mm sniping rifles. In 1970 Mitchell WerBell, the President, decided to enlarge his military equipment activities and formed the Military Armament Corporation at Powder Springs, Georgia, and it is with this company that Ingram worked until very recently.

Ingram produced a SMG which is entirely different from his previous weapons. It is very short, very compact, solidly built and easy to control in spite of its light weight. There are no projections to catch in undergrowth and the gun can be operated equally well by left handed firers. The Model 10 is chambered for 9mm Parabellum or .45 ACP. The model 11 uses the 9mm short (.380 automatic) and so has been made lighter and smaller. Special high velocity ammunition in .380 ACP was loaded by Winchesters with the headstamp 'MAC 380 SMG'. The action of both models is the same, using blow back with a wrap round bolt. This gives the short body length and the control obtainable at full auto. Both models are screw threaded at the muzzle to take the Military Armament Corp suppressor. This does not completely silence the gun but makes it extremely difficult to determine the point of origin. The great advantage of this equipment is that the muzzle velocity is not reduced because the gases enter the suppressor after leaving the barrel and so the bullet velocity is not affected. The suppressor consists of helical channels going forward from the muzzle end and others coming back from the front end. The gases therefore dissipate their energy within the suppressor to reduce the emergent sound to a very consider-able extent.

The cocking handle is located on top of the body and therefore a slot is cut in it to allow the firer to see through his sights. The cocking handle, when rotated through 90deg, locks the bolt in either the forward or rear position. This automatically blocks the sight line and so the firer is fully aware his gun is set to 'safe'. There is also a manual safety slide near to the trigger guard. The Model 10 **43** and Model 11 **43** are similar in appearance and both have the same neat two step retracting butt. Both models are very suitable for Commandos, Airborne troops and in fact also for any soldier who has to carry equipment such as a wireless set. Crews of armoured fighting vehicles who work in confined spaces and need a weapon to provide quick accurate fire whilst outside their vehicle could well find it ideal. Another role in which it would be ideal is that of the Naval or Commando swimmer who can use the weapon to achieve a slight negative buoyancy whilst below the surface. About 10,000 Model 10 and Model 11 guns have been produced so far.

Ingram has carried out further development work on these guns. The Model M10A1 is shown **44** with a canvas covered suppressor. [The Model 10 has a rubber covering.] The entire gun – except the barrel – is made of sheet metal stampings. Even the bolt **45** is made of sheet metal, filled with lead, and rivetted. Both the sheet metal bolt (lead filled) and the standard bolt have the same dimensions. The sheet metal bolt was filled with lead only enough to give it the same weight as the standard bolt. The firing pin too is a sheet metal stamping. The Model M11A1 is similar.

The standard M10 and M11 have been extensively tested in many countries. MAC's very energetic Vice-President, Lt Col Hugh McWhinnie (USAR) has

40 The Ingram Model 6. This was produced by the Police Ordnance Co in 1948 in .45. The picture shown is the first produc-tion model.

41 The Ingram Model 7 in cal. .38 Super – Police Model. (*top*). The Ingram Model 6 in cal 9mm Parabellum – standard Military Stock.

55

42

43

42 Long barrelled Ingram carbine designed after Ingram left the Police Ordnance Co. Only one was ever made.

43 The Ingram Models 10 and 11. The Model 10 (*top*) is in .45 ACP, the Model 10 (*centre*) is 9mm Parabellum and the Model 11 (*bottom*) is 9mm short. All weapons are shown with the M.A.C. suppressor.

44 The Ingram Model 10A1.

45 The bolts from the Ingram Model 10A1 (*top*) and M11A1 are made of sheet metal – lead filled. The firing pin is also a stamping.

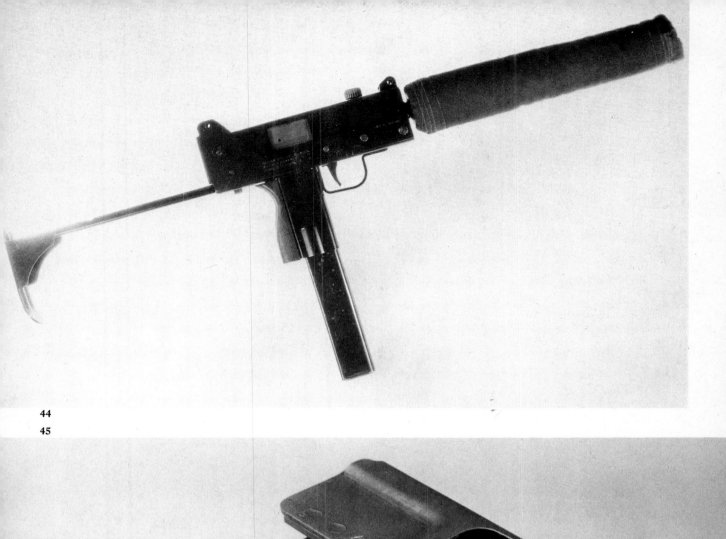

44

45

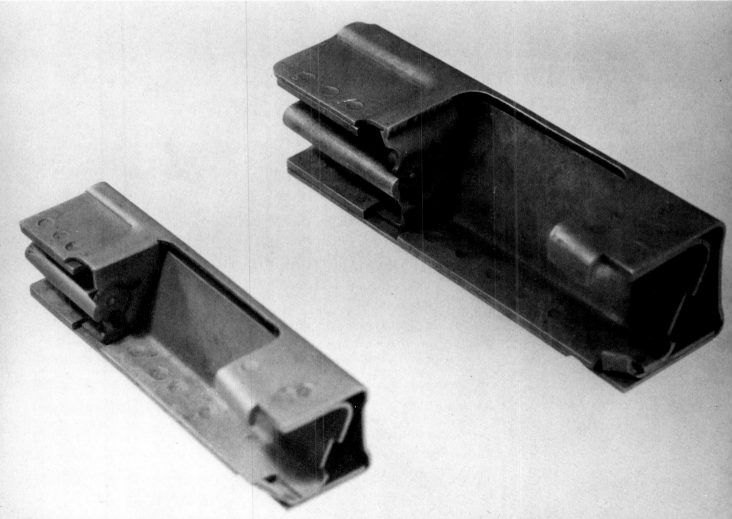

travelled extensively from the Phillipines to England demonstrating the weapons and everywhere they have been received with great interest.

THE COMPACT SMG

The Compact SMG **46** was designed around features of the Ingram Model 6, utilising a trigger mechanism giving single shots when pulled half way back and full automatic when completely retracted. One of the original members of the Police Ordnance Company – see page 53 – Jack Purcell, was responsible for the sponsoring of the design by the Interstate Engineering Corporation of Anaheim, California, in 1954. The Interstate Corporation provided the drawings and three demonstration models were made by local machine shops. Although the US and Canadian Armies and several police forces witnessed the gun firing, no orders were placed and it was never put into production.

The barrel jacket and body were of steel tube and the butt stock could be telescoped in to reduce the overall length. The straight through action demanded a high sight line. The magazine housing and trigger housing were stampings and the trigger guard could be unsprung and laid flat against the pistol grip to facilitate the use of arctic mittens. One feature of the gun was its short length of 24in. [This led to the adoption of the name Compact.] The pistol grip was mounted at the point of balance and it was claimed that the gun could be fired with one hand like a pistol.

THE COOK SMG

This gun was designed by Loren Cook in 1950 **47.** It will be seen that it bore a superficial resemblance to the German Erma EMP44 **158** in its straight through action, tubular butt stock and shoulder piece. The prototype shown had no sights but these obviously must have been high mounted. The short length of the Cook SMG of 23¼in was obtained by having a bull-pup design with the trigger forward of the magazine and the return spring in the shoulder stock tube. The magazine housing which was at the point of balance, was also the hand grip and there was a forward tubular steel grip suspended below the unjacketted barrel.

THE HILL SMG

This gun was designed in 1952 by John L. Hill of Houston, Texas **48**. It is a blow back operated weapon firing 9mm Parabellum ammunition and incorporates a reduced diameter bolt. The revolutionary feature of the gun is the feed system. The plastic magazine is prepacked at the factory and is disposable after use. The magazine lies in the top of the body of the gun and the cartridges face to the right across the weapon. A thin plate holds the magazine from contact with the bolt. When the bolt moves to the rear it extends a spring which rotates a turntable, holding the leading round, through 90deg. The cartridge is thus lined up with the bore and is fed into the chamber by the bolt moving forward. The turret (turntable) then rotates back to its original position and accepts the next round which is impelled forward by the magazine spring. When the bolt is blown back the fired case is ejected downwards through the pistol grip and the turntable is rotated again to position the next round for feeding.

The advantages of this system appear to be several. The ammunition is pre-packed and remains clean since there is no magazine opening in the gun. The

46 The Compact 9mm SMG, Model 55. This weapon was designed by Jack Purcell, who was with the Police Ordnance Co with Ingram, and is internally much like the Ingram Model 6. It was made for easy production.

47 The Cook 9mm SMG. This was a prototype gun with the magazine in the pistol grip and the trigger forward of the magazine.

48 The Hill 9mm SMG. The very unusual feature of this gun is the expendable magazine placed on top of the body and a turntable to align the cartridge ready for feed.

49 The Colt .223 Commando SMG. This is a shortened version of the direct gas action M16A1 rifle, firing from a locked, closed breech.

46

47

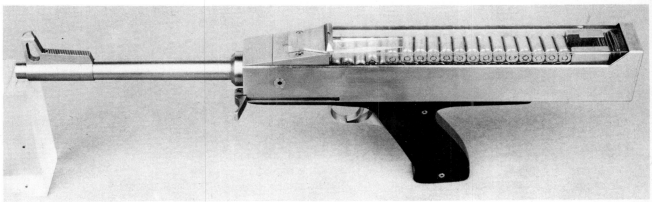

48

49

empty magazine is discarded. There is no side projecting magazine and so the centre of gravity remains unchanged in the vertical plane as the ammunition is expended. The disadvantages of a magazine placed below the gun – ie the spring lifting ammunition against gravity and the likelihood of grounding the magazine in the prone firing position – are overcome.

Against this must be set the complexity of the feed system which has yet to be proved to be 'soldier-proof'.

The weapon is still in the development stage.

THE COLT COMMANDO

The adoption of the M16A1 as the standard US Army rifle introduced a new cartridge – the .223 Remington, based on ideas put forward by Eugene Stoner the gun's designer. The Colt Commando introduced this cartridge into the SMG field. The Commando **49** is a direct action gas operated SMG which for all practical purposes is a shortened version of the M16A1 rifle with a telescoping butt, and having its cocking handle immediately behind the carrying handle and sights. The gas operated SMG is rare and this particular weapon is even more unusual in that there is no piston system but the gas is tapped off near the muzzle and led back through a stainless steel tube into the hollow interior of the bolt carrier. There is no gas regulator. The bolt, with its seven locking lugs, is secured to the barrel extension; the bolt carrier moves back and a cam slot cut in it causes the bolt to rotate and unlock. The combined carrier and bolt then move to the rear together to compress the return spring and start another cycle. The gun can be fired at either single shot or at the full automatic cyclic rate of 750rpm. Due to the low muzzle impulse the 5.56mm M193 ball with a 25 grain charge, can be fired in short bursts with some degree of control. The light, 55 grain, bullet is fired at 2,700ft/s and with a muzzle energy of 905ft.lb, it is an effective close quarter weapon. The gun was used extensively in the Viet Nam campaign by the Green Berets – the US Army's Special Force.

THE AR-18S

This is a shortened SMG version of Armalite's AR-18 rifle using the .223 Remington cartridge. The gun is gas operated using a piston and operating rod to unlock the rotating bolt and drive it rearwards. There is no gas regulator. Both the Ar-18 and 18S are extremely cheap to produce, using sheet steel pressings and automatic screw machine parts and the design specifically requires few close tolerances. With an order of 100,000 guns the AR-18S would cost substantially less than $105. The gun was designed by Arthur Miller **50**.

The gun can be fired either at full automatic or single shot and some remarkably accurate and penetrative shots have been demonstrated at ranges out to 600m which is an extremely long shot for a short barrelled weapon.

THE ERQUIAGA SMG

The MR 64 9mm SMG **51** was the joint work of Juan Erquiaga Azicorbe and Gordon Ingram. It was a typical 9mm SMG of the 'Sten type' utilising simple blow back. The Sten magazine was used. No shoulder stock was fitted. Production at the Erquiaga Arms Co, City of Industry, California exceeded 1,000.

Azicorbe was a Peruvian. He made SMGs for Castro and had to flee to South America.

50 The Armalite .223 AR–18S SMG. The Armalite AR–18 rifle has been shortened to produce a locked bolt, closed breech SMG.

51 The Erquiga MR64 9mm SMG was a Sten type weapon jointly designed by Juan Erquiga Azicorbe, a Peruvian, and Gordon Ingram. About 1,000 were made.

52 The Stoner .223 SMG. This was part of the Stoner 63 system using common parts in a number of weapons extending from the SMG to a medium machine gun.

ERQUIAGA ARMS COMPANY
CITY OF INDUSTRY, CALIFORNIA
U.S.A.

MR-64 SUB-MACHINEGUN
CAL. 9MM PARABELLUM

THE STONER SMG

Eugene Stoner worked for Armalite Inc from 1954 until 1961. He then acted as a consultant for Colt's and in 1963 he produced a complete weapon system known as the Stoner 63 System, marketed by Cadillac Gage Ltd. The idea was to meet the varying tactical requirements of the troops by a variety of weapons all based on a common body, bolt, piston and return spring, and a trigger group, and all firing the .223 Remington cartridge. Thus a SMG, rifle, magazine and belt fed light machine gun, a medium machine gun and a tank machine gun could be built on the common components using a variety of barrels, stocks and feed systems. The idea was not received well commercially and Cadillac Gage in USA and NWM in S'Hertgenbosch, Holland, later concentrated on improving the Stoner 63 rifle and the light machine gun as separate weapons in their own right. Both are excellent guns.

The Stoner SMG was a gas operated gun with a fully locked rotating breech block and a conventional piston system, firing from a closed breech position. The block and piston as well as the body were quite substantial, because in the Stoner 63 system, they had to undergo the stresses imposed on a medium machine gun. Thus the gun **52** was sturdy and reliable but somewhat heavy for a .223 SMG. With the fibre glass butt folded it was quite handy. As far as is known no substantial orders were placed.

THE IMP (Individual Multi Purpose Weapon)

Like several other small calibre, light weight systems, the Imp developed from studies aimed at producing a better survival rifle for aircrew. In this concept the weapon is shortened by eliminating the butt and it is controlled by laying it on top of the right forearm with the left hand resting quite lightly on the rear of the body, steadying it. To ensure that the 30 round magazine, fitted below the gun, clears the forearm, the forward pistol grip can be rotated from the central position through 45deg, either to the right – which ensures the magazine lies on the inside of the right forearm – or to the left for a left handed firer using his left arm. The fact that the gun can be swivelled into three positions means three sets of aperture sights. The gun fires single shots or full auto at 550rpm using a delay device, acting on the hammer pivot, to keep the rate of fire down. The bolt has an 8 lug forward locking system and a bolt carrier with a curved cam slot is driven back by the gas piston to rotate the bolt out of engagement. The Imp is one of few SMGs firing from a closed breech position with a locked bolt and using gas operation **53**. The cartridge selected was a commercial round – the .221 Fireball which has a bullet weighing 52 grains fired at a muzzle velocity of 2,500ft/s. The inventor of this weapon, Mr Dale M. Davis of the United States Air Force Armament Laboratory at Eglin, Florida, has plans to amend the prototype in the light of development experience. The trigger mechanism may be altered to give single shots from a partial pressure and full auto from complete trigger operation and the selector dial, now at the rear of the body, may be replaced by a lever near the trigger. Four prototypes have been made by Colt's Patent Firearms Corp at Hartford but at the time of writing (July 1972) it is too early to say what its eventual future will be. Colt's are now investigating the survival rifle in .223 and .17 calibres. This weapon has now received the official designation 'Rifle calibre .221, GUU-4/P'.

FOOTE SMGs

John P. Foote worked with the Military Armament Corporation, of Powder

62

53 The .221 Imp. The Individual Multi Purpose Weapon uses the firer's arm as a butt and gives good accuracy, firing from a closed breech. It is a gas operated weapon, invented by Mr Dale M. Davis of the USAF Armament Laboratory at Eglin, Florida.

54 The Smith and Wesson 9mm Light Rifle was tested in 1940 and 2,000 were purchased by the Royal Navy. It was never used in action.

55 The Light Rifle was fitted with an alloy butt stock as an experiment at Enfield. The magazine can be seen, the ejection chute lies behind the magazine.

56 The Smith and Wesson 9mm Model 76 SMG. This is a commercial SMG. It is shown here in its silenced version.

57 The Foote MP970 9mm SMG. This is a very simple weapon, easily manufactured with a minimum of machinery. Without the butt it is very compact and measures only 15 inches long.

56

53

54

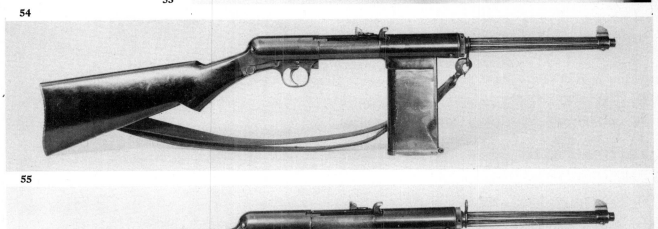

55

57

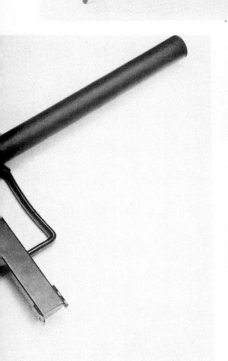

Springs, Georgia, in the final development of a new .223 assault rifle. He has previously produced prototypes of two very interesting SMGs.

The MP 970 SMG **57** is in 9mm Parabellum. The main frame of the weapon is constructed from rectangular welded tubing which has resulted in a simple design, easy to manufacture, and very suitable for construction in under developed countries with a minimum of tooling. The gun is very compact and is often used without a butt. It has been kept to a thickness of only $1\frac{1}{4}$in. It utilises a fixed firing pin with a short bolt design somewhat similar to the Italian Luigi-Franchi **211** and produces full auto only.

The MP 61 SMG **58** is in .45 ACP. Again the designer has concentrated on simplicity, ease of manufacture and a minimum number of parts. The body of the gun is made of seamless tubing. The magazine is that of the M3 'grease gun' and the action is simple blow back using an orthodox (non wrap round) bolt. The gun is 26in overall with an 8in barrel. When the stock is folded its total length is reduced to 15in. The weight is 8.25lb with a 30 round magazine.

ATCHISSON SMGs

Maxwell G. Atchisson also worked with the Military Armament Corporation. He has been involved in a number of projects including the design of a replacement bolt for the M16A1 rifle allowing .22 LR rounds to be fired in training.

His interest in weapons for training was continued in his .22 SMG **59** which takes either a box magazine or an extremely ingenious 70 round drum magazine.

The Atchisson Model 57 9mm SMG **60** is of the conventional blow back type with the bolt, non reciprocating cocking handle and return spring, all built into one integral unit that can be withdrawn for maintenance with a minimum of time and trouble. The gun is extraordinarily light – weighing only 4lb 10oz. It is 24in overall with stock extended, $15\frac{1}{4}$in when folded. The 32 round MP–40 magazine is used.

THE SCAMP

This is the title of Colt's Small Calibre Machine Pistol **61**. It is designed to be carried by those soldiers whose duties do not allow them to carry a rifle or conventional sub-machine gun. The wireless operator, mortar crewman, driver are obvious examples. The Scamp introduces several unique features. It consists of a relatively light barrel and receiver assembly containing all the moving parts of the mechanism. The receiver assembly is contained within a housing, forming the pistol grip and trigger guard, made of glass reinforced high strength plastic. All the metal parts are made of stainless steel alloy. Unlike most SMGs the bolt is locked before firing, using a locking link similar to that of the Browning Automatic Rifle. It is gas operated using an operating rod connected to a gas piston concentric with the barrel – ie wrapped round the barrel – located close to the muzzle. The return spring is also concentric with the barrel and is located between the gas piston and the body (receiver). The gun fires either at single shot or in three round bursts at a cyclic rate of 1,500 rounds a minute. To preserve the essential concept of lightness a special low impulse .22 centre fire cartridge has been developed. This has a bullet weight of 40 grains with a 9 grain charge producing a muzzle velocity of 2,100ft/s and a muzzle energy of 392ft.lb – almost exactly that of the 9mm Parabellum firing a 115 grain bullet at 1250ft/s.

The Scamp is still in the early stages of development but should provide a

useful and technically interesting SMG when it is ready for service.

59

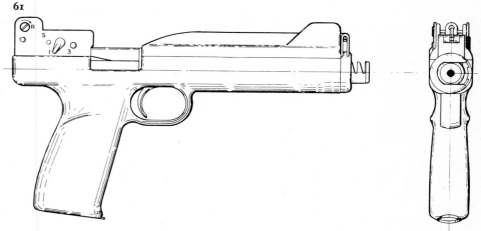

61

58 The Foote MP61 .45 ACP SMG. This is a very neat and simple weapon using the M3 magazine to feed a straight forward blow back action.

59 Maxwell G. Atchisson firing his .22 SMG. This has a 70 round drum and cuts training costs considerably.

60 The Atchisson Model 57 9mm SMG weighs only 4lb 10oz. It is of conventional blow back design.

61 The Scamp. This is Colt's lightweight personal weapon firing from a locked bolt and gas operated. It uses a special .22 centre fire cartridge which is fired either in single shot or in bursts of three for a single trigger operation.

REFERENCES

[1] *The Gun that made the Twenties Roar* by W. J. Helmer.

[2] *The World's Sub-Machine Guns* by Nelson and Lockhaven.

[3] *Sub-Machine Guns 1921 through 1945*, by Davis and Gleason.

[4] Aberdeen Proving Ground Partial Report No 109 dated 28 November 1939.

[5] Aberdeen Proving Ground Partial Report No 141 dated 11 October 1942.

[6] Aberdeen Testing Ground Partial Report No 197 dated 20 May 1942.

[7] Aberdeen Proving Ground Partial Report No 231 dated 24 November 1942.

[8] Obituary notice in the 'American Rifleman' February 1964.

[9] Aberdeen Proving Ground Partial Reports Nos: 134 dated 30 August 1940, 161 dated 28 July 1941, 174 dated 25 November 1941.

[10] Aberdeen Proving Ground Partial Report No 138 dated 23 September 1940.

[11] Aberdeen Proving Ground Partial Report No 176 dated 10 December 1941.

British Sub-Machine Guns

SMGs 1914–39

The first test of a SMG in the United Kingdom took place on 7 October 1915 at the School of Musketry at Hythe when the Villar Perosa **180** was demonstrated by Mr D. Bernachi from Italy. The experimental officer in charge of the trial hardly knew what to make of it and in his report[1] to the Small Arms Committee (SAC) he described it as 'two long barrelled automatic pistols connected together, very suitable for trench work'. The same weapon was tested at the Royal Small Arms Factory (RSAF) Enfield on 18 October 1915 and described as the 'Villar Perosa Machine Gun'. In spite of a favourable report from the trial, GHQ in France said, on 29 January 1916 'it was not proposed to further increase the number of types of weapons now in use by asking for a supply of these guns'.

The Bergmann MP 18.1 **141** was tested on 12 September 1918. The actual weapon was no 214 and was described[2] as 'a German Machine Pistol firing a .35in pistol cartridge'. The SAC recommended that GHQ France be asked if they required a weapon of this type. The reply came 11 months later, 9 months after the war ended, and sums up the British attitude well:[3] 'A really penetrating bullet is necessary to ensure that the enemy's problems in regard to penetration shall remain difficult and to prevent the use of body armour. A heavy high velocity bullet of small calibre is also required to obtain a flat trajectory. It follows therefore that no weapon of the pistol nature can ever replace the rifle as the Infantryman's main arm. Its issue will be limited to those who, for some reason or other, cannot carry a rifle. No 'Pistol gun' resembling this particular German weapon is required therefore in the British Army since it is apparently designed as a substitute for rifles and auto rifles and this violates the principles already stated in this minute.'

The American Thompson SMG **13** was demonstrated at Enfield on 30 June 1921 under the personal direction of the inventor, Brigadier-General John Taliaferro Thompson, and reported on in SAC Minute 407 dated 7 September 1921 which stated: 'The gun is an entirely new type. Its special features lie in the general arrangement and in the method of locking the breech. General Thompson stated that the principle was first thought of owing to an accident which occurred to a naval gun when the breech only opened partially instead of being blown out. The gun functioned correctly horizontally and up or down at an angle of 75deg. The recoil of the gun was found to be 1.44ft.lb. The gun was fired under safety precautions with the locking wedge removed. Two rounds were fired and the condition of the spent case was identical with that of the spent cases fired with the wedge assembled to the gun.' The Committee noted the report but took no further action. The Thompson was demonstrated at the National Rifle Association meeting at Bisley on 11 July 1921. It was described by Major Hardcastle – probably the greatest living authority on Small Arms in Europe, who in his report on the Bisley Meeting of 1921,[4] stated: 'On 11 July 1921 there was a public demonstration of the Thompson sub-machine gun. The firm asked for a marksman to fire the pistol prone with automatic firing of the 100 round magazine at 200yd. Sergeant A. G. Fulton, DCM, assistant foreman at CIA range, volunteered and after a few trial shots by single fire he started automatic fire and hit or nearly hit the 200yd target for the whole magazine. Some hundred people saw him do it. Without the prone position the full automatic firing is very erratic and dangerous.' The firer, of course, was Arthur Fulton who before his death on 26 January 1972 aged 84, shot for Great Britain on 22 occasions and 44 times for England. He captained Great Britain twice. He appeared in the King's/Queen's Final 28 times. He won the King's Prize in 1912, tied in 1914, won again in 1926 and 1935, a record never equalled.

In April 1928 a trial was carried out to test the Cutts' Compensator fitted to the BSA produced model of the Thompson SMG. Mr Norman of the Birmingham company demonstrated the device which the SAC said 'had no appreciable effect'. The improved Villar Perosa 9mm SMG in single barrel form and known in England as the Revelli Automatic Rifle was demonstrated at Enfield on 27 April 1928 by Count Revelli and Colonel Davies but the SAC found nothing to recommend in the weapon **183**.

In 1932 the SAC received details of the Vollmer 'machine gun pistol' made by the German firm of Erma. They noted that there was an increasing interest in this type of weapon on the Continent and suggested that two should be bought for trial.[5] However the General Staff once again positively stated 'a weapon of the machine gun pistol type is NOT required by the Army'.[6]

In December 1934 there was a demonstration at Enfield of the Swiss Solothurn S1-100 **149**. This firm was German owned and gave German manufacturers the chance to design, produce and export an SMG. The Committee purchased one gun, at a cost of £18, for trial and together with a long barrelled version of the same gun and a Bergmann 9mm SMG it was fired at wooden targets at 500m. It was noted that at this range penetration was slightly greater than that of the .380 revolver cartridge at 50m.[7]

On 29th September 1936 the Suomi 9mm SMG Model 1931 **269** was demonstrated. The report said 'This is probably one of the best "gangster" weapons we have seen'. This is the first recorded instance of this term 'gangster' which occurs frequently in subsequent reports. One Suomi was purchased for £31.5.2. [SAC Minute 1697 of 15 September 1937.]

The American Hyde .45in Automatic Carbine **20** was demonstrated on 23 June 1937. It did well and the Committee were particularly impressed with the double magazine consisting of two independent 20 round compartments side by side in one casing which could be slid across the gun.[8] In December of the same year the results of a demonstration of the Spanish Star 7.65 SMG **310** were published.[9] It was considered inferior to the Suomi, Hyde and Solothurn.

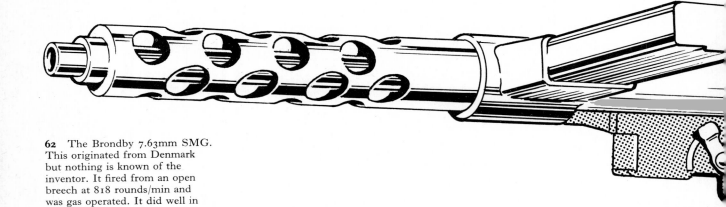

62 The Brondby 7.63mm SMG. This originated from Denmark but nothing is known of the inventor. It fired from an open breech at 818 rounds/min and was gas operated. It did well in trials in March 1938 but nothing was done to develop it.

63 The Biwarip 9mm SMG. After trials in August 1938 this was considered too light for adequate control. The general design was very advanced for its time.

64 The BSA-Kiraly 9mm SMG. Kiraly brought incomplete drawings to BSA who made up this prototype. The magazine did not fold under the gun but the general similarity with the Hungarian M39 **177** is obvious.

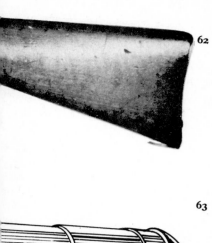

62

63

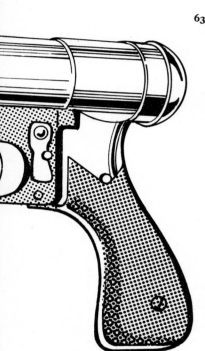

64

The Japanese Nambu **302** with a very long magazine was investigated in 1938. It was considered worth looking at because it weighed only 6.17lb with a magazine holding 50 8mm cartridges. It fired at 500 rounds a minute. Although only 24.4in long, it was 11in deep.

The Brondby series of weapons – LMG, Rifle and SMG were tested on 8 March 1938.[10] They were all gas operated weapons. The SMG had the gas cylinder located above the barrel and fired from an open breech, using a dropping block locking system **62**. The magazine holding 15 7.63mm cartridges was located beneath the gun. The cyclic rate was 818 rounds a minute. After the trial the Committee said 'it shows promise of being an efficient weapon of the gangster type'. Trials were arranged to compare the Suomi 9mm Sako, the Hyde .45 SMG, the Solothurn 9mm SMG, the Schmeisser MP 28 9mm SMG, the Bergmann 9mm SMG and the Brondby 7.63 mm SMG. The Suomi and Bergmann fired 9mm Parabellum and the Solothurn and Schmeisser fired 9mm Mauser. The trial was partly intended to compare the ammunition as well as the weapons but was accorded a low priority and there is no record of it ever taking place.

In August 1938 the Biwarip SMG **63** was examined. This was a remarkably modern looking SMG. It had a perforated barrel casing very much like the modern Sterling SMG and had a left side mounted 30 round magazine. It fired 9mm Parabellum ammunition using the blow back system. The Committee considered it to be too light for accurate control and did not recommend further action.

In October 1938 a later version of the Suomi was tried. This was the type used by the Estonian Army and had a 50 round magazine consisting of two boxes in a common case, mounted side by side, with two platforms and two springs. The dividing wall between the two sections ceased near to the top so that the cartridges from both sections came together to feed into the weapon through a single opening. The Committee liked the gun, particularly the magazine, and asked the Chief Superintendent of Design to consider making a Bren Light Machine Gun magazine on the same lines.[11] In November 1938 the General Staff informed the Director of Artillery[12] that 'the policy as regards the provision of a machine carbine has again been under consideration. It has been decided not to introduce a weapon of this nature into the Army. Work on the design of a machine carbine can therefore be closed down.'

It should be noted that the term 'machine carbine' was used in Britain until 1954 to describe the weapon generally referred to as a sub-machine gun.

In May 1939 Messrs Dinely and Dowding – a firm of importers – drew the attention of the War Office to the SMG designed by Kiraly and manufactured by Danuvia at Budapest.[13] The Ordnance Board – which now carried out the work previously done by the Small Arms Committee – was interested and two versions of the gun, one long barrelled and one short barrelled, were tried. The long barrelled gun used SIG parts from the MKMO SMG **283** including their 20 or 40 round magazines and BSA was licensed to produce this gun. They produced a small pilot batch **64** and claimed that it would cost only £5 to manufacture;[14] the Superintendent of the Royal Small Arms Factory agreed this figure was reasonable. The weapon was Kiraly's early version of what was later to become the Hungarian M39 but differed in some respects to the final service gun. Firstly it had a fixed magazine housing which took 40 9mm Mauser cartridges. This made the weapon somewhat unwieldy and Mr Dinely suggested to Kiraly that the MKMO type pivoting housing should be employed. The two

69

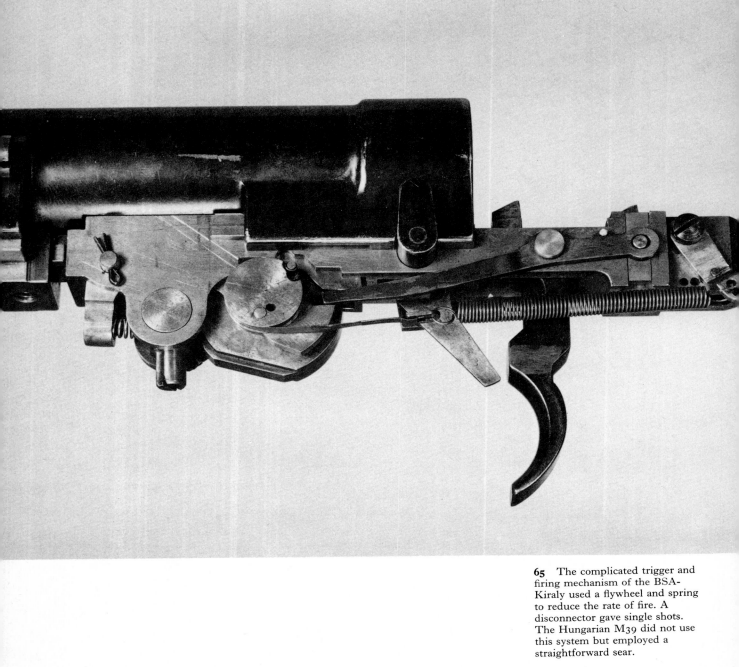

65 The complicated trigger and firing mechanism of the BSA-Kiraly used a flywheel and spring to reduce the rate of fire. A disconnector gave single shots. The Hungarian M39 did not use this system but employed a straightforward sear.

66 The Dinely .32 ACP SMG. This was made up by Mr Mark Dinely using a cut down Ross rifle barrel. It never went beyond the experimental stage. It was blow back operated and with the compensator was easy to control.

66

part block and lever of the Hungarian M39 **177**, described in some detail on page 136, was used with an additional spring lock which kept the two parts of the block apart until it was released by a projection in the body as the round was chambered. Lastly the trigger and firing mechanism was astonishingly complicated for a SMG. There was a rate of fire reducer consisting of a flywheel around which was wound a steel tape connected to a spring **65**. As the bolt reached the rear it struck a flat on the flywheel and caused the flywheel to rotate. The spring was extended and after a delay it returned the flywheel to its original position and the flat forced down a lever to release the bolt and let it go forward. There was a disconnector superimposed for single shot fire and a safety, locking the sear. No soldier could ever have coped with this watchmaker's dream. Kiraly agreed that if BSA manufactured the gun a simple orthodox sear would be adequate.

The weapon behaved quite well and no reason can be found for the complete lack of interest that followed, especially considering BSA were ready to produce it so cheaply.

The next SMG to be tested was the German Erma **151**. It is interesting to note that at this date (4 May 1939) the Director of Artillery wrote to the Secretary of the Ordnance Board saying 'although we are not particularly interested in this type of weapon, in view of the fact that 1,000 of this make could be procured at very short notice, we would like it investigated'.[15] Britain went to war with Germany on 2 September 1939.

WARTIME SMGs

Ordnance Board Proceeding 3,947 dated 22 December 1939 revealed a complete reversal of attitude towards the SMG. 'A request has been received from the British Expeditionary Force in France for an immediate supply of machine carbine or gangster guns'. Seven samples of guns were sent to France for trial. These were not listed but since they came from specimens already tested in the UK they were presumably the Thompson, Solothurn, Hyde and Suomi. The Ordnance Board did not wish to introduce a new cartridge and said any weapon taken into service must fire the .303, .38in or the 7.92mm round then being manufactured for the BESA machine gun. Instructions were given for trials of the Melville Johnson, the Czech ZH 29 and the YSC self loading rifles modified to give automatic fire. The stripped Lewis, Soley converted Lewis, and the Bren were also fired from the hip. The OB minute concluded by saying that the Thompson SMG in .380 calibre would be the best selection for immediate supply and BSA were contacted about the Thompson.

In January 1940 the Ordnance Board tested the 'Schmeisser' SMG in 7.63mm calibre[16] **142**. There is no doubt that the weapon used was the Schmeisser MP 28 which was described as 'similar to the Bergmann'. The gun was thought to be satisfactory in functioning and gave accurate shooting. In July 1940 the Board tested the German MP 38[17] **153**. This gun was described by the Board as the 'German parachutists' machine carbine' and subsequently as 'the Schmeisser' – although it was manufactured in fact by Erma. These two trials were of considerable importance in determining British policy later. The question of the SMG for the Army in 1940 was now given urgent consideration.[18] The OB said 'The Thompson is the most costly of its class costing £50 a gun and involves dollar exchange. Also it is the most complicated and elaborate as regards manufacture. It shoots high unless fitted with a special muzzle compensator which costs $20. With all these disadvantages it is only a pistol ammunition

weapon with corresponding limitations of range and accuracy'. The Board assumed that the Suomi, which it considered to be the best of the SMGs, was unavailable and the Thompson, the least desirable on technical grounds, was likely to be available. The decision was made to adopt the .45in Thompson to meet immediate needs.

THE LANCHESTER SMG

After the British Expeditionary Force had been evacuated from Dunkirk in June 1940, the situation in Britain was desperate. German parachutists were expected to attempt to seize and hold airfields for the landing of gliders and Junkers JU 52 troop carriers. The Air Staff decided to adopt a British made copy of the 'Schmeisser' for the defence of aerodromes.[19]

On 12 August 1940 a meeting was held at the Ministry of Supply 'to co-ordinate the requirements of the three services for the home production of a machine carbine'.[20] The Army requirement was satisfied by USA production of the .45 Thompson SMG. The Admiralty had ordered 2,000 Smith and Wesson self loading carbines **54** and now asked for 10,000 British copies of the Schmeisser MP 28 **142**. The Air Ministry had tested the German Parachutists' SMG – the MP 38 **153** – with a collapsible butt and wanted 10,000 copies of this gun. Eventually it was agreed that 50,000 Schmeissers of the MP 28 pattern would be produced, starting in 4 months' time – which was the minimum required for the production of prototypes, testing and tooling up for production. These 50,000 were to be divided equally between the Navy and the RAF. The question of ammunition for these guns also was discussed. ICI ammunition was not satisfactory[21] and it was decided that the first deliveries of the 110 million rounds ordered from the USA would be tested in the 'British Schmeisser'.

On the 8 November 1940 the first two pilot models of the British Schmeisser, made by Sterling Armament Co, were tested. The sights were altered slightly and the rifling was relieved at the leed to make the weapons less sensitive to variation in ammunition dimensions.[22]

On 13 November 1940 these two pilot guns PG1 and PG2 were tested again.[22] Unfortunately the modification made to PG1 resulted in a failure to fire using Winchester flat nose ammunition and unsatisfactory functioning with ICI ammunition. PG2 functioned satisfactorily with 9mm Parabellum ammunition made by Winchester (both flat nose and round nose), ICI, Bergmann, Beretta, and German issue 1936. The general performance of PG2 was considered to compare favourably with the German MP 38 Parachutists' model.

On 28 November 1940 the first limited endurance trial of the British Schmeisser was carried out using PG4[23] **68**. Present at the trial was Mr Lanchester of the Sterling Armament Co and also Major R. V. Shepherd of the Design Department. The gun passed proof and functioned well. There were 26 stoppages in 5,204 rounds fired and nearly all of these were ammunition defects. The gun passed accuracy tests, sand and mud tests, penetration tests and functioned satisfactorily with 7 types of ammunition. It would not fire any 9mm Beretta ammunition. This had a cartridge case with a mean increase of 0.004 over the ICI case and 0.002 over the Winchester. The British Schmeisser was eventually named the 'Lanchester' after its designer George Herbert Lanchester who was employed by the Sterling Armament Co at Dagenham, and all production was given to the Navy.

The Lanchester Mk I **68** was a typical piece of Naval equipment. It was large, heavy, sturdy, solidly made and even had the magazine housing made of

67 Lanchester 9mm prototype. Pilot Gun 3. No sights were used on this gun during its test firings. Note the form of the bayonet lug and position of selector lever in front of trigger guard.

68 Lanchester 9mm prototype PG4. The first endurance trial was fired with this gun. There were 26 ammunition stoppages in 5,204 rounds fired. Note different front sight and bayonet lug. The Mk 1 gun was unchanged from this prototype.

brass. It looked what it was – a copy of the Schmeisser MP 28 II. It differed in slight detail. The change lever giving selective fire was located in front of the trigger guard instead of above it; the catch used to strip the gun, located on top of the rear of the body, was larger and more prominent.

A Mk I* was produced in 1941. This fired only at full automatic and new guns had no selector lever. Some Mk I guns were modified to Mk I* at Base Workshops. The Mk I* also had a simplified rear sight enclosed within protectors **69**. In 1942 the trigger mechanism which had given trouble was redesigned.

LANCHESTER PROTOTYPES

Model 1: After adoption of the Lanchester Mk I and whilst the Sten was being developed, George Lanchester worked at Sterling Armament Co to produce a lighter, all metal SMG. His first model **71** consisted of a Lanchester body with a modified trigger mechanism held to the body by screws. Since the Lanchester cocking slot provided a rear safety position to hold the bolt when retracted, the fire selector lever had only two positions giving 'auto' and 'single shot'. Note in the photograph the location of this selector in the front of the trigger housing. The magazine housing was welded to the body. The bolt was from the Lanchester with the long one piece extracter of that gun and a separate firing pin. The cocking handle was on the right with a curved hook for the firer to grip. There was a cylindrical foregrip made of Tufnel. In short with the comparatively minor differences mentioned (chiefly in the selector lever) it was a Mark I Lanchester lightened and adapted. Although there was no butt stock there were drilled and tapped holes at the rear of the body for one to be fitted.

Model 2: This gun **72** had a different body which was clearly new. The cocking slot was on the left. This continued straight back to the end cap with no safety slot. The bolt was new. It was shorter than the Lanchester bolt by one inch and was a lot lighter. It had a small multi-piece extractor consisting of a claw and spring. It had a separate firing pin around which fitted the return spring, bearing on a collar at the front. The cocking handle was a milled knob integral with the bolt. The trigger housing was welded to the body. The selector lever had *three* positions. Its location was changed to below the housing. The forward grip was of wood, shaped for the firer's fingers. The pistol grip was of Tufnel. There was a single, curved, tube behind the body for a shoulder stock.

Although these models functioned well enough they had no advantages to offer over the Sten and were relegated to the store room at Sterling's where they remained until 1972.

THE STEN GUN

Whilst the Lanchester was still being developed, the Design Department announced[24] in January 1941 that a greatly simplified model had been designed and prototypes produced. These were demonstrated at Enfield on 10 January 1941 and 21 January 1941 and tried at the School of Musketry at Hythe. The gun had immediate and obvious advantages in terms of size, weight and ease of manufacture.

A prototype was given a limited endurance trial of 5,000 rounds.[25] It passed all the required tests of functioning both normally and under adverse conditions of mud and sand. Its firing rate of 520rpm was satisfactory and its penetration acceptable. The sights needed improvement and the bent of the breech block was too soft and blurred rapidly, but the consensus of opinion was very much in its favour. Thus was born the STEN. The name came from the initials of

74

69 Lanchester Mk I*. Note selector lever is not in front of trigger guard but has been removed to give full auto fire only; sights are simplified.

70 Lanchester Mk I modified to give full auto fire only. Many guns were modified locally but not marked 'Mk I*'.

Major R. V. *S*hepherd who was in charge of the Small Arms Group and H. J. *T*urpin the designer, and the first two letters of *En*field. Major Shepherd had retired from the Army in the mid 30s and was a Director of BSA. When war came he went back to the Army and subsequently became a Colonel.

The Mk I Sten **73** incorporated a wooden forestock and a tubular wooden front handgrip that swivelled down when required. It had a bent tubular skeleton stock and a long half cone flash hider. The bolt was a simple cylinder with a fixed firing pin and the weapon used the blow back system. The Mk I* which appeared at the end of 1941 was the first of many attempts to simplify production. The flash eliminator was removed, together with the wooden fore end and tubular grip **74**. Considerably more than 100,000 Mk I and Mk I* guns were made.

The Mk II Gun **75** simplified production even further. Whereas the Mk I had a six groove fixed barrel, the Mk II had a detachable 2 groove barrel. Later 6 groove barrels were used but Mk II barrels were not interchangeable with those of the Mk I gun. There was no wood in the Mk II Sten. In most production models the butt was a single tube with a welded-on cross bar for the shoulder piece, although there were some double tube skeleton stocks. The magazine housing could be rotated through 90deg to close up the ejection slot against sand and dust. The perforated barrel nut could be used as a forward grip. Eventually over 2,000,000 Mk II Stens were produced. On 7–25 August 1941 a trial was held at Pendine[26] of the Mk I and Mk II Stens. Both guns in themselves functioned well but here, right at the very beginning, was revealed the great weakness of the Sten which persisted throughout the War.

The magazine was a stamped sheet metal box with a single position feed. The lips of the magazine deformed readily and a life of 300–400 rounds could rarely be exceeded. The lip angle was critical and any departure from 8deg caused the bolt to ram the nose of the round against the barrel face thus pushing the bullet back into the cartridge case and stopping the firing. Any grit, dirt or sand that entered the magazine could not find a passage through the rounds and the friction soon stopped feed. This trial also revealed that a cartridge with the wall thickness at its maximum permitted dimension at the mouth would not enter the 0.380 chamber. The fixed firing pin caused cap initiation with the case unsupported and resulted in a blowout in the feed way. The low chamber dimension was at once increased to 0.3835in and to prevent cap blow back, the ammunition design was altered to secure the cap by ringing or stabbing.

The Mk II Sten was first used by British and Canadian troops in the abortive raid on Dieppe on 19 August 1942.

In the quest for simplicity the Mk III Sten **86** was produced in 1943 by Lines Bros – the toy manufacturers. The body of the gun was a formed sheet metal tube, rivetted, and a long weld was made along the top. A finger guard was introduced to prevent a firer putting his finger in the ejection opening. The barrel was not removable and only projected about an inch from the barrel casing. The butt stock was similar to that of the Mk II. The gun was manufactured both in UK and in Canada at Long Branch Arsenal.

The Mk IV Sten was developed from the Mk II in 1943 for Airborne Troops and was made shorter, more compact and with a folding stock. There were two variations which were referred to in correspondence of the time as Mk IVA and Mk IVB. The Mk IVA **89** had a wooden pistol grip at the rear of the body and a very large trigger guard intended for use with arctic mittens. The steel shoulder butt could be rotated to the forward position to produce an overall

71 Lanchester Prototype 9mm Model 1. This was produced shortly after production started on the Lanchester Mk 1. This has a Lanchester Mk 1 body, modified screwed on trigger mechanism, and selector lever gives auto and single shot. Safety comes from the cocking slot.

72 Lanchester Prototype 9mm Model 2. This followed the previous prototype and had a new body, with cocking on the left. A three position selector was fitted as there was no safety recess in the cocking slot. A new bolt was fitted.

73 Mk 1 Sten. This is recognised by flash hider, wooden fore grip and wooden stock.

71
72

73

length of 27½in compared to the Mk I length of 35¼ and the 30in of the Mk II and III.

The Mk IVB **90** had its wooden pistol grip further forward towards the centre of gravity to allow firing with one hand. It had a different trigger mechanism, enclosed in a smaller, neater, housing and the trigger itself was crescent shaped with a conventional trigger guard. There was a support from the rear of the body which came down and then forward to connect up with the pistol grip. The collapsed length was 24½in. In both models the barrel was only 3.85in long and had a long flash hider. The Mk IV Sten did not fare very well in trials and also was considered to be uncomfortable to fire. It was never adopted.

The Mk V Sten **93** came into service in 1944. It had a wooden butt and a wooden pistol grip. On early models there was also a wooden forward pistol grip **92**. The front sight came complete from the No 4 rifle. To accommodate the pistol grip the trigger housing, of the same shape as that on the Mk II –was moved forward 1¼in. This required a modification to the bolt to provide a cutaway to clear the disconnector at automatic fire since the entire bolt came back over the sear and disconnecter. This model of the Sten was extremely well built and is considered to be one of the best SMGs in service in any country during World War II. Unfortunately the magazine was never up to the standard of the gun and was the major cause of stoppages. This gun was used extensively in Europe after D Day and its successful employment by Airborne Forces was a major reason for the cessation of work on the Mk IV.

A requirement for a silenced weapon to deal with sentries, advance guards or outposts was expressed as early as 1940 when Commandos operating from Britain found such a gun to be essential to the success of their raids. Early efforts to meet this need were concentrated on the Thompson .45 SMG with which the Commandos were initially armed and an effective muffler was devised **18**; it was never taken into large scale use. When the Sten gun came into service a silenced version of the Mk II, known as the Mk IIS, was developed. The barrel, which was drilled, was surrounded by a jacket which extended well forward of the muzzle. A series of metal cups was placed around the barrel and forward of it, so that as the gases emerged through the sidewall of the barrel their energy was dissipated and the bullet, after it left the muzzle, went through these metal cups and finally penetrated a rubber sealing plug, at the end of the jacket, which prevented gas following it out. The jacket surrounding the cups was itself perforated and surrounded by an outer jacket. The hot gases heated the outer casing and so the outside of the silencer was wrapped in a canvas sleeve to protect the firer's hands. The bolt weighed only a pound and the last two coils of the return spring were cut off to reduce its strength. Troops were instructed to fire single shot and only use automatic fire in extreme emergency. The sole noise discernible 50ft in front of the muzzle was the clatter of the bolt. The silencer also reduced muzzle flash at night. The effect of the silencer was to cut down the effective range of the weapon to about 100m.

The Mk IIS was used by Commandos, Special Forces, SOE and was parachuted in large numbers to Resistance Fighters all over Europe. It was extremely efficient and reliable and was probably used in greater numbers than any other silenced weapon during World War II **85**.

After the Mk V Sten was adopted a silenced version called the Mk VI was made **96**. The principles employed were exactly the same as those used in the Mk IIS.

78

74 Sten 9mm Mk 1*. This came at the end of 1941 and reduced weight and production time by removing the flash hider, fore grip and wooden stock.

75 Sten 9mm Mk II. Note length of projecting barrel. Magazine housing rotated to seal ejection slot against dirt. 2,000,000 were produced.

76 Experimental Sten Mk II with wooden butt.

74
75

76

77 Experimental Sten Mk II
with 5in barrel – known as T42.
Note design of the folding butt.
There was an experimental single
column magazine and some
variation in the trigger mechanism.

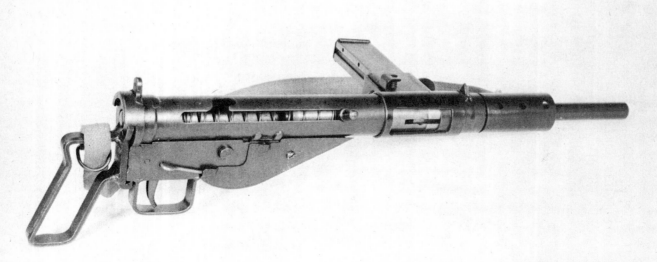

78 Experimental Sten Mk II
with short rear grip. Originally
intended for firing by parachutists
whilst descending.

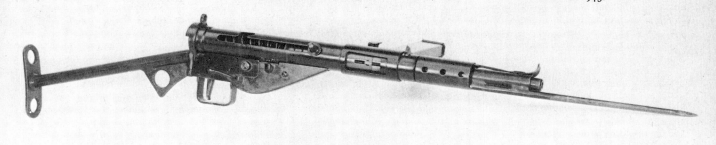

79 Sten Mk II with bayonet. Made at Longbranch Arsenal, Canada in 1943.

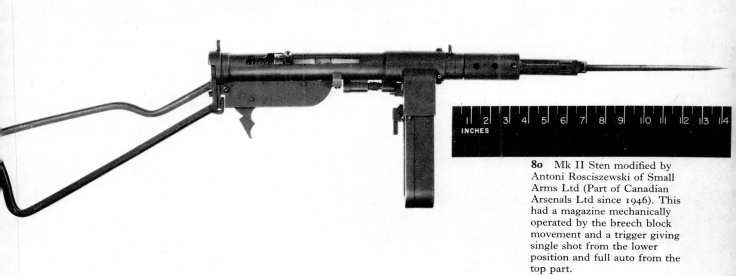

80 Mk II Sten modified by Antoni Rosciszewski of Small Arms Ltd (Part of Canadian Arsenals Ltd since 1946). This had a magazine mechanically operated by the breech block movement and a trigger giving single shot from the lower position and full auto from the top part.

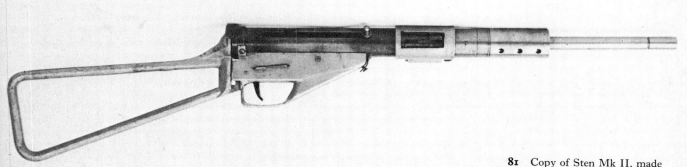

81 Copy of Sten Mk II, made by Danish Resistance in 1944.

82 Early silenced version of the Mk II Sten.

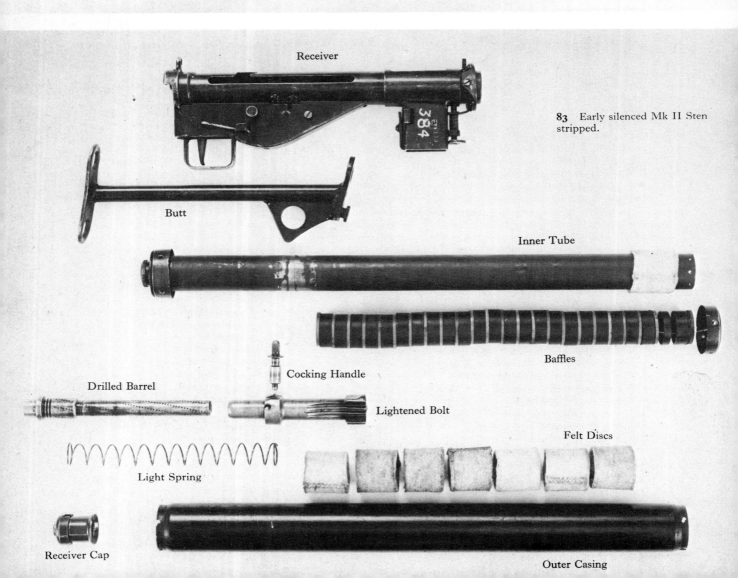

Receiver

83 Early silenced Mk II Sten stripped.

Butt

Inner Tube

Baffles

Cocking Handle

Drilled Barrel

Lightened Bolt

Felt Discs

Light Spring

Receiver Cap

Outer Casing

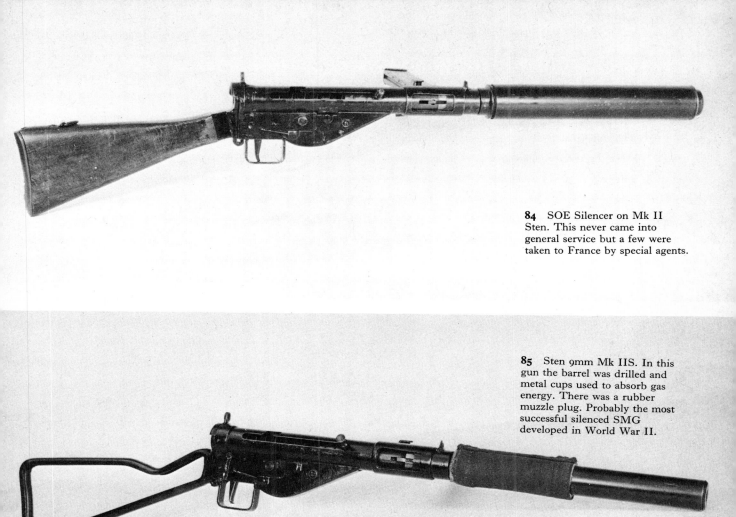

84 SOE Silencer on Mk II
Sten. This never came into
general service but a few were
taken to France by special agents.

85 Sten 9mm Mk IIS. In this
gun the barrel was drilled and
metal cups used to absorb gas
energy. There was a rubber
muzzle plug. Probably the most
successful silenced SMG
developed in World War II.

86 Sten 9mm Mk III. This was
produced to cut production time.
The body was a formed metal
sheet welded at the top. The
barrel was fixed.

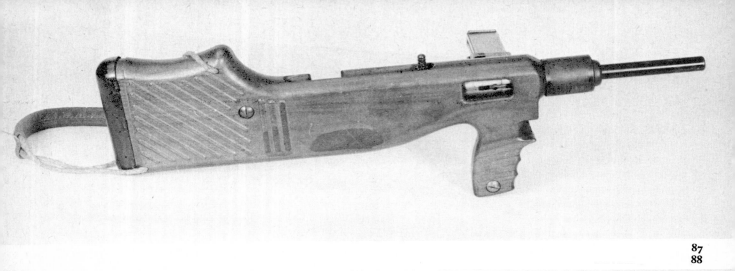

The Sten guns were specifically designed for ease of production. The firm of BSA set up production in September 1941 at Tysely and in that month produced 200 Mk I guns. In October 1,000 were produced, 2,000 in November, and by July 1942, when 100,000 had been produced, production was 20,000 a month. The final figure for BSA was 404,383 Stens with 350,000 spare barrels. The Royal Ordnance Factory at Fazackerly produced Stens at a rate rising to 20,000 a month during 1943–44. The Long Branch Arsenal in Canada also produced large numbers.[27] The British Army, Commonwealth Forces, the Resistance Forces in Europe, all used the Sten gun. When America evaluated the current series of SMGs on entering the war the Sten gun came out on top.

This simplicity and ease of production made the Sten an ideal weapon for production by underground groups who had only the minimum of simple tools available and examples made in Denmark **81**, France, Holland, Israel, and Cyprus, have been recorded. The Germans made several varieties of the Sten both for the last ditch defence of their country and for guerrillas operating behind the Russian lines **159–161**.

The cost of a Mk I, II and II made in UK was £3 and a Mk V cost £5. The Canadian Mk II cost $13.55.[27]

OTHER BRITISH SMGs IN WORLD WAR II
The early and continued success of the Sten gun and the immense numbers produced made the adoption of any other SMG unlikely. Its technical performance would have had to be far superior to that of the Sten to make worthwhile the dislocation of production that must inevitably have resulted from the adoption of a different weapon. All the same, throughout the war years, SMGs

87 Sten 9mm Mk III wooden covered. This was an experimental straight through action Sten. Just why it was wood covered is totally unknown.

88 Sten 9mm Mk III. Experimental version with wooden butt, bayonet, and sling swivels.

89 Sten 9mm Mk IV Model A. Note position of pistol grip and shape of trigger housing.

were constantly being offered to the Ordnance Board for trial. Many came as very roughly prepared sketches and a description, others were supplied in prototype form. All had faults and all needed trials, development, further trials, and still more development. All of this put the Proof and Experimental Establishments – particularly Pendine – under extreme pressure and took up resources to improve weapons already accepted. Amongst the wartime trials were those of weapons which had great potential but could not be adopted. The accounts of these trials are contained in Ordnance Board Proceedings. They make very interesting reading but in themselves they do not give a complete picture because the decisions to reject or modify came from the General Staff, the War Office Directorates, the Ordnance Factories, the Design Department and the Master General of the Ordnance. The decisions taken by these bodies who had to take the broadest view were expressed in OB Proceedings only as 'No further action.'

On 17 June 1940 the Ordnance Board discussed[28] a proposal by Major R. Brown (late W Yorkshire Regt) who was a well-known writer and enthusiast. He saw the urgent need for a sub-machine gun and designed an adaptor to fit the No 1 and No 4 Lee-Enfield rifles. There is little detail available but it seems clear that it was a system similar in principle to the US Pedersen device in 1917 which was a replacement for the bolt of the Springfield rifle allowing semi-auto fire using a .30 calibre pistol cartridge. Unlike the Pedersen device 7 which could be inserted into the rifle when the tactical situation demanded, this was a modification which permitted only automatic fire of a small calibre round from the rifle. The Board considered that the time spent on developing such a project would be better spent on a new weapon and dismissed Brown's suggestion together with a machine gun he submitted at the same time.

90

91

90 Sten 9mm Mk IV Model B. Note shape of trigger and straight sides to forward located pistol grip.

91 Sten 9mm Mk IVA – silenced. Only one was ever made

92 Sten 9mm Mk V. Early version with forward pistol grip.

92

93 Sten 9mm Mk V – production model. This was considered to be one of the best SMGs in service in any army in World War II.

93

94

94 Sten 9mm Mk V – early version issued in 1944 to parachutists, without the butt stock.

95

95 Sten 9mm Mk V with blank firing attachment.

96 Sten 9mm Mk VI. The silencer was much the same as that used on the Mk IIS.

96

THE HOWARD FRANCIS SL CARBINE

The drawings of this SLC were made by a member of the Naval Ordnance Inspection Staff at Simonstown in West Africa and forwarded to London for appraisal together with a specimen gun. The Ordnance Board were asked to test the gun[56] and did so. The Howard Francis SLC **97** was adapted from the No 1 Mk III .303in rifle barrel and body. The chamber was plugged and then drilled to take the Mauser 7.63mm pistol cartridge. The barrel was shortened but the bore and rifling were left unchanged. The rifle bolt was removed and replaced by a heavy breech block operating on the blow back principle and incorporating a moving spring loaded firing pin. The rifle magazine was replaced by a 12 round magazine.

The weapon was not intended for automatic fire. The firing pin was held up as the bolt went forward and came to rest. Operation of the trigger released the firing pin in much the same way as in the No 1 rifle.

When the gun was tested the bolt would not feed the top round from the magazine. In the end several groups were fired, loading singly by hand. The grouping was good but the MPI was consistently high and left. The weapon weighed 8lb 1½oz, was 32in long with a 12¾in barrel weighing 1lb 7oz. After this trial it was not considered worthwhile to develop the arm.

THE VESELEY 9mm SMG

In August 1940 the Chief Inspector of Small Arms received two sets of drawings of a machine carbine, the V40, designed by Mr Joseph Veseley, a Czech, who came from Brno to help BSA tool up for manufacture of the BESA MMG. The V40 contained certain novel features, particularly the magazine feed, and on 27 December 1940 the drawings were passed to the Ordnance Board who stated[29] that the British Schmeisser had been accepted in principle by the Navy and Air Force and a much simplified machine carbine had been produced by the Chief Superintendents of Design which might be acceptable to all three services and any introduction of another gun would mean delay. No further action was recommended.

However Mr Veseley was not discouraged and went ahead and produced at his own expense, a prototype SMG. This was submitted to the Chief Inspector of Small Arms in October 1942 and the Ordnance Board arranged trials at RSAF Enfield on Thursday 12 November 1942. This SMG was known as the V42 **98**. It was a blow back operated 9mm weapon, wooden stocked with a perforated metal fore-end. The magazine was in two compartments, one in front of the other, each containing 30 rounds. Whilst there was ammunition in the front compartment its magazine follower held down that in the rear part and the bolt passed over the rear compartment and fed from the front half. After 30 rounds, feed was from the rear compartment. The weapon functioned well at Enfield but did fail the mud test. The Chief Inspector of Small Arms in his report dated 18 November 1942[30] described it as a 'quality' weapon whose functioning under normal conditions was faultless. He considered its automatic rate to be too high and that this should be reduced by increasing the mass of the breech block. The Navy expressed interest and trials were arranged at HMS *Excellent*. These found the action violent. The British Graphitised Metals Co Ltd who sponsored the project sent the drawings to the Design Department. Nothing occurred until June 1944. The gun was now controlled by VAP Holdings Ltd who produced six guns (made by BSA) (three infantry and three parachutist) of a modified design intended to meet the new General Staff

97 The Howard Francis SL 7.63mm Carbine. This was made from the No 1 Mk III .303 rifle barrel and body with the bolt replaced by a breech block. The 12 round feed system was poor and the weapon was rejected.

98 The Veseley V42 9mm SMG. The chief feature of interest was the magazine which had two 30 round compartments one in front of the other. Feed was initially from the front box and the rear rounds were held down. When the front magazine was empty, feed was from the rear half. The V43 was the same gun with a collapsible butt.

99 The Mitchell 9mm SMG came from New Zealand. It was very light and the effective barrel length was only 2½ inches. The trigger gave a lot of trouble.

Specification published in OB Proc Q 1798 dated 7 January 1944. This called for a gun weighing not more than 6lb, cyclic rate not more than 500rpm, holding 30–60 rounds of 9mm ammunition. The Board purchased four guns at £12 each with 12 60 round magazines; the Infantry gun was the V42 and the collapsible butt type was the V43. Veseley also offered light barrels as an alternative to the normal barrel. The V42 gun weighed 6lb 10oz and fired at 700 rounds a minute. It carried an attached bayonet. Trials were carried out at Pendine and also at Valcartier in Canada. The results were not unsatisfactory but the Board decided to take no further action in October 1945[31] as other designs looked more promising.

THE MITCHELL 9mm SMG

On 10 December 1943 the Director of Artillery (SA) asked the Secretary of the Ordnance Board to organise trials of the 9mm Mitchell SMG **99** which had just been received as a pilot model, from New Zealand.[32] The trial was passed to the Inspection Department who carried out an investigation. The weapon was described[33] as all metal except for the pistol grip, having a weight without

magazine of 4lb 12oz. The Sten magazine was used located below the gun. The total barrel length was 5in, made up of 2½in of rifled bore and 2½in of unrifled tube acting as a flash eliminator. In spite of this latter feature there was a great deal of flash which got worse as the barrel got hotter. The rate of fire was 700rpm. It fired well from the hip but was too light and short to be controlled from the shoulder. The trigger mechanism gave trouble, the butt came detached from the body and it was considered that there was great danger of the firer's left hand slipping over the muzzle when firing. It was decided it should be returned for re-design.

THE PATCHETT 9mm SMG

On 25 September 1942 Mr George William Patchett demonstrated his new carbine to representatives from the OB, Artillery 3 and the Chief Inspector of Small Arms. The carbine was described[34] as 'essentially, with the exception of the trigger mechanism, a Lanchester without butt or sights'. It was intended for firing from the hip only. The trigger mechanism was self contained and incorporated a change lever giving single, automatic, or safety when operated by the thumb of the right hand. When set at 'safe' the breech block was locked in the forward position. The trigger mechanism was situated half way along the casing near the point of balance. At the trial it functioned well. Mr Patchett was advised to fit a butt and sights and the weapon was later re-submitted so modified. Meanwhile the trigger mechanism produced adverse comment in that if the safety catch was forced home to 'safe' with the bolt partly cocked, the entire mechanism was broken. It was decided to subject the Patchett to a trial with other SMGs.[35]

On 24 February 1943 the Director of Artillery (SA) informed the Secretary of the Ordnance Board that a new SMG called the *Welgun* had been designed and that it should be tried against the Sten Mk IV.[36] The Welgun was designed by Mr Norman of BSA at the request of Special Operations Executive (SOE) who were then located at Welwyn. From this the gun was called the Welgun. It should be noted that this was not the same Mr Norman of BSA who has been mentioned earlier as working on the BSA–Thompson SMG in 1928 and who had long since retired. The Welgun **100** had some noteworthy features. It was cocked by gripping grooves machined around the bolt. The bolt had two forward extensions lying alongside the barrel. These were connected by a removable ring which formed the forward housing of the return spring which was wrapped round the barrel. When the bolt was cocked, the spring was compressed. The firing pin was spring retracted and operated by a pivotted rocking plunger which protruded, above the firing pin, from the bolt face. When the bolt closed the plunger was pushed in and the firing pin was pivotted forward. The gun normally fired single shots but a long rocking lever on the left of the body gave automatic fire when it was depressed by the firer's right thumb. The safety catch was a similar long lever, on the right, with a hook at the end. When the bolt was closed the hook came up behind it to prevent retraction. When the bolt was cocked the hook came up into a recess at the front to hold it back. The steel butt frame could be folded over.

The trials of the Patchett, Sten Mk IV and the Welgun took place in late February 1943 at the Proof and Experimental Establishment at Pendine. Lanchester Mk I and Sten Mk II were used as controls and the SMGs tested were: 9mm Welgun Nos, 3, 5, and 6. 9mm Sten Mk IV Nos, 2, 3 and 5 and one unnumbered Patchett SMG. Firing was conducted at 50, 150 and 250yd. The

100 The Welgun 9mm SMG is shown with the folding butt over the barrel. The bolt is forward. It was cocked using the milled surface as a hand grip. Note the hook on the right of the body that locked the bolt either forward or back.

101 The Andrews 9mm SMG. This was a private venture produced for the Australian inventor by BSA. The two return spring guide rods passed through the breech block and were located one above the chamber and one below. The spare mag was the butt stock.

order of merit for accuracy was Welgun, Sten Mk IV, Patchett. The Welgun failed the cold temperature firings but the Board considered the Welgun was best under clean, temperate conditions with the Sten Mk IV best for service use under unfavourable conditions. The Patchett required further development.[37] It was inaccurate over 150yd and performed very badly in the mud test.

From 22 September 1943 to 5 October 1943 a trial was conducted[38] at Pendine of: 9mm Welgun No 1 (modified), 9mm Patchett No 001 **120**, 9mm Special Sten Mk IV (modified) (this was a type B Mk IV), 9mm Austen Mk II, No 2 **239**, 9mm Owen Mk II No 43 **235**, and a 9mm *Andrews* **101**. Of these guns the Owen and Austen were Australian and are described elsewhere. The Sten was a modified Mk IV, the first of the type known as type B. The Andrews was a private project and had some interesting and unusual features. It was designed by an Australian and made up by BSA. The spare magazine formed the shoulder stock, the pistol grip was a plain metal tube and the two return springs were mounted on rods which came through the bolt and emerged from the barrel casing above and below the barrel. The body was very short and fat and firers complained about the casing being too thick for a comfortable hold. The magazine type butt also was liable to come loose. The feed was from the right side. The trial gave an order of priority of (1) Owen Mk II (2) Patchett, Austen Mk II, Andrews (3) Sten Mk IV (4) Welgun.

In November 1943 the same weapons were fired again at Bisley by the Small Arms School who also simultaneously tested another weapon, the Veseley VAP SMG Type V43. Of the seven weapons the SAS reckoned the V43 was the best.

After these trials it was announced that production limitations precluded any requirements for this type of weapon but the Patchett seemed the most nearly to meet a future requirement.

On 7 January 1944[39] the General Staff at the War Office issued a set of new specifications for weapons including that for the SMG. In brief it stipulated a 9mm weapon, weight of 6lb, capable of putting 5 shots fired singly into a square 12in × 12in at 100yds. The cyclic rate of fire should not exceed 500rpm. No bayonet was required. The Patchett SMG went some way towards meeting the requirement, and a new bolt, with helical ribs to improve its performance in mud and dust, was tested at Pendine.[40] As a result of the success of this trial 20 Patchett SMGs were ordered from Sterling Armament Co on 12 January 1944 and delivered in April 1944. These were tested by a brief functioning and accuracy firing conducted by the Inspectorate and then they were sent to Pendine for endurance firings. At the same time the Board announced that a special order of 100 Patchett SMGs had been produced for troop trials. The Pendine Trials were carried out in September 1944 and the Ordnance Board reported 'with regard to accuracy, functioning, endurance and penetration, it is considered the Patchett machine carbine is suitable for Service'.[41] The Board also announced that they had tested the Patchett SMG with the No 5 rifle bayonet. They further said they had tried the Patchett machine carbinette which was a telescoping body version of the Patchett SMG intended principally for parachutists **119**.

POST 1945 SMGs

In April 1945 a new General Staff Specification for the post-war SMG was published.[42] The gun was to weigh not more than 6lb without its magazine, fire at not more than 600rpm, a bayonet of the type used on the No 5 rifle was preferred and the magazine capacity was to be 30–60 rounds.

102 The 9mm carbine was designed by Mr Norman of BSA for SOE. He also designed the Welgun **100** and the similarity of cocking and fire selection is clear. The forward grip was for the *left* hand which passed under the barrel and was protected by a guard in a manner similar to Dinely's SMG **66**.

103 The Norm carbine is here shown cocked, stock detached and forward grip folded.

THE 9MM MCEM (Military Carbine Experimental Models)

At this time in addition to the Design Department's own British designers headed by Turpin, there were teams of Polish designers working on SMGs and Belgium designers, headed by Lalou and Saive, working on rifles. It appears from the recollections of people working at Enfield at the time that there was considerable rivalry between the British and Polish designers.

The EM1: 105 This was designed by Turpin. It was a neat design with a machined steel body having a cocking handle on the right with a slide attached which sealed off the cocking slot. The trigger mechanism was that of the Sten. When the bolt reached the end of its rearward travel, the back end entered a spring cylinder which it forced open. This gripped the bolt until overcome by the force of the return spring and this served to reduce the rate of fire. It had single shot and full auto from a push-through selector just above and forward of the trigger. The wooden butt could be slid off to the rear leaving a shaped metal grip. There was no fitting for a bayonet. The safety catch was well forward on the left of the trigger housing. The gun had a double side-by-side magazine which was slid through the weapon to use the second compartment. Work was stopped on the EM1 when it was found at Enfield that the EM3 performed better.

The EM2: 107 This was the work of Lt Podsenkowski of the Polish section. It was only 14¼in long, with the pistol grip, into which the magazine was inserted, well forward at the point of balance so that it could be fired with one hand like an automatic pistol. The holster had a skeleton steel frame, canvas covered, and could be connected to the rear of the body by a simple 90deg turn, to become a shoulder stock. The bolt was of advanced design. It was half a hollow cylinder 8¾in long, with the fixed firing pin 1½in from the rear end. When the gun fired, 7in of the 8½in barrel were inside the bolt. Behind the bolt

104 The 9mm ROF Sten was produced at ROF Fazackerley in 1944. It had two return spring rods, one on each side of the bolt, and a buffer between them. It cocked by pulling a ring at the rear and a wire cable pulled back a cocking slide. Note the flash eliminator. There were no funds to develop the gun.

was another semi-cylinder carrying a fixed rod ejector which protruded through the bolt face as the bolt came back. The return spring lay behind the rear of the bolt. There was a slot above the muzzle and the firer inserted one finger to cock the gun in the manner of the USA M3A1 SMG. The magazine had to be taken out of the gun before the end cap could be removed for stripping. The capacity of this magazine was only 18 rounds and the rate of fire was 1000 rounds a minute.

The EM3: 106 This was Turpin's improved version of the EM1. It had a single, curved magazine holding 20 rounds. The friction-type reducer was eliminated. The safety catch was moved to the rear of the right of the trigger housing. There was a fitting for the No 9 bayonet.

The EM6: 108 Lt Podsenkowski, assisted by Lt Ichnatowicz, produced this improved version of the EM2. The barrel and the jacket were lengthened by one inch, it was cocked from a finger entry further back, a bayonet lug was fitted. The weight of the bolt was increased over the EM2 by 2oz to 1lb 12oz and the return spring was made both heavier and $1\frac{1}{2}$in longer. This brought the rate of fire down to 600–700rpm. Little is known of the EM4 and EM5. The EM4 may well have been designed by Kulikowski and was tested in a silenced version against the Mk IIS Sten.[43] The EM5 could have been the Sparc but the records remaining are very few and the memories of people who worked in this field thirty years ago are no longer as clear as they were. The Design Department requested trials of the EM2, EM3 and EM6.[44] The EM2 was rejected in September 1946 because its rate of fire of 1,000rpm was excessive. The EM3 was considered 'to show considerable promise as being a both efficient and reliable carbine, worthy of more intensive trials'.[45] The EM6 was then withdrawn so that effort could be devoted to the EM3.[45] The EM3 was tested in June 1947 with the BSA SMG. It weighed $7\frac{1}{2}$lb and was thus $1\frac{1}{2}$lb

105 The 9mm MCEM1 was designed by Turpin. It had a double, side by side, 40 round magazine. The cocking slot was covered by a slide attached to the handle. The wooden butt could be withdrawn leaving the shaped metal grip for the right hand. There was no provision for a bayonet.

106

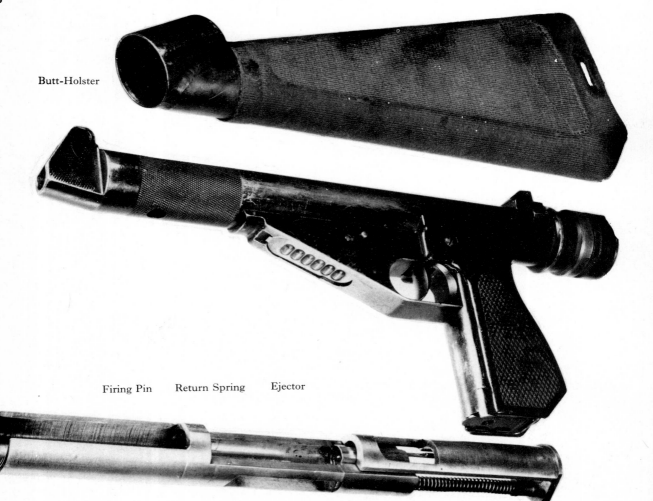

107

Butt-Holster

Firing Pin   Return Spring   Ejector

over the specified weight. It was designed to be manufactured by traditional Enfield machining methods and would have been expensive. It fired at 650rpm – whereas the specification stipulated not more than 600rpm – and its magazine held only 20 rounds instead of the 30–60 demanded. In its final trials on 8–16 September 1947 it got so hot that the handguard could not be gripped and further development was terminated.

THE VIPER 9MM SMG

In 1945 tests were conducted of a new SMG, designed to meet the recent GS Specifications, called the Viper **109**. It was designed by Mr Hutton-Williams who was then working under the Director of Ordnance Factories. Mr Hutton-Williams retained his interest in Small Arms and in 1964 he became Superintendent of the Royal Small Arms Factory at Enfield.

Three models of the Viper were made. The first had a 4.7in barrel, was $21\frac{1}{4}$in overall and weighed 4lb 13 oz; the second had a 6in barrel, was $22\frac{1}{2}$in overall and weighed 4lb 14oz; the third had a 7.5in barrel, was 24in overall and weighed 5lb. Only the 4.7 and 7.5in barrels underwent trial. The gun was designed to be fired using only one hand. It took a standard German 32 round magazine from the MP38 and MP40. It had an unusual arrangement for the fire selector system. The change lever on the left hand side of the body was pressed in to the full extent for automatic fire. For single shot it was pushed halfway in. In addition to this conventional system it was also possible to fire single shots when the gun was set to 'automatic' by depressing the trigger for only half its full travel. The breech block had a fixed firing pin and a rubber buffer was fitted to the rear; a dead weight plunger located inside the stock was designed to reduce the rate of fire to 692rpm.

The Ordnance Board pointed out that the rate of fire was excessive. They also implied that the full permitted weight of 6lb should be used. No further action was recommended.[46]

THE 'NORM' 9mm CARBINE

102 This design was instigated by SOE and was the detailed work of Mr Norman of BSA who was also the designer of the Welgun. There are certain similarities in the two guns. The 'Norm' breech block had milled cocking slots which enabled the firer to grip the breech block and pull it back over a telescoping steel tube containing the return spring. The firing pin was spring retracted and positively controlled by a projecting plunger on the bolt face. The bolt face was recessed to take the cartridge. The entire bolt was open to the elements and had no protection against the entry of dirt. The change lever was again a large pivoting lever which had to be held down by the right thumb to produce automatic fire. The holding arrangements of the Norm were very unusual. The forward grip for the left hand projected horizontally sideways to the *right* of the muzzle and so the firer's left hand passed under the barrel and a special heat guard was provided to rest on his left forearm. The foregrip could be folded flat along the barrel and the butt stock tube was easily detached **103**. There is no record of the gun being used in action.

THE ROFSTEN 9mm SMG

This was designed and prototypes produced at the Royal Ordnance Factory (ROF) Fazackerly **104**. It was well made and extremely well finished. The barrel was of original design with a large flash hider at the muzzle, taking a No 5

106 The 9mm MCEM3 was developed at the same time as the EM1 above. Turpin used a single 20 round box magazine and changed the buffer arrangement. It became excessively hot when firing.

107 The 9mm MCEM2. Lt Podsenkowski was the designer. The bolt was of unusual design and was a very early 'wrap round' type. The holster formed a butt.

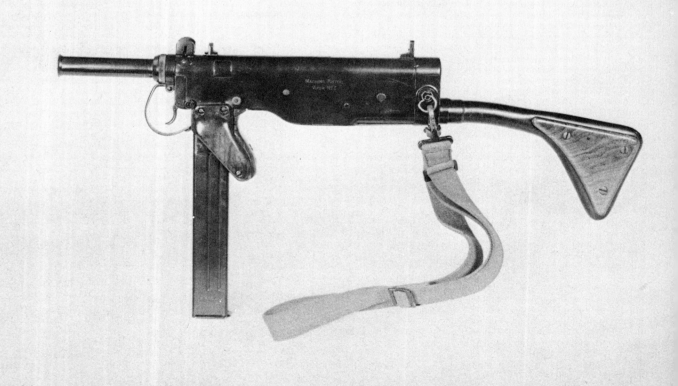

110

111

108   The 9mm MCEM6. Lt
Podsenkowski was assisted by
Lt Ichnatowicz in producing this
improved version. It fired at a
more controllable rate than the
EM2 but work on this design was
stopped in favour of the EM3.

109   The Viper 9mm SMG was
designed by Mr Hutton-Williams.
Note that the artic trigger guard
is forward of the pistol grip –
magazine housing. Only three
models of this gun were made, all
with different barrel lengths.

110   The 9mm Jurek SMG Mk 2.
This was tested for the OB in
October 1946. It fired at 350rpm
and was very accurate. In June
1962 the gun was sold to a Mr
Becket who in turn sold it to the
Services Armament Corp in
USA.

111   The 9mm Jurek with the
holster attached as a butt.

bayonet, and a flange around the chamber to position the barrel against the
front of the body. A large milled barrel nut was screwthreaded to the body. The
bolt was cylindrical, of uniform diameter, and a groove was cut on each side to
house return spring rods. These return spring rods were located, at the forward
end, in recesses on each side of the chamber. They were connected at the rear
end by a flat steel strip and between them was a heavy spring buffer. The gun
was cocked by pulling on a steel ring behind the breech, which pulled out a wire
cable attached to a slide under the body which engaged in a recess in the bottom
of the bolt. Above the trigger was a fire selector lever. When set to 'safe' a
plunger came up under the bolt and fitted into one of two holes corresponding
to the forward and cocked positions. This gun, of original and unusual design,
was never tried in competition with other SMGs available in 1945 because no
funds were available to the Ordnance Factory for development work.

99

112

113

114

THE RUSSEL S. ROBINSON 9mm SR MODEL 11

This **243** was designed by Mr. Russel Robinson, an Australian, at the Shepherd Robinson Arms Development Company in Woolwich, Nr Sydney, Australia. Prototypes were built at the Commonwealth Small Arms Factory, Lithgow, New South Wales, and sent to Enfield in 1944. This weapon is described in detail in the Chapter on Australian guns and is mentioned here because the inventor's theory of producing balanced forces was of great interest. The Board recommended further work on the gun but the SR Model 16 which eventually resulted was never adopted. The SR Model 11 weighed 2.9lb empty, fired at 600rpm and had a barrel which rotated to balance the applied bullet torque.

THE JUREK 9mm SMG

Dr Jurek was a graduate of Cracow University in Poland. His training was basically that of a chemical engineer but he was extremely interested in metallurgical problems and acquired a considerable knowledge of mechanical engineering. He was a national rifle shot and retained his interest – and ability – for many years after he left Poland. When war with Germany seemed inevitable, Dr Jurek became Research Manager at the Wytworni Ammunition Factory at Warsaw. When the Germans and Russians occupied Poland, Jurek fled to Rumania, then France and finally to Britain. The Polish troops were nearly all stationed in Scotland. After posting to the 14th Polish Lancers and the 2nd Polish Tk Regt he became Workshop Officer of 16 Polish Armoured Brigade Workshops. In 1942 he was asked to design a weapon which did not have the safety problems of the Sten. He made a SL carbine which had a good performance. This gun was blow back operated with an effective range of 150yd. 17,000 rounds were fired through the barrel which was taken originally from a Sten gun. Later it was developed to fire full automatic but had a rate of fire of over 1,000rpm. The gun had no fixed butt. It was carried in a steel holster, canvas covered, which could be attached to the rear of the body to form a butt. It had a 20 round magazine. In 1945 Jurek was posted to Germany. Here he designed his second SMG. This was produced quite quickly and tested. In October 1946 Colonel Shepherd sent for Jurek who reported to him at Cheshunt to demonstrate his gun. It was tested and performed well[47] **110**. It has certain interesting features. It was of the blow back type but had a heavy 4oz, spring loaded hammer which assisted in the delay. The hammer could not fall onto the spring retracted firing pin until the breech block was fully closed and the weak hammer spring, housed in the pistol grip, produced a delay at single shot which allowed the vibration caused by bolt closure to die away before firing occurred. This system produced accurate single shot fire and also a slow rate of fire at full automatic of 350rpm. Safety could be applied with the hammer either forward or cocked. In the firing trials it was particularly successful when fired as a pistol, using only one hand. Weighing only 5lb 7¼oz it showed great promise but the Board whilst agreeing the Jurek SMG could be developed to meet the GS specification, considered that other SMGs under development had reached such a stage as to make it not worthwhile. Jurek planned to provide an alternative rate of fire device for the SMG. The hammer, as provided, was to be changed and two hammers substituted. The inner hammer alone would fire the round when the high rate of fire of 800rpm was required. Another hammer fitting around the light hammer would be held back at the high rate of fire and play no part. When the low rate of 350rpm was selected the two hammers would be locked together and the increased mass would slow down the rate of rearward

112 'Type A'. The Jurek SMG Mk 1 after Becket added a butt before selling to the USA. A Sten mag has been fitted in lieu of the original.

113 'Type B'. The Jurek SMG Mk 2 after similar treatment.

114 The BSA 9mm SMG is shown in the position immediately after cocking. The handgrip would then be withdrawn again. This was a very early version with the straight magazine and unable to take a bayonet.

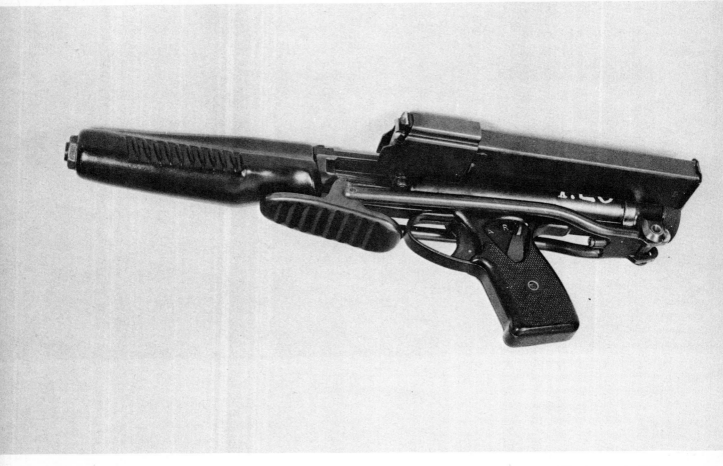

The same early BSA 9mm
SMG with magazine and butt
folded. Its overall length was then
18.9 inches.

travel of the bolt; the weak spring would cause a long time lag after breech
closure, before firing, and so the rate would be low.

When I spoke to Dr Jurek in April 1972, he made it clear that he did not
consider the Ordnance Board would ever have passed one of his designs. After
the War ended he came back to England and worked for Webley & Scott where
he played an important part in their pistol development. He also continued his
shooting and fired for England. His last appearance was in the 3 position match
team in 1957.

When Jurek came back to England he brought his two SMGs with him.
Because he had no licence for a fully automatic weapon he removed the trip
levers from both guns and sold them as SL weapons to a Mr Becket in
Birmingham. Becket fitted Sten magazines and made butts for the weapons.
When I spoke to him in April 1972, he remembered selling the two guns to the
Services Armament Corporation in USA. These two guns are shown in the
'World's Sub-Machine Guns' as Experimental Models Types A and B **112** and
113. Dr Jurek confirmed they were his work – except for the butts – but would
not agree that he used the No 4 rifle barrel for his second gun. Both, he insists,
were made from Sten barrels. Becket however says the Model B used a No 4
rifle barrel cut down. Jurek gave the drawings of his gun to a Mr Stevenson of
Birmingham, Alabama, who is now probably the only judge of the barrel's
origin. The official report describes it as a modified Mk V Sten barrel.[47]

116 Later BSA SMG with curved magazine and cylindrical grooved cocking handle.

THE BSA 9mm SMG

On 12 April 1945 a demonstration of the new 9mm SMG **114** developed by Birmingham Small Arms Co Ltd was given at Enfield.[48] It was of conventional blow back operation but cocked by pushing the foregrip forward. The magazine housing could be swung rearwards to clear a stoppage. All openings were closed when the breech block was forward. Four weapons Nos, 4, 6, 7 and 9 were subsequently tested at Enfield. Each fired some 950 rounds and functioned satisfactorily. Further trials – carried out between 1 and 30 October 1945 – were exhaustive. The Board considered that the gun, although slightly overweight, showed great promise.

There was a lull until June 1947 when trials were arranged[49] against the MCEM3. The comments on the MCEM3 have already been noted (page 95). The BSA at 6⅛lb was overweight but fired at 530rpm which gave greater control than the 650rpm MCEM3. Messrs BSA meanwhile had made some alterations and offered a curved magazine holding 30 rounds, a folding butt and two alternative methods of cocking. The Board arranged another trial of the BSA against the MCEM3 and also included the Australian Experimental model No 1 **241**.[50] This was a further development of the Kokoda **240** (qv), designed by Major S. E. M. Hall.[51] The trial took place at Pendine on 8–16 September 1947. The guns used were: Sten Mk V – 2 weapons as control. MCEM3 – No 2. Patchett Mk 2 – No 006. Australian EM1 – No 2. BSA ¬ modified.

117 Final version of BSA SMG, able to take a bayonet. This was called the BSA Machine Carbine Mk III and prototype No 3 is illustrated.

118 No 1 of the 5 Experimental Patchett 9mm SMGs tested. It will be seen that this gun was produced before the helical grooves were put on the bolt to clear sand, mud etc. Note muzzle cap and straight magazine. No sight protectors.

119 The Patchett 9mm Carbinette or Machine Pistol. The rear part of the body slid forward and the entire body shortened for airborne use. The bayonet was spring loaded and flew into position when the catch was released.

120 Patchett Machine Carbine 9mm Mk 1. This is gun No 001. Note no sight protectors. Barrel does not protrude.

121 Patchett MC 9mm Mk 1. This gun No 62, introduced a different muzzle, new shape and location for cocking slot, new ejection slot, different sights, different pistol grip.

122

123
124

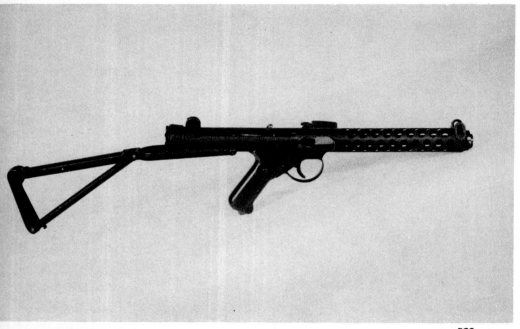

122 The Patchett Pioneer Mk 1.
This was a 9mm commercial
version of the Mk 1 with a
different butt stock, and trigger.
It is shown here with a blank
firing attachment.

123 Patchett MC 9mm Mk 2.
This is gun No 001. Note that
the straight magazine was used
on this gun.

124 Patchett 9mm MC Experimental. This is No 251 of a
batch produced for evaluation.
Note the magazine. This gun
became the L2A1.

125 SMG 9mm L2A2. This is
the same gun as the Sterling
Mk 3. Note the butt stock. The
top plate is a modified version of
that first used on the Pioneer. A
new blank firing attachment is
shown.

126 SMG 9mm L2A3. This is
the same gun as the Sterling
Mk 4. Note trigger and folding
stock and compare with the
Pioneer 122.

None of the guns was ready for production. The MCEM3 got very hot; the Patchett trigger gave trouble; the Australian EM1 suffered fractures of the welds in the trigger housing; the BSA (modified) needed a lot of development.

A further trial[52] of Patchett, BSA and MCEM3 gave the BSA the best report and it was considered fit for troop trials. An order was placed for 100 guns but the cost of tooling proved so high that this was reduced to an order for 6. These 6 were tried[53] and returned to BSA for re-design of the trigger mechanism.

The GS specification for the SMG was now changed and made a bayonet mandatory. Due to the cocking sleeve passing forward over the barrel when the gun was cocked, the BSA in its current form could not take a bayonet and had to be modified. A further trial was carried out in 1951 of the new BSA with a bayonet and the Patchett Mk 1 and Mk 2 guns. The BSA exhibited trigger faults, stiff cocking and some fractures due to poor cocking sleeve design. It also needed a special tool to strip it.

In May 1951 further trials of BSA, Patchett and Australian MCEM1 and the Madsen Model 50 **281** were carried out. These were very comprehensive and the report showed the BSA cocking was still stiff and it did not function in sand. The Board considered that even if modified it would not be better than the Patchett. The Patchett functioned well, the Madsen was very good but its magazine would not cope with sand or mud. The Australian MCEM fractured badly and there was a total failure to eject. A last trial was arranged in 1952, chiefly to satisfy the BSA Company who felt that the change of the specification halfway through the testing programme had prejudiced their chances. The

127 This is a SMG 9mm L2A3 modified and stamped L2A4. It was never adopted.

Madsen had a new magazine and was better than the BSA which was then rejected.

THE PATCHETT 9mm SMG

The Patchett SMG was first tested in 1942. It was developed steadily and improved in reliability by the addition of the new ribbed bolt in 1944. The Mk 2 gun (No 006) was tried against the BSA, the MCEM3, the Australian MCEM1. For this trial in September 1947 it was modified from the earlier version by having a fixed striker in place of a separate firing pin. To make up the weight in the block a secondary recoil spring was fitted which pushed up the rate of fire to slightly over 600rpm. The main fault was in the trigger mechanism. The sear was in contact with the trigger and when firing single shots, the blow of the breech block bent against the sear was transmitted to the trigger and the firer's finger was badly bruised.

The trigger mechanism was quickly re-designed and the weapon was tried again against the BSA and MCEM3. On this trial the rate of fire went up to well over 600rpm and the BSA was favoured.

In May 1951 the trials were repeated with the Madsen, BSA and Australian MCEM2 **242**. This time the Patchett was clearly the best gun. The secondary return spring had been taken out and a slightly stiffer main spring substituted. The separate firing pin was restored. The net effect was to reduce the rate of fire. The sand and mud tests were passed and in the 'stripping in the field' test it gained marks by requiring no tools.

128 SMG 9mm L2A3 fitted with the Singlepoint Sight which was evaluated both in the UK and at the Jungle Warfare School at Kota Tingi in Malaya.

After this test the Ordnance Board recommended the Patchett for adoption by the British Army[54] if the new British 7mm rifle, the EM2, could not serve in the SMG role. If the EM2 was acceptable they considered the Madsen should be adopted by non-tooth arms ie Line of Communication troops. In the event, the EM2 was never taken into service, the FN based L2A1 SL rifle could not carry out the SMG role and the Patchett was adopted.

The Patchett was approved for service as the SMG L1A1 on 18 September 1953. It was manufactured by the Sterling Armament Co, and is generally referred to as the 'Sterling' in British service.

There has been a lot of controversy about the correct nomenclature for the SMG since it came into service. In the Army Estimates 1953–54 the Secretary of State for War said 'The Patchett machine carbine has been designed and is undergoing wide scale troop trials. This is intended as a replacement for the Sten and has so far passed all its trials extremely well'. In the Army Estimates 1954–55 Antony Head, Secretary of State for War, said 'The new sub-machine gun known as the Patchett has been adopted as a replacement for the Sten gun'. Yet in spite of this the name 'Sterling' has been widely used. The problem was settled, at least in part, by the use of the official designation 'SMG L2A1'. The L2A1 was approved for production on 18 September 1953 and declared obsolescent on 12 April 1955. The L2A2 which differed only in minor detail was approved for production on 12 April 1955 and declared obsolescent on 10 May 1955 (one month later). The SMG L2A3 was approved for production on 10 May 1955 and is still current. It is the basis of the Canadian SMG the C1 130.[55]

In 1956 work started on a silenced version of the L2A3. A prototype of a modification to the L2A3 produced by the Design and Development Department RSAF Enfield, is shown at 132. Another L2A3 was modified to a design produced by Saben and Harts in 1958. This is shown at 133.

Patchett put up drawings for a mechanical silencer with a flap over the muzzle which closed when the bullet passed 134. A very limited number of prototypes were produced and tested at the Inspectorate of Armaments at Woolwich. These performed well but after subsequent OB tests it was decided to use a conventional design similar to that used on the Sten Mk IIS and Mk VI but retaining the full barrel length. The Tool Room of the Sterling Armament Co made up the weapons for test and it was decided a little later to adopt this as the L34A1 136. It was approved for production on 20 January 1967. The Patchett/Sterling Mk 5 Silenced SMG is to the same design.

The table shows the production of Patchett's SMG.

Patchett Mk I	Approx 110 manufactured in 1944. They were used by 6 Airborne Division at Normandy and by 1st Airborne Division at Arnhem.
Patchett Mk II	Manufactured 1944 to April 1954.
L2A1 (Sterling Mk 3)	First manufactured October 1953. Last manufactured February 1955.
L2A2 (Sterling Mk 3)	First manufactured February 1955. Last manufactured March 1956.
L2A3 (Sterling Mk 4)	First manufactured June 1956. In current production as the Sterling Mk 4.
L34A1 (Patchett/ Sterling Mk 5 (Silenced))	First preproduction manufacture May 1966.

129 Experimental Canadian C1 9mm SMG based on the L2A3.

130 The Canadian C1 9mm SMG made at Longbranch. Blank firing attachment is shown.

131 Experimental Canadian C2.

132 Prototype L2A3 Silencer produced by the Design and Development Department RSAF Enfield 1956.

133 Silenced SMG 9mm L2A3. Designed by Saben and Harts in 1958. Made by the Enfield Tool Room.

129

130

131

132

133

The total production for Her Majesty's Government at the ROF Fazackerly and elsewhere was:

SMG 163,475.

Magazines 1,723,623 incl 227,262 by Rolls Razor and 309,800 by Mettoy.

Manufacture of the Patchett and SMG L2A2 and L2A3 by Sterling for the Ministry of Defence totalled approximately 22,000. The weapons were numbered as follows:

US 55A 1 to 2909
US 56A 1 to 2772
US 57A 2773 to 8592
US 58A 8593 to 14250
US 59A 15001 to 16000

(The first group of two figures denotes the year of manufacture.)

In addition to the above there were approximately 3,000 Patchett and pre-production weapons manufactured.

Sterling prefer not to disclose the total number of the various marks of their guns that have been made but say that it is 'far into the six figure mark'.

The Ministry of Defence used Patchett's Patents in the guns made at Fazackerly. They refused to pay for the use of these and in 1955 Patchett felt compelled to issue a writ against the Crown through the Ministry of Defence.

134 Drawing of mechanical silencer produced by Patchett. A flap controlled by a linkage from the breech closed the muzzle after the bullet passed.

135 Prototype L34A1 – modified L2A2 by Patchett in 1964.

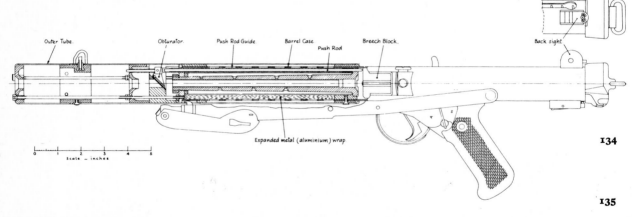

Outer Tube.   Obturator.   Push Rod Guide   Barrel Case.   Push Rod   Breech Block.   Back sight.

Expanded metal (aluminium) wrap

Scale – inches

134

135

The Ministry tried to use the Official Secrets Act to prevent disclosure of the numbers involved but these eventually came to light and are quoted above. Patchett won his case after a long struggle and in June 1966 he was awarded £116,975. The Sterling Arms Co are still selling the Sterling Mk 4 abroad. In 1970 their Chief Designer, Frank Waters, introduced the prototype of an improved version which would be much cheaper to produce. The present Mk 4 consists of a tube – bought from Accles and Pollock, already perforated with cooling holes – on to which are silver brazed the various attachments such as the magazine housing, the ejection slot lips, finger guard etc. Waters' model was made of pressings. It had a neat folding butt and incorporated a grip safety, very similar to that of the Steyr MPi69 **176**.

There was only the one prototype which is shown at **138**. An effort was made to design a Sterling Mk 4 for sale as a police weapon in the USA. To meet USA legal requirements a 16in barrel was required. A preliminary model was made by welding three standard barrels together. This is shown at **139** and the final result is shown at **140**. The actual rifled portion only extends for about 9in and the remainder is opened out to produce a 7in flash hider. The gun was not very accurate and sales were very limited.

In 1972 the Sterling Arms Co was purchased by Paul Escaré Engineering Ltd. The new Chairman, Mr John Edmiston, appears to have every determination to produce a number of firearms to be sold in Sterling's traditional overseas markets and to this end is evaluating a number of weapons.

136 SMG 9mm L34A1. This is identical to the commercial Patchett/Sterling Mk 5.

136

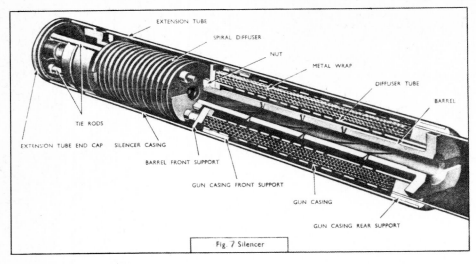

EXTENSION TUBE
SPIRAL DIFFUSER
NUT
METAL WRAP
DIFFUSER TUBE
BARREL
TIE RODS
EXTENSION TUBE END CAP   SILENCER CASING
BARREL FRONT SUPPORT
GUN CASING FRONT SUPPORT
GUN CASING
GUN CASING REAR SUPPORT

Fig. 7 Silencer

137

138

137 Sectioned view of the L34A1.

138 Prototype SMG produced by the Chief Designer of Sterling Armament Co, Frank Waters, in 1970. It utilizes stampings and would be cheaper to produce than the current Sterling Mk 4.

139 Prototype police model destined for sale in USA. It has three standard barrels welded together.

140 Sterling 9mm Police Model for USA. Only 9 inches of the 16 inch barrel were rifled. It was not accurate and did not sell well.

REFERENCES

1 SAC Minute (S) 103 dated 15 September 1916.
2 SAC Minute 133 dated 18 September 1918.
3 SAC Minute 214 dated 27 August 1919.
4 SAC Minute 415 dated 26 October 1921.
5 SAC Minute 1240 dated 26 October 1932.
6 SAC Minute 1282 dated 16 February 1933.
7 SAC Minute 1576 dated 8 April 1936.
8 SAC Minute 1680 dated 21 July 1937.
9 SAC Minute 1725 dated 15 December 1937.
10 SAC Minute 345 dated 2 June 1938.
11 Ordnance Board Memo 1682 dated 25 October 1938.
12 Memo 2034 dated 29 November 1938.
13 OB Proceeding 1979 dated 4 July 1939.
14 OB Proceeding 4324 dated 17 January 1940.
15 OB Proceeding 2166 dated 21 July 1939.
16 OB Proceeding 4055 dated 1 January 1940.
17 OB Proceeding 7661 dated 26 July 1940.
18 OB Proceeding 4450 dated 24 January 1940.
19 OB Proceeding 7960 dated 12 August 1940.
20 OB Proceeding 8228 dated 26 August 1940.
21 OB Proceeding 8189 dated 23 August 1940.
22 OB Proceeding 9671 dated 29 November 1940.
23 OB Proceeding 10117 dated 3 January 1941.
24 OB Proceeding 10410 dated 22 January 1941.
25 OB Proceeding 10672 dated 12 February 1941.
26 OB Proceeding 14174 dated 24 September 1941.
27 *The World's Sub-Machine Guns*, Nelson and Lockhoven.
28 OB Proceeding 7299 dated 8 July 1940.
29 OB Proceeding 10411 dated 22 January 1941.
30 OB Proceeding 20747 dated 7 December 1942.

[31] OB Proceeding 32342 dated 15 October 1945.

[32] OB Proceeding 25905 dated 22 December 1943.

[33] OB Proceeding 30311 dated 12 February 1945.

[34] OB Proceeding 19930 dated 12 October 1942.

[35] OB Proceeding 21596 dated 8 February 1943.

[36] OB Proceeding 21867 dated 24 February 1943.

[37] OB Proceeding 22349 dated 26 March 1943.

[38] OB Proceeding Q1755 dated 20 December 1943.

[39] OB Proceeding Q1798 dated 7 January 1944.

[40] OB Proceeding Q1810 dated 12 January 1944.

[41] OB Proceeding 30171 dated 31 January 1945.

[42] OB Proceeding Q3270 dated 13 April 1945.

[43] OB Proceeding Q1377 dated 9 July 1943.

[44] OB Proceeding Q4353 dated 4 June 1946.

[45] OB Proceeding Q5128 dated 3 June 1947 and Q4668 dated 11 October 1946.

[46] OB Proceeding Q5319 dated 23 September 1947.

[47] OB Proceeding Q4859 dated 3 January 1947.

[48] OB Proceeding Q5232 dated 1 August 1947 and OB Proceeding 33036 dated 1 February 1946.

[49] OB Proceeding Q5232 dated 1 August 1947.

[50] OB Proceeding Q5278 dated 26 August 1947.

[51] Major Hall came to Enfield and took part in the .280 rifle project.

[52] OB Proceeding Q5545 dated 6 April 1948.

[53] OB Proceeding 6233 dated 4 October 1949.

[54] OB Proceeding Q6975 dated 27 July 1951 and Q7058 dated 16 October 1951.

[55] OB Proceeding 39606 dated 9 December 1960.

[56] OB Proceeding 21975 dated 5 March 1943 and 26372 dated 31 January 1944.

German Sub-Machine Guns

SCHMEISSER AND BERGMANN SMGs

Although the Italian Villar Perosa was the first SMG to go into service in 1915, it was not typical of the type of weapon that has since been developed. It operated on the delayed blow back principle.

In 1916 work started at the Bergmann factory on the first German sub-machine gun. The designer was Hugo Schmeisser. Some confusion exists about Hugo Schmeisser and his father Louis. Louis designed the Bergmann automatic pistol and the Bergmann Model 1901 machine gun whilst working for the Theodore Bergmann Small Arms Factory at Suhl. In 1902 Louis Schmeisser left the Bergmann concern to become the chief designer for the German firm of Dreyse at Sömmerda in Thuringen which had just been acquired by Rheinmetall, a Dusseldorf firm and one of Germany's greatest small arms concerns. In the 1890s Hugo Schmeisser also joined Bergmann and he remained with the firm when his father left. He is credited with the basic design of the Bergmann Model 1910 machine gun and was responsible for the design of the MP18. The production version was designated the MP18.1 ie the first modification to the MP18.

The MP18.1 **141** was a blow back operated weapon of simple construction, firing from an open breech, at full automatic only, with a cyclic rate of 400rpm. It contained in one form or another nearly all the features which were used in subsequent generations of SMGs all over the world. The bolt was cylindrical in shape with the cocking handle permanently fixed on the right hand side. The barrel, 7.88in long, was that of the Luger pistol. The magazine housing on the left of the body was inclined rearwards at 45deg and took the 32 round snail magazine also originally produced for the 9mm Luger pistol.

The first guns reached the front line in the early summer of 1918. Like all new weapons the tactical organization of the troops had to be found by a process of trial and error. The original concept was to issue it to all officers and NCOs. Each company was to have a squad with six guns, six gunners, and six ammunition numbers with three handcarts to carry ammunition. It appears that the mobility of the squad – limited by its handcarts – would hardly allow it to keep up with a fluid battle.

Some 35,000 MP18.1 SMGs were manufactured before the end of the war in

November 1918. When the Treaty of Versailles was signed, the German Army was limited to 100,000 men for internal security and border defence. The Army was not permitted any SMGs but the police forces were allowed such weapons on a scale of 1 gun per 20 men.

The first police weapon of this category was a modified MP18.1. The snail magazine was discarded and a new housing fitted taking a straight, single column magazine, which was mounted at right angles from the left hand side of the body. The modification was designed by Hugo Schmeisser and made by the C. G. Haenel firm of Suhl. Some of these modified MP18.1 SMG had a system of locking the bolt in either the forward or cocked positions. The bolt was positively locked when forward by a lug engaging in a slot. The lug blocked the cocked bolt. Hugo Schmeisser further modified the MP18.1 in the late 1920s and C. G. Haenel produced it as the MP28.11. The MP28.11 **142** differed from the MP18.1 in firing both automatic and single shot. The tangent back sight was improved and the bolt had a separate firing pin contained within it. The general configuration and furniture remained unchanged. The gun was made in Spain and adopted in Belgium in 1934. Although manufactured in 9mm Bergmann Bayard, 7.65mm Parabellum, 7.63mm and .45 ACP, the 9mm Parabellum was most widely sold. The gun was used in some numbers in the Spanish Civil War in 1936 **308**.

In the mid 1930s Hugo Schmeisser designed the Mk 36 SMG. Only prototypes were made because the telescopic main return spring infringed a patent held by Vollmer who was an Erma designer. Two of these prototypes are now in the Pattern Room at the RSAF Enfield. One is stocked for the Mauser 98K with a German bayonet lug **145** and the other is stocked like the Hungarian rifle with, again, an appropriate bayonet lug for the Hungarian bayonet **146**.

The Bergmann concern designed a new SMG in 1932 and the prototypes were made by Schultz and Larsen in Otterup, Denmark. [The gun was later adopted by the Danish Army.] This gun was designed by Theodor Emil Bergmann and an engineer named Müler[1] at Suhl but due to a lack of manufacturing facilities, construction was subcontracted to the Carl Walther Company at Zella-Mahlis. It had a wooden stock and fore-end, a perforated barrel casing and a compensator. The MP34 **147** as it was called, had several unusual features which allow easy recognition. The 32 round box magazine was held horizontally from the *right* hand side of the body; the cocking handle did not reciprocate with the bolt; there was a double trigger. When the forward trigger was pulled half way back, a single shot was fired. To fire at full automatic the front trigger was pulled right back and this in turn forced the rear trigger rearwards to give continuous fire. The standard MP34/1 had a 7.8in barrel; a limited number of guns with 12.6in long were also made. There were approximately 2,000 standard weapons produced. These were taken by the German Police, Bolivia, Ethiopia and Abyssinia. The MP35/1 **148** was used by the Waffen SS between 1940 and 1945.

STEYR-SOLOTHURN SMGs

The Versailles Treaty greatly restricted the overt activities of the small arms firms and subterfuges of various kinds were used to conceal activities from the supervisory commission. For example Rheinmetall established a subsidiary in Switzerland in 1929 at Solothurn and through them obtained control of the Steyr works in Austria to manufacture weapons ordered through Solothurn.

The Steyr-Solothurn concern produced a number of weapons. The earliest, in 1920, was the S1–100 **149** which was designed by Louis Stange of Rhein-   117

metall, who in the early 1900s had worked under the direction of Louis
Schmeisser. He also produced a machine gun, the S2–200, for Rheinmetall at
Sömmerda and this was produced by Solothurn. The parachute FG42 was
also his design. The S1–100 had a wooden stock and fore-end and a perforated
barrel casing. It was blow back operated with the return spring in a tube in the
butt. The standard barrel was 7.8in (200mm) and a longer barrelled version
with a bayonet was also offered. The early versions had a straightforward
magazine housing into which a 32 round magazine was placed horizontally
from the left. Later versions of the housing had a charger loading guide cut
into the top and a cut-away in the bottom to hold the magazine for loading
from Steyr or Mauser type stripper clips. The weapon was machined and
proved to be costly but it was sold to several countries in South America,
Portugal and was taken up by the Austrian Police and Army as the MP34 **150**.

An unusual design, the S17–100 was also produced in limited numbers in the
30s by Steyr-Solothurn. It had no butt and was intended to be used either in a
vehicle or on a tripod. The 30 round magazine was located horizontally on the
left into a conventional housing and the gun fired single shots from the top half
of a centrally pivotted trigger and full automatic from the lower half.

141 The MP18.1 9mm SMG
was designed by Hugo Schmei
and produced by the Theodor
Bergmann factory at Suhl. It
was issued in early summer 19
and 35,000 were in service by
11 November 1918. This was tl
first genuine blow back SMG.
The barrel and magazine came
from the Luger pistol. Note tha
the magazine housing on the lef
of the gun, slopes back.

142 The MP28.11 was a modification of **141** firing selective
fire. The 30 round box magazine
fits at right angles to the body.
The fire selector button is above
the trigger and the catch behind
the body end cap is for stripping.
Compare this gun with the British
Lanchester Mk 1. **68**

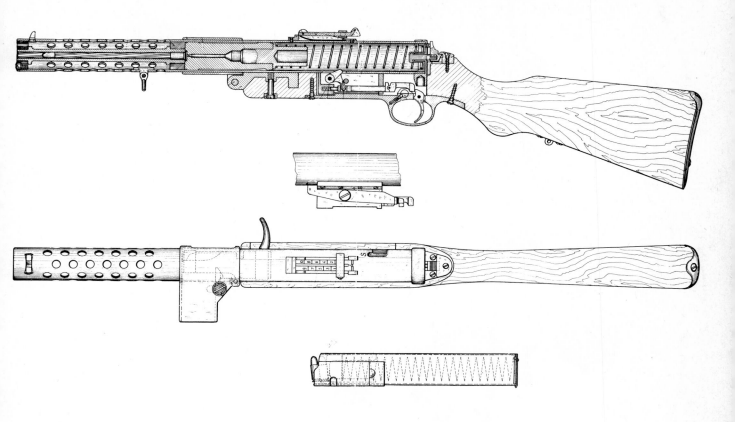

143   Drawing of the MP 28.11.

ERMA SMGs

The first Erma was designed by Heinrich Vollmer in the mid 20s and was named after him. The earliest Vollmer had a 12.6in barrel with no barrel casing. It had a wooden butt and the wooden foregrip had a telescoping metal monopod below it. The later model had a 9.9in (250mm) barrel enclosed within a slotted jacket and had no monopod but was otherwise the same. The gun took a 32 round magazine placed horizontally on the left. The Vollmer patented return spring was held in a steel tube which telescoped into the bolt when the latter came back. The next gun was the Erma (EMP) which was a development of the Vollmer. This gun existed in three models.[1] The model 35, which was sold to Jugo-slavia, had a long, jacketted barrel on which was mounted a bayonet. The second model, which sold widely, is usually called the standard model 151. It had the wooden butt and foregrip of the Vollmer. The short 9.9in barrel was jacketted but had no bayonet lug. It had a bolt locking safety screwed to the upper right side of the body behind the ejection slot. This was similar to that used in the modified MP18.1. It had a 'flip' rearsight giving 100 and 200m. The action was the same as that of the Vollmer.

The third type had the MP18.1 grooved forestock and no wooden pistol-type

119

144 The toggle joint Heineman Model 32 in 9mm Parabellum was produced in limited numbers but a licence was taken out by FN to manufacture in 1935 **248**.

145 The Mk 36 II designed by Hugo Schmeisser. The gun used a Volmer return spring patent held by the firm of Erma and was produced only in prototype. This gun is stocked like the German Mauser 98 rifle and takes that bayonet. It has *left* hand cocking.

146 This Mk 36 II is stocked like the Hungarian rifle and takes the Hungarian bayonet. It has *right* hand cocking. Both these guns are shown with MP28.11 magazines taking 30 9mm rounds.

147 The Bergmann MP 34 I. The box magazine is on the *right* and slopes forward. Pulling the front trigger half way back fires one shot; further movement forces back the rear trigger and gives automatic fire. The gun shown was made for Abyssinia.

148

148 This gun inscribed 'Theodor Bergmann and Co GmbH' is the MP 35 I and was one of the few taken into German military service, and was used exclusively by the Waffen SS.

149

149 The Steyr-Solothurn S1–100 was designed by Louis Stange in 1920 for Rheinmetall but made by Steyr-Daimler-Puch in Steyr in Austria. The gun shown is the short barrelled version evaluated in England in 1934.

150

150 The Steyr-Solothurn S1–100 with modified magazine housing. The empty magazine could be held below the gun and filled from clips. The gun shown was adopted by the Austrian Army as the MP 34.

151

151 This is the standard Erma 9mm SMG generally known as the EMP. (Erma machine pistol). It is inscribed 'Erma MP 34'.

foregrip. It usually had a tangent back sight and no bolt locking safety – although some were adapted later to fit this feature.

In 1938 Berthold Geipel, director of the Erma factory at Erfurt, demonstrated a new SMG intended for use with armoured and airborne forces. The designer of this gun, the MP38 **153** is not known but contrary to popular belief it certainly was not Hugo Schmeisser who was then working at the Haenel plant in Suhl. Nevertheless this gun and its successor were known to the Allies as the 'Schmeisser' throughout World War II.

The MP38 ushered in a new concept in SMGs. Gone was the conventional wooden stock and fore-end, together with the perforated jacket surrounding the barrel which had characterised the SMG to date. Instead the body of the gun was made from steel tubing with longitudinal machined slots along its full length to reduce weight. The cover below the body, was made of cast anodised aluminium with the foregrip and pistol grip of phenolic resin using paper fibre as a filling. The double rod stock could be swung down and forward when released by pressure on a knurled button above the left side of the pistol grip. The shoulder piece pivotted at its centre to lie horizontally below the gun. The stamped sheet metal magazine, holding 32 9mm Parabellum cartridges, was located below the gun and had no fullering grooves. Underneath the plain barrel was a solid metal bar with a hook like projection at the front. Some authorities say this was a cooling bar, others say it was a barrel rest for use principally when firing through a fire port with the 'hook' designed to prevent the weapon being pulled into the vehicle – still firing – if the soldier lost his footing as the vehicle traversed uneven terrain. A threaded nut at the muzzle could be removed to fit a blank firing attachment and in front of the hooded blade foresight was a muzzle cover/cleaning rod guide. The cylindrical bolt carried a spring retracted firing pin. The return spring had a three piece telescoping tube with the forward section enclosing the firing pin. The one piece cocking lever was mounted on the left. The gun was costly both in its material and manufacturing time and so was not produced in large numbers by its sole manufacturer – Erma.

The next model the MP40 **154** was basically the MP38 modified for cheaper and more rapid production. The body was made of stamped sheet steel, brazed and spot welded. The magazine and trigger housings were also spot welded steel stampings and the magazine was now fullered. The magazine housing had five horizontal ribs to increase its strength. This provides a ready identification since the MP38 housing was smooth – sometimes with a hole in the centre. The use of plain carbon steel in these stampings allowed for ready subcontracting as well as conserving alloy steels which were already available in quantities less than ideal. The cocking handle was a two piece assembly which could be used to lock the bolt in either the cocked or forward positions. The barrel had no muzzle cover and the bar below was no longer solid but a steel pressing.

During the fighting against the Germans during 1942/43, the Russians used the PPD40 and PPSh 41 with 71 round drum magazines and in an effort to increase firepower the MP40 was modified in 1943 to take two 32 round magazines side by side, inserted into a sliding magazine housing. After firing one magazine and cocking the gun, the housing could be moved over to line up the second magazine with the chamber. The gun with two loaded magazines weighed 12lb and was somewhat cumbersome. This modified gun was known as the MP40/11 **156**.

In 1939 when the Germans went to war over Danzig, they found that the

152 The silenced Erma. The barrel was not drilled. Aluminium alloy discs fill the jacket and gases from the muzzle enter through holes in the interior wall. The muzzle has a rubber plug. Used only by French security police working with the Germans.

153 The MP 38. This was NOT designed by Schmeisser although it is generally so called together with the MP 40. Note muzzle cover-cleaning rod guide. It has a one piece cocking handle which will set back if jarred and fire a round. Magazine has no fullering. Bar below barrel is solid.

154 MP 40. Note magazine housing ribs, fullering on magazine, muzzle cap, two piece cocking handle. The cooling bar under the barrel is a pressing.

MP38 was unsafe with the bolt forward and a loaded magazine on the gun. Any jar set back the bolt sufficiently to fire a round. To prevent this the MP38 was modified by substituting the cocking handle from the new MP40 and cutting a forward locking position in the cocking handle slot in the body. This was done at base workshops. The resulting weapon was called by the Germans the 'mixed' model and designated the MP38/40 **155**. The MP38 and MP40 were used by German troops in every theatre in which they fought. The MP40 was produced in large numbers as shown in this table.[1]

1940	113,700
1941	239,300
1942	231,500
1943	234,300
1944	228,600

These figures show not only the quantities involved but also how the Speer organisation managed to maintain production under the constant hammering of the RAF by night and the 8th USAAF by day.

Erma-Werke also produced a silenced SMG **152** of interesting design. Instead of using steel gauze to absorb the gases, the barrel was surrounded by a series of aluminium discs which deformed under pressure until eventually the gases were held between the foremost discs and fed back beyond the barrel, through the radial holes bored in the casing. This gun was never used by the German Army but was employed by the French Security police who collaborated with the occupying troops and the Gestapo.

The MP41 was designed by Schmeisser and the model illustrated **157** is marked 'Schmeisser Patent, C G Haenel, Suhl' on the top surface of the body. The gun has the action of the MP40, the body of the MP40 but with a rear closure cap and the wood stock and fire-selector cross bolt action of the MP28.11. The bar under the barrel of the MP40 was removed. This weapon was not accepted by the German Army and was only manufactured in small numbers.

During 1942–43 the Erma factory at Erfurt developed the EMP44. This would appear to have been designed for simplicity and ease of manufacture. The butt stock, body and barrel casing were all formed from a single straight steel tube. The shoulder piece and pistol grip were two pieces of similar tube. The shoulder piece was T-shaped and the top formed an end closure for the body, holding it by means of a spring loaded plunger. The double side by side magazine of the MP40/11 was used with separate magazine catches. The tubular muzzle brake and compensator was welded on to the barrel casing. One such gun examined in England after the war had the shoulder piece mounted at its centre point to the body thus giving a straight-through butt arrangement calculated to prevent the muzzle rising at automatic fire. It is probable that this would have been the production version because the design made special provision for the raised sights that would have been required, as is apparent from the photograph **158**.

OTHER GERMAN SMGs

The Germans manufactured large numbers of copies of the Sten gun. These were made for two purposes. Firstly the equipping of the Volksturm and secondly to arm German guerrillas who were expected to operate behind the Allied lines. A number of German firms produced these copies. Mauser produced, at great expense, some 25,000 copies of the Mk II Sten, known as the

155 MP 38/40. Known by the Germans as the 'mixed model' since it has MP 38 muzzle, magazine housing, and cooling bar with MP 40 cocking handle and magazine.

156 The MP 40/11 had a dual side by side magazine giving 64 rounds. This was incorporated after German soldiers said the Russian 71 round drum magazine on the PPSh 41 gave them superiority of fire. The MP 40/11 weighed over 12lb with its loaded magazines.

157

158
159

'Gerat Potsdam', in about six weeks.[1] They also produced, and subcontracted, a Sten gun using the MP40 magazine mounted below the body. These were known as the MP3008 **159**. The aircraft firm of Blohm and Voss also produced considerable numbers of Stens **160**. The usual German system of allocating code numbers to firms who thus identified their products was not always used on these Stens, and many have been found which it has not been possible to identify. One such is illustrated **161**. This is similar to the MP3008 but has left hand cocking.

The Germans used some remotely controlled guns in their fortifications on the Western Wall. One was the Fest machine pistol **162**. The action resembled the MP28 but as can be seen the body is quite different. The gun is marked FMP1.

POST WAR GERMAN SMGs
ERMA SMGs

When the Russians moved westwards in 1944 the Erma factory was overrun and when the East German Republic was formed the factory was in the Communist zone. The German management staff and key workers got away before the Russians occupied the factory. On 1 January 1951 the Erma Werke was officially relocated at Dachau in Bavaria. During the intervening years, research and development had been curtailed due to the control exercised over German munition production, but correspondence with former German officers had been maintained. These were added to when the Dachau factory was established. Two sources of value to Erma were Colonel Butz and the weapons Engineer Dipl Ing Echart.

In 1955 Erma took up the French SMG the MGD **266**. This is often referred to as the PM9 and it was advertised for sale by the Societé Pour l'Exploration des Brevets MGD of Grenoble – a company formed to exploit patents. This SMG had a unique flywheel mechanism which permitted a short bolt movement thus reducing the body length. It also allowed a wide variation in the rate of fire by means of a small adjustment in the flywheel mechanism. Erma apparently looked on this enterprise principally as a training exercise for their young engineers, allowing them to make design changes and gain production experience. Few of these guns were sold because the cost – quoted at $150[1] – was too high.

After this trial run Erma engineers were given the task of producing a weapon with a length of $15\frac{3}{4}$in, a weight of about 7 to $7\frac{3}{4}$lb and a cyclic rate of 500–550rpm. The resultant SMG was called the Erma MP56. Ten models were sold in 1956. The designer was Louis Camillis. It appears that the weapon existed in two forms. The first had a collapsible shoulder stock, a pistol grip, incorporating a grip safety, and took the MP40 32 round magazine. The other model had a shaped grip attached to the barrel casing very near to the muzzle and no shoulder stock. It was intended for police work **163**. No further development was carried out and it is said[1] that the financial controller of the weapon, Fenner Achenbach, transferred the project to Mauser who modified the design into their Model 57. Some of the more interesting features of the MP56 were the wrap round bolt and the location of the return spring which was attached to the bolt, wrapped round the chamber, and was compressed between the forward part of the wrap round bolt and the barrel flange as the bolt moved back. It fired only at full automatic.

In 1958 Erma Werke and another firm collaborated in the design of a SMG which was conceived as a multi-purpose weapon to fire rifle grenades. The

157 The MP 41 was a mixture of the body and action of the MP 40 with the fire selector and wooden stocking of the MP 28.11 It was designed by Schmeisser and made by Haenal but was never accepted into service.

158 The Erma EMP 44. The butt stock, body and barrel casing are all one tube. The double magazine of the MP 40/11 was used. It was very cheap to produce but was never developed

159 MP 3008. This was a copy of the British Sten with the magazine below the body. This particular model was well made by Mauser.

160 A German Sten made by Blohm and Voss in 1945. This has the standard MP 40 magazine. It is unique amongst German Stens in having a pistol grip, a different trigger mechanism and housing and a perforated jacket over a very long barrel.

161 This German Sten is of unknown manufacture. Note that it cocks on the left – unlike all the similar models. The barrel retaining nut is also unique.

prototypes of this weapon, **164** firing from a closed bolt, and known as the Erma-Panzer 58 or sometimes as the 'Smart' – was tried at the Bundeswehr Testing Centre at Meppen and achieved good results both with ball ammunition and grenades. However the German army did not show any interest and requested a simple cheap SMG at a cost of DM60 to DM80 (about £9 to £11) and Erma started work on this project. In the spring of 1959 Erma presented the first test models of the MP58 **165**. It met the official requirements of a total length of 16in, a barrel length of 7.4in, a weight of 6.8lb and a cyclic rate of 650–680rpm. It used the MP40 magazine and made use of sheet metal stampings and the telescopic return spring of typical Erma design, located conventionally behind the bolt. The wire stock folded forward over the barrel.

However the German Army asked for various changes and the MP59 **166** was designed to meet them. The chief issue was the rate of fire which was now set at 400–450rpm. Erma found that with a light bolt and a weapon length of $22\frac{1}{6}$in this rate of fire could not be obtained without a buffer. A novel hydraulic buffer was designed which functioned without trouble, at any rate of fire from

162 The Fest SMG was probably developed to cover blind approaches in the coastal fortifications of the West Wall. It was remotely controlled. The action is that of the MP 28.II.

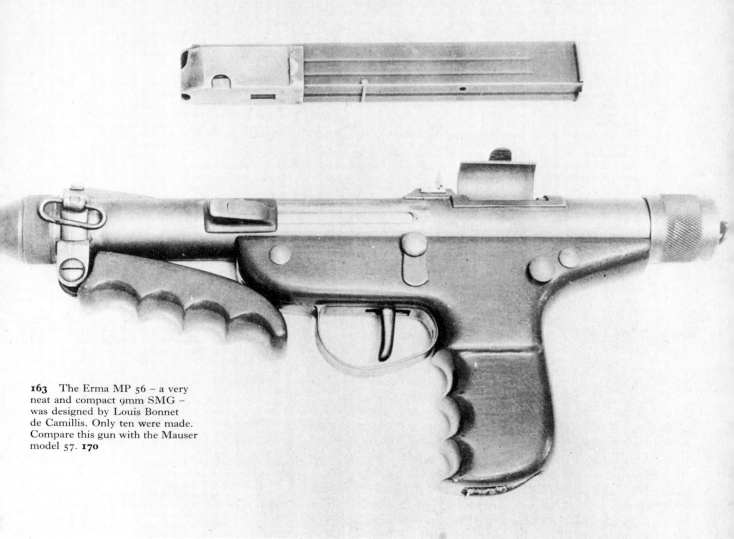

163 The Erma MP 56 – a very neat and compact 9mm SMG – was designed by Louis Bonnet de Camillis. Only ten were made. Compare this gun with the Mauser model 57. **170**

100 to 600rpm. Unfortunately the seals did not last and a new approach had to be found. The prototype had a barrel lengthened from 7.3 to 10.3in, a longer body and a straight retracting metal stock. The MP40 magazine, which was a double column feed merging to a single column at the mouth, was abandoned and a new staggered double feed type adopted in which the round was picked up from each column in turn. When this weapon was tested Erma once more experienced the infuriation of finding that the requirement had been changed with the replacement of personnel in key posts in the Bundeswehr.

In the spring of 1960 Erma Werke decided to try yet again to meet a specification which seemed to shift like sand under their feet. The resulting weapon, the MP60 **167**, was quite different to anything they had produced before. The body and barrel casing were stamped as one integral fabrication. The butt stock swung to the right of the body. The Vollmer return spring assembly was discarded and two rods carrying springs were passed side by side through the bolt to the front of the body, after the fashion of the USA M3 SMG. The new magazine developed for the MP59 was discarded and the Swedish Carl Gustav magazine with two separate compartments separated by a plate extending two-thirds of the way up was adopted.

Twenty MP60 SMGs were delivered to the Bundeswehr in September 1960 as troop test models. Within 8 weeks a further twenty models were built. All these forty weapons were hand built and the short time gap between the two orders prevented the incorporation of improvements in the second batch. Although Erma were very confident that this design would satisfy the German army, no further orders were placed. The Erma design team under the Chief Engineer, Josef Eder, continued to improve the MP60. First a MP61 **168** was produced and finally a MP64 **169**. After this the SMG programme was terminated.

MAUSER SMGs

MP57: In 1956 Erma produced four prototypes of a SMG, known as the Erma MP56, **163** designed by Louis Bonnet de Camillis. Camillis was a Frenchman who worked on this gun in the early 1950s. The sponsor of the weapon, Fenner Achenbach, decided to transfer development to Mauser and their first post war gun – the Mauser Model 57 – was a modified version of the Erma gun. The gun embodied the 'wrap round' bolt principle and fired from the open bolt position. The return spring was wrapped round the barrel and was extended as the bolt went back. The Mauser MP57 differed from the Erma gun in firing both single shot and full automatic. There was a forward grip which hung below the muzzle and could be folded back under the barrel when not required. The 32 round magazine fitted into the rear pistol grip. The double wire stock could be rotated over the barrel giving a short overall folded length of slightly under 17in. The body was made up of stamped pressings **170**.

The MP57 has been successfully demonstrated but has not sold.

Model 60: The Model 60 **171** was designed by Vorgrimmler and Kimmick. Only prototypes have been produced. It would seem that it was a Mauser equivalent to the Erma Panzer MP58 – or Smart – and was intended to fire anti-tank and rifle grenades. Guide and sealing rings were machined on the barrel just forward of the body and a muzzle thread took a muzzle brake which served the dual purpose of reducing the heavy recoil when a grenade was fired and also acted as the forward guide when the grenade was positioned over the barrel. Since the entire gas energy was required to launch the grenade it was necessary to be able to lock the bolt. To do this the axis of the selector lever had

164 The Erma-Panzer 58 – sometimes called the 'Smart' – was designed to fire anti-tank grenades out to 100m as well as ball ammunition. It was evaluated at the Bundeswehr Testing Centre at Meppen but although it did well it did not meet official requirements.

165 The Erma MP 58 9mm SMG was made at Dachau to meet the requirement for a cheap but effective SMG with a short overall length and a rate of fire of 650–680 rounds/minute. It utilized many features of the MP 40. Only a few were made.

166 The Erma MP 59 9mm SMG embodied further changes required by the Army. These were a rate of fire of 400–450rpm, longer barrel and a new two position feed magazine. The gun is sometimes called the MP 40/59.

164

165

166

167

168

169

170

171

167 The Erma MP 60 9mm SMG was quite different in design from its predecessors. The body and barrel jacket came from one stamping and the double return spring was similar to the US M3.

168 The Erma MP 61 was a detail improvement of the MP 60.

169 The last design produced by Josef Eder for Erma was the MP 64. This was a further development of the MP 60 utilizing the large one piece stamping. The gun was smoother in action and easier to control. By the time this gun appeared the German Army had adopted the Uzi and the programme was terminated.

170 The Mauser MP 57 9mm SMG was designed by de Camillis and is a Mauser produced version of the Erma MP 56 **163**. The gun used a 'wrap round' bolt and – unlike the EMP 56 – had selective fire. The gun was never sold.

171 The Mauser Model 60 9mm SMG was Mauser's answer to the Erma Panzer 58, firing anti-tank and rifle grenades. It was very accurate.

a D section which entered a recess in the bolt when set to 'grenade'. The gun fired at all times from a closed bolt using a spring retracted firing pin and a hammer. This closed bolt firing produced extremely accurate and consistent fire, as immediately before the firing the bolt was closed and the barrel vibrations had time to subside before the hammer fell on the firing pin.

WALTHER SMGs

The firm of Carl Walther at Ulm, Donau, is well known for its pistols, SL rifles and its part in the development of the Assault Rifle. In 1963 it introduced two versions of a SMG known as the Model MPL (long) and MPK (Kurz or short) **172**. The two guns vary in barrel length, overall length and weight. The mechanism is identical. The open bolt position is used with a design that seems to be based on the Italian Beretta Model 6 (qv) designed by Domenico Salza in 1953. The bolt is ⌐ shaped with the fixed firing pin, extractor and feed horn on the face of the lower arm. The return spring guide rod passes right through the long arm of the bolt to the front of the body and its forward housing lies above the barrel.

The body and magazine housing are stamped. The butt stock can be swung forward on either side of the body. The cocking handle runs in a slot high on the left of the body, engaging the upper part of the bolt. It does not reciprocate with the bolt. Only full automatic is possible.

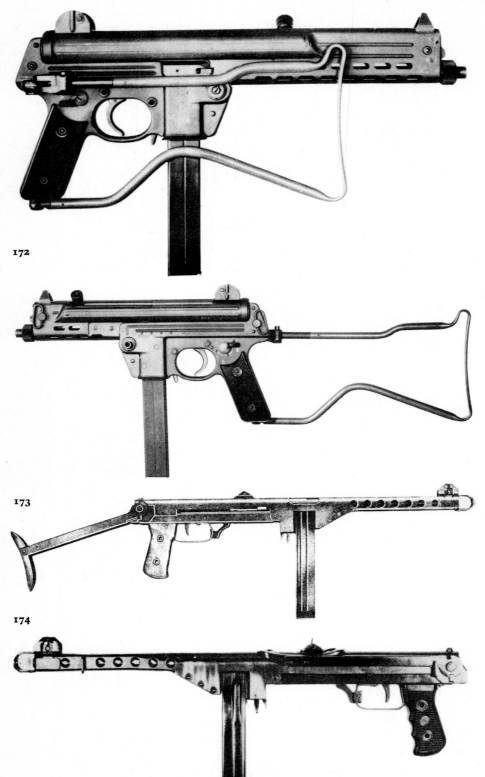

172

173

174

172 The Walther 9mm SMG was made in two models. The long barrelled version was the MPL (*top*) and the short barrelled type was the MPK (Kurz— short). The gun was made from stampings and the butt folded on either side of the body.

173 The Dux 51 9mm SMG was based on the Finnish M44 **272** which itself was derived from the Russian Sudarev PPS–43 **229**. It was made at Oviedo in Spain.

174 The Dux 53 9mm was an improvement in detail only. It was made at Oviedo and **100** were sold to the German Border Guard.

DUX SMGs

The first Dux model – the 51 **173** – was based on the Finnish M44. The designer was the well known Mauser engineer, Ludwig Vorgrimmler and the Dux 51 and the Dux 53 which followed were produced at Oviedo in Spain. The German Border Guard took 100 Dux 53 SMGs in 1954 and when Germany came into NATO, the Bundeswehr examined this design. Specimens were modified by Mauser, Sauer and Sohn, and Anschutz and these modified weapons were tested by the German Army at Meppin. Finally the Anschutz pattern seemed most nearly to meet the official requirement and a development contract was placed with that firm. They evolved several variations ending with the Dux 59. Nelson and Lockhoven state that the gun was never produced for the German Army because of difficulties between the original sponsor Willi Daugs, who brought the M44 design from Finland – where he was manager of the Tikkakoski Arsenal – and Anschutz. The Dux 53 **174** was based on the Finnish model M44 which itself was a 9mm version of the Russian 7.62mm PPS43 using Suomi magazines. It looked almost identical with the Sudarev design even to the sheet metal muzzle brake and was made from stamped heavy gauge steel sheet.

The Dux 59 **175** was a considerably modified version of the 53. The body was still a flat sided pressing incorporating the magazine housing. The barrel jacket was of circular section, perforated, with a hooded foresight. There was no muzzle brake. The Suomi magazine was not used but was replaced with a curved 32 round 9mm magazine. A new sliding safety was located above the left hand side of the pistol grip.

THE STEYR MPi69 SMG

After World War II the Steyr-Daimler-Puch concern in Austria re-entered the SMG field in 1965. An extremely simple and effective 9mm weapon was produced that became standard for the Austrian Federal Army in 1969.

The gun fires from an open breech with a bolt that strongly resembles the Uzi in its wrap round action. The entire weapon was designed for cheapness in production consistent with maintaining accuracy and reliability. The design team was led by Hugo Stowasser and the very short while available for preliminary studies and early mock ups was very well spent. The gun consists of a square section medium gauge steel receiver pressing; a nylon moulded receiver cover fitting under the body and carrying the trigger mechanism, pistol grip and magazine housing; and the barrel and breech block with return spring. The butt is a telescoping spring steel pattern modelled on the USA M3.

The barrel which is 10in long is made by the cold forging process. The bolt is a machined casting with the firing pin located half way along its length to allow complete envelopment of the breech before firing. The 25 round magazine fits into the pistol grip. Both single shots and full automatic fire are obtained from the same trigger without having to use a selector lever. Partial pressure produces semi automatic fire and full rearward movement of the trigger provides continuous fire. The gun is cocked by using the sling to retract the cocking lever. To prevent accidental feed a bracket is welded to the receiver which blocks movement of the cocking lever unless the sling is held out at right angles to the body of the gun. The gun has two sighting systems offered as alternatives in commercial weapons. The first is a simple cheap orthodox aperture back sight with two leaves giving aperture ranges of 100 and 200m. Zeroing is carried out on the foresight which has an eccentrically mounted pillar which can be raised or lowered for elevation on a screw thread and then locked in the required position. This sight is used by the Austrian Army.

The second sight offered is the British Singlepoint sight **176**. This is a collimater sight producing a small spot of green light, from a Beta source, which is parallel to the axis of the bore and is directed back into the firer's master eye. The user keeps both eyes open and places the spot on the target. The sight has been extensively tested by the British Army in England and in Malaya and some success recorded in trials with SMGs.

The bolt has three bents located successively back from the front edge of the block and ensuring that the block cannot bounce if dropped and also that using ammunition of low impulse a 'run away gun' cannot occur.

The Steyr MPi69 is a good example of modern technology producing a cheap effective weapon.

THE HUNGARIAN M39 AND M43

The M39 **177** was designed by Pal de Kiraly and produced by Danuvia in Budapest. The M39 and its successor the M43 incorporated an original delay

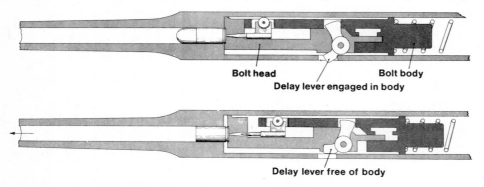

Bolt head   Bolt body

Delay lever engaged in body

Delay lever free of body

Fig III Delayed Blowback Action of the Hungarian M 39 SMG

blow back system using a two part bolt. The bolt head carried a vertical lever, one end of which engaged in the bottom of the body and the other end pressed against the bolt body. When the base of the cartridge pressed against the bolt head, the rearward motion was curtailed until the lever was rotated out of the body. The rotation was resisted by the bolt body and the return spring which were forced back. The lever was not centrally pivotted and the long arm acted on the bolt body which was accelerated rearwards whilst the bolt head held up the cartridge. Since a parallel sided case was used a small rearward movement of the bolt head was acceptable as obturation was still complete. This system allowed a light breech block – about 1lb – with the powerful Mauser 9mm cartridge. The gun fired when the rear part closed up to the breech head, rotated the lever into its recess in the body – and only then drove the firing pin forward.

The gun fired at full auto or single shot with a rotatable selector ring at the rear of the body.

The magazine – holding 40 rounds – could be folded forward into a deep groove cut in the underside of the wooden fore end. The Hungarian M35 rifle bayonet could be fitted under the barrel. The original drawings for the M39 were imported into England in 1938 by Mr Mark Dinely and manufacturing rights were obtained by BSA who estimated that it could be produced for £5 (see page 69 and a photograph of the BSA produced weapon at **64**).

    Only some 8,000 of these weapons were produced by Danuvia.

175

176

177

175 The Dux 53 9mm SMG was developed by Mauser, Sauer and Sohn and Anschutz. The latter design was known as the Dux 59 and is shown above.

176 The Steyr-Daimler-Puch firm returned to SMG design in 1965. The MPi 69 9mm SMG was designed by Hugo Stowasser. It is a very efficient SMG with a wrap round bolt. It cocks by holding out the sling and pulling it back. The gun shown has the Singlepoint sight which is offered as an alternative to the simple aperture back sight used by the Austrian Army.

177 The Hungarian M39 9mm (Mauser) SMG was a delayed blow back SMG using a two part bolt. It was designed by Pal de Kiraly and should be compared with the BSA Kiraly **64**. The 40 round magazine folded under the body after the fashion introduced in the Swiss MKMS SMG. The M43 which followed was the same gun with a folding butt.

178 The Heckler and Koch MP5 9mm SMG. This is produced at Oberndorf. It is a delayed blow back weapon using the same system as the G3 rifle and HK machine gun. The action is illustrated on page 139.

178

137

The M43 had a folding metal stock, a shorter barrel and used a 40 round magazine which was not interchangeable with that of the M39.

HECKLER AND KOCH MP5 SMG

The CETME rifle designed at the Centro de Estudios Tecnicos de Materials Especiales in Spain and eventually adopted by the German army as the G3 7.62mm rifle, used a delayed blow back action breech which was subsequently employed by Heckler and Koch, its makers, at Oberndorf in a SMG called the MP5. This 9mm SMG was adopted in the autumn of 1966 by the Police Forces of the Federal Republic of Germany and by the German Federal Border Police.

The MP5 **178** uses a two part bolt consisting of a bolt head and a much heavier bolt body behind it. The bolt head carries two rollers. When the gun is ready to fire these rollers are forced out into recesses in the barrel extension by a wedge shaped extension of the bolt body which pushes forward between them during the chambering of the round. When the cap is struck the gas pressure tries to force the bolt head back but movement is limited until the rollers are forced in by the reaction of the recess walls. The inward movement of the rollers is resisted by the wedge shaped extension of the bolt body backed up by the return spring. As the rollers are forced in, the bolt body is accelerated rearwards as the rollers drive the wedge back. Thus the bolt body moves rapidly whilst the bolt head is held up and withstands the gas pressure. By the time the rollers are fully in, the bullet has left the muzzle and the two parts of the bolt are able to move back together under the residual gas pressure. The operations of extraction and ejection follow as the return spring is compressed. The bolt is then driven forward to feed and chamber the round; the rollers are forced out again.

If the selector lever is at 'auto' and the trigger is pressed, the hammer is then released and the gun fires. If the selector is at 'single shot' the disconnector makes it necessary to release the trigger before it can be operated again to fire another shot.

This leads to closed breech firing and the attendant risk of 'cook off' on the one hand and increased consistency on the other. The gun fires either single shot or fully automatic and can additionally be fitted if required with a burst control mechanism. These are usually 3 round devices but Heckler and Koch offer 3, 4 or 5 round burst controllers. This makes a very useful feature for the SMG. The gun normally has a rigid butt stock and is then known as the MP5A2 but a telescoping wire stock can also be offered with the MP5A3. The magazines take 10, 15 or 30 rounds.

A very similar weapon **179** designed to fire the .223 cartridge is known as the HK53K.

REFERENCE
[1]*The World's Sub-Machine Guns*, Nelson and Lockhoven.

179

179 The Heckler and Koch HK 53K is a SMG using the .223 Remington cartridge used in the M16A1 rifle. It uses the same delayed blow back action as the MP5.

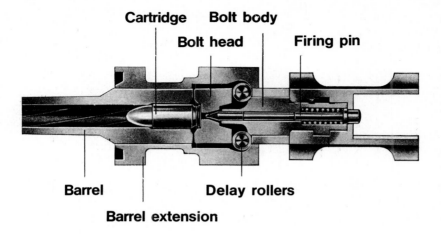

Cartridge **Bolt body**

Bolt head **Firing pin**

Barrel **Delay rollers**

Barrel extension

SMG loaded ready to fire

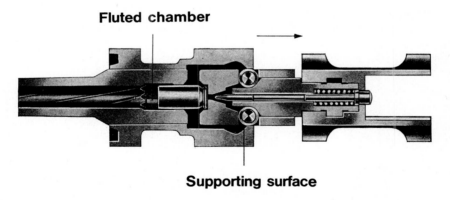

Fluted chamber

Supporting surface

Cartridge fired – rollers fully in

Fig IV The Heckler and Koch MP 5

Italian Sub-Machine Guns

THE VILLAR PEROSA SMG

The Villar Perosa **180** was the first weapon of the type to enter service. It was not constructed specifically to meet the characteristics of the modern SMG but was designed by an engineer called Abiel Botel Revelli as a light weapon to produce bursts of automatic fire. No single shot mechanism was incorporated.

The cartridge of the 9mm Glisenti pistol, which had been standard in the Italian Army since 1910, was used. This cartridge was not the 9mm Parabellum but, although of the same external dimensions, was less powerful and the 9mm Parabellum was never used in the Villar Perosa during World War I. As a matter of interest an experimental model was made for the British .455 Webley and Scott pistol cartridge and this gun **181** was brought into England and tried at Enfield in 1916. It is now in the Pattern Room of the RSAF.

The Italian Army tried the gun in various roles. It was used with a shield in defensive positions as a LMG; it was mounted on the sidecar of a motor-cycle combination, fitted on motor cars and used in the mountain fighting against the Austrians in a conventional LMG role. The most unusual way of using it was to hold it on a wooden tray slung round the firer's neck, in the assault role. It was also used as an observer's gun in aircraft and on light naval patrol boats.

It was initially manufactured by Officine di Villar Perosa, at Villar Perosa in Italy and then by Fiat. As a result the gun had various names. Its official title was the Model 1915 but it was referred to as the Revelli from its designer and as the Fiat. It was also manufactured by the Canadian General Electric Co of Toronto for the Italian Government in 1917–18 and called by them the 'Revelli Automatic Machine Gun' and supplied with a complex tripod. It is now universally known as the Villar Perosa (VP).

The VP consisted of two weapons, built together, without a stock but fitted with two brass spade grips like a medium machine gun. Above these handles was fitted a lever type safety catch which when pushed to the right, could lock the breech blocks in the rear position. Under the safety catch were two thumb operated push button triggers which could be operated together or singly. The two tubular body frames were joined by two collars. On the right of each of the bodies was a cocking lever slot and a connecting rod allowed both levers to be retracted simultaneously. Above each weapon was a curved 25 round magazine with the rear end open to allow the firer to observe how many cartridges were available. Many models had no sights but some were fitted with a pivotting plate, mounted above the rear connecting member, which could be moved to bring a series of V notches, giving ranges from 50 to 400m, into position. The foresight was a broad aperture – almost a ring – mounted above the forward connecting bar.

The rate of fire was 1,200–1,500rpm from each barrel. Thus using the two barrels together could produce up to 3000rpm and the magazines were emptied in one second of firing. This rate of fire resulted in the gun spending more time unloaded than firing. The cause of this high rate of fire was a very light breech block and a very heavy return spring.

The breech block of each gun had a lug riding in a track and at the end of the forward stroke the track was curved to cause a 45deg rotation of the bolt. The striker moved also in the track but never reached the curved portion. Only when the bolt had rotated could the striker emerge from the front face of the bolt to contact the cap of the cartridge. This occurred whilst the bolt still had forward motion. Thus the curved track in the body of the gun served two purposes. During the feed stroke it ensured that safety was provided before firing by controlling the striker. During the rearward movement of the bolt the friction between the lug of the bolt and the track provided a slight delay in the breech opening. It will be seen therefore that this was a delayed blow back operated weapon and was not of the straight blow back system developed subsequently. The VP is now comparatively rare since most models were used to provide parts for a later Beretta SMG.

After the War ended the original manufacturer, Officine di Villar Perosa, produced a single barrelled version with a conventional rifle type wooden stock **182**. The original bolt action and 25 round vertically mounted box magazine with the open rear wall, were retained. The barrel was shortened by 4cm and given an unperforated jacket extending half-way to the muzzle.

The cocking lever was replaced by a cylindrical metal sleeve located around the body behind the magazine. This was knurled to provide a grip and cut away on the underside to slide round the trigger housing. The firer pulled this cover to the rear to cock the bolt and then slid it forward again to the forward position. Both single shots and automatic fire could be used. This OVP SMG remained in Italian service for 20 years and was used in the North African campaign in 1940.

BERETTA SMGs

The firm of Pietro Beretta at Brescia has achieved a very high reputation for its pistols and SMGs and remains today one of the great arms producing concerns of the world.

Model 1918: The first SMG produced was the Model 1918. Towards the end of World War I the Italian High Command asked Beretta to examine the possibility of developing a lighter weapon which would be more effective than the Villar Perosa and easier to handle. The task was entrusted to Tullio Marengoni, a young engineer. Marengoni subsequently designed many weapons for Beretta all of which showed his skill and meticulous attention to detail. He remained as a consultant to Beretta for some years after his official retirement in 1956.

The Marengoni Model 1918 used the Villar Perosa action, barrel, body and feed system. A new trigger mechanism – similar to the Italian rifle – was developed and a new stock was produced. An ejection chute was added under the

ejection slot. Two components from the Carcano military carbine were added –
the bayonet catch and the folding bayonet **183**.

This weapon was called the Beretta Moschetto Automatico 1918 model and
was issued to the Arditi (assault units) of the Italian Army. It came into service
before the Schmeisser MP18.1 was adopted by the German Army and remained
in general use until the start of World War II.

Model 1918-30: This was not a genuine SMG but a semi-automatic carbine.
It had a butt stock and barrel taking the folding bayonet of the M-1918. Alterations included a new body with a ring shaped cocking handle at the rear end.
The ammunition was fed in from a box magazine holding 15 rounds underneath
the weapon and a feed cover was fitted. Ejection was through the top of the
gun. The back sight was adjustable for ranges of 100 to 500m **184**.

Firing was from a closed breech with a hammer operated firing pin. The
cocking ring did not come back towards the firer's eye during action, and there
was a holding open device.

The weapon was designed for police use and was never mass produced. A
quantity was sold to the Argentine Police Force.

Model 1935: This was another SL carbine with the same action as the M 1918–
30. It had a different shape which was standardised in the very famous Model
1938 which followed. Without its magazine it looked very similar to the Bergmann
MP34 **147** in shape with a cooling jacket with long oval perforations. The M35
underwent limited production but was soon ousted in favour of the Model 38.

Model 1938A: This was Marengoni's most successful SMG. It was developed
from the M1935 and was produced throughout World War II. After the war
production continued and lasted until 1950.

The M1938A was produced in three variants. The first version **186** which was
produced in January 1938, had a jacket with long cooling slots and a simple
compensator with two large ports separated at the top by a central bar. A folding
bayonet was standard. Two triggers were fitted, the forward to produce semi-
automatic fire and the rear to give automatic fire. The safety catch was located
on the left of the body above the triggers.

The second version **187** had a barrel jacket with smaller, circular, perforations,
but the same compensator and bayonet. In addition to the safety catch an
additional blocking bar was fitted in the rear of the trigger guard which when
pushed across to the right, blocked the automatic trigger, enabling only single
shots to be fired **188**. This version was mass produced.

The third version appeared at the end of 1938. The bayonet was removed
and the compensator changed to a pattern consisting of four slots cut at a
forward sloping angle on top of the muzzle. This model was mass produced
from 1938 to 1944 for Italian and German forces; in 1939 for Rumania and in
1947 for the Argentine **190**. The third version was further modified in 1949–50
and a cross bolt safety incorporated **198**. This safety was taken from the Model
38/49 SMG (qv).

The Model 1938A was an extremely reliable and accurate gun but since nearly
all its parts were machined it was costly to produce. Later production models
had a stamped barrel jacket and some had a fixed firing pin. A prototype was
also tested with an aluminium jacket **185**.

The gun fired from the open breech position and was cocked by a handle on
the right attached to a slide which engaged the bolt. The handle was pushed
forward after cocking was completed and was held forward by a catch. The slide
then acted as a dust excluder. It did not reciprocate during firing.

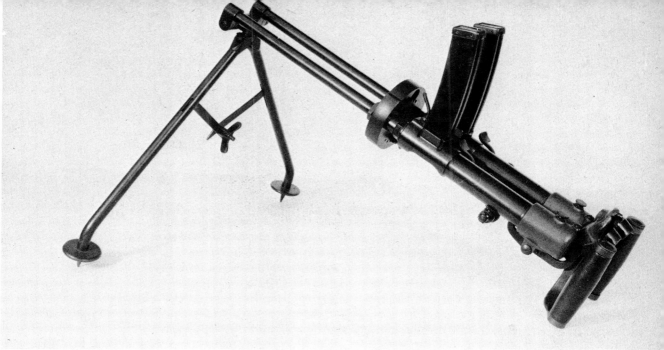

180

180 The Villar Perosa was the first SMG to go into service. The design by Abiel Revelli was issued in 1915 and used in many roles including aircraft, motor cycle and tripod mountings. It was a delayed blow back operated weapon firing at 3000rpm from two 20 round magazines, using the 9mm Glisenti cartridge.

181 A unique VP chambered for the British .455 cartridge and tested in England in 1916.

182 The Officine di Villar Perosa produced the OVP after World War I, using the action and parts of the Villar Perosa. It was still used by the Italian army in the North African desert in 1941. The weapon is shown here cocked.

181
182

183 The Beretta Model 1918 was developed by Tullio Marengoni from the VP and was probably in use before the German MP 18.1. It remained in service throughout World War II.

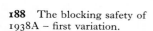

184 The Beretta 1918–30 was a self-loading carbine derived from the Model 1918 for police work. A number were sold to the Argentine.

185 An early prototype of the Beretta 1938. Note the aluminium fins.

186 The original Model 1938A – sometimes called the 1938. It is distinguished by the open compensator and long cooling perforations in the jacket. Few were produced and many of those had a folding knife bayonet.

187 The first variation of the 1938A retained the open compensator but had numerous circular cooling perforations of the jacket. It had a safety which blocked the rear automatic trigger. This gun was mass produced.

188 The blocking safety of 1938A – first variation.

186

187

188

189

190

191

The firing arrangement was complex for a SMG and added considerably to the cost. When the bolt was fully forward a cam came into contact with the ejecter stud and was revolved to drive the firing pin forward. The return spring was of small diameter and entered the bolt to bear on the firing pin. The other end went into a tube which fitted into a recess in the end closure cap. The magazine opening was sealed with a sliding plate to keep dirt out, when no magazine was in place. The 1938A used a higher powered cartridge than most 9mm Parabellum SMGs, known as the M38. To provide ready identification a 1mm groove was cut two thirds of the way up the case which permitted recognition by touch alone. Since the current Italian pistol was the Beretta model 34 taking the short 9mm (.380 ACP) the SMG and pistol did not take the same cartridge. The SMG ammunition was loaded into the magazine from Mannlicher type clips holding 10, 20 or 40 rounds.

Model 1: This was designed by Tullio Marengoni in 1941 and was intended for parachute troops. It showed some similarity with the German MP38 and 40, especially in the folding stock. It's construction was considered to be excessively complicated and it was shelved in favour of the Model 38/42 (qv) and never came into production.

The Model 1 **191** had the same double trigger mechanism, body and cocking arrangements of the Model 1938A. The breech block was fitted with a fixed firing pin but retained the small diameter return spring with its guide tube and rod of its predecessor. The barrel which was reduced in length by 15cm, had no perforated cooling jacket but had longitudinal grooves machined on its surface for cooling. The compensator consisted of two large slots in the top of the muzzle. The 40 round magazine fitted into the forward grip. The pistol grip, trigger guard and trigger housing were all made of an aluminium alloy.

Model 38/42: The Model 38/42 **192** was designed and produced for the Italian Army and was both easier and cheaper to produce than the Model 1938A. It was designed by Marengoni in 1942. The body was the same as the Model 1 and stampings were used for the body and the magazine housing. The bolt had a fixed firing pin and the return spring of the Model 1938A. The spring guide rod projected to the rear of the end closure cap and provides a ready recognition feature. The wooden buttstock was shortened and the forestock terminated at the magazine housing which did not follow the pattern of the Model 1 and was not extended below the body to make a handgrip. The barrel was the fluted design of the Model 1 with the same two cut compensator; later production models had no grooved barrel and this version with the smooth barrel was sometimes known as the Model 1938/43. The Model 1938/42 was used by the Italians and Germans in the last years of World War II and some were sold to Rumania in 1944.

Model 1938/44: This SMG – again by Tullio Marengoni – was a simplified version of the 38/42. The 38/44 **195** had the length of the bolt reduced from 7.1in to 5.9in and replaced the small diameter return spring with its guide tube by a large diameter spring similar to that used in the Sten SMG. This resulted in a plain end closure cap at the rear of the body and so allows ready distinction from the 38/42.

The 38/44 went into production in February 1944 and in December 3,000 were being produced each month. These were sold to Syria, Iraq, Pakistan and Costa Rica.

Model 38/49: The Model 38/49 **199** was a modified version of the Model 38/44 with a cross bolt safety located above and forward of the double trigger. It

189 The bolt, firing pin, return spring and the cam which held up the firing pin of the 1938A until the bolt was fully home.

190 The second variation of the 1938A had a 4 groove compensator. It had no bayonet.

191 The Beretta Model 1 was intended for airborne forces. It had a fixed firing pin giving floating firing. The folding stock and pistol grip came from the German MP 40. It never went into service.

192 The Beretta 38/42 was the first Italian SMG to go into mass production with a fixed firing pin. This is a prototype. Note the 'step' at the breech of the thick barrel and the deep grooves.

193 Early production 38/42 with a narrow, contoured barrel and shallow grooves.

195

196

194 Late production 38/42 with a smooth barrel. Usually known as the 38/43. Note all 38/42 series have a projection in the end cap to house the return spring rod.

195 Beretta Model 38/44. Note end cap has no projection.

196 Beretta 38/44 modified by Eoka in Cyprus in their struggle against British troops. The butt was cut short and a Bren carrying handle was used as a forward grip.

197 Prototype Beretta Model 38/49. This had the firing mechanism of the 38/44 and no cross bolt safety.

197

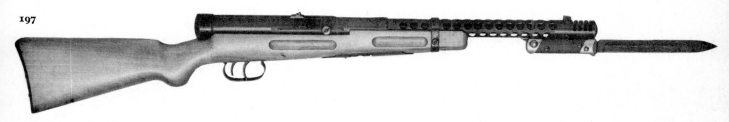

locked the bolt in either position and with it a secondary safety locked the sear whilst the cross bolt was in transition from 'fire' to 'safe'. In 1949–50 the cross bolt safety was fitted to the Model 38A **198**.

The Model 38/49 has been a commercial success. It was used by the Italian Army and was ordered by the West German Border Police in 1951 and 1961 as their MP1. In 1956 the Model 38/49 was re-designated the 'Model 4' to assist in sales promotion since it was seen that the date classification was causing potential customers to regard it as 'dated'. This has led to some confusion amongst collectors because Marengoni designed a model in 1956 which was also called the Model 4. It was produced only in prototype form and the name then was given to the Model 38/49. The 'original' model 4 is described later in this chapter. Some of the commercial Model 4 were fitted with a folding bayonet similar to that of earlier Model 1938A and were sold to Egypt. West Germany ordered the 38/49 in 1951 and re-ordered in 1961. These were used by the Border Police.

Model 2: This was produced in prototype by Marengoni in 1951 **200**. It had a folding stock and the fore-grip magazine housing of the Model 1. The smooth barrel, cross bolt safety, bolt and return spring came from the Model 38/49.

Model 3: This was a design from Marengoni in 1955. It had the smooth barrel and compensator of the Model 38/49 and the magazine housing of the Model 1. The new features were the cocking lever on the left of the body and the incorporation of the rear pistol grip and trigger housing in one single stamping. The cross bolt safety of the Model 38/49 was eliminated and replaced by a grip safety behind the pistol grip. No other safety was fitted. The buttstock was a telescoping wire type which when fully forward stopped some 2in behind the grip safety resulting in a rather uncomfortable grip for the firer's right hand **201**.

Model 4: This was Marengoni's last design for Beretta. He was responsible for all their models from the Model 1918 and the Model 4 appeared as a prototype in 1956. He probably produced more successful weapons than any of his contemporaries and his work included some of the finest designs produced anywhere.

The Model 4 was an improvement of the Model 3. The buttstock was re-shaped to allow it to go further forward around the pistol grip and allowed the gun to be fired with comfort with the stock in its closed position. The folding bayonet from the Carcano carbine was fitted to lie below the barrel **202**.

Model 5: This was a modified version of the Model 1938/49 – the Model 4. It was engineered by Domenico Salza who succeeded Tullio Marengoni in 1957. The Model 5 was fitted with a new safety device consisting of a grip safety positioned in the finger groove on the right of the forestock. This had to be depressed with the fingers of the left hand to permit the gun to be fired; it had also to be pressed in before cocking was possible; when released it locked the bolt in either the forward or cocked positions. This was the only difference from the Model 1938/49. The Model 5 was still in production in 1970 for the Italian Carabinieri **203**.

The SMGs designed by Marengoni were extremely successful and sold well but they were all of a similar basic pattern which embodied only minor changes. In 1952 a research team was set up, led by Domenico Salza, to undertake a study of the next generation of SMGs. The team was given as its guidelines the following requirements for a SMG:

    a. it had to be strong and compact;

    b. it had to be manufactured as economically as possible.

    c. it had to be inherently accurate and stable in automatic fire.

198 Long barrel version of the 38/49. This is a modified 1938A with a cross bolt safety added.

199 Standard Beretta 38/49. The name was changed to 'Model 4' in 1955 to assist sales promotion.

200 The Beretta Model 2 in 1951 was a folding stock version of the 1938/49 using components from the Model 1.

198

199

200

201

202

203

The need for economy in a highly competitive market was found to be best met by all metallic construction using stampings and spot welding.

The early Berettas had attempted to achieve stability and prevent the muzzle from rising by using compensators. Salza adopted a different approach by attempting to place the centre of gravity of the weapon on the axis of the bore. This entailed lowering the barrel within the body. At the same time he endeavoured to reduce the change of the centre of gravity induced by the reciprocating breech block. To do this a 'wrap round' bolt was produced which had the firing pin near the rear end and so enveloped the breech. As the bolt moved backwards and forwards its centre of mass remained further forward above the fore grip.

The first prototype designed along these ideas was designed in 1953 and came out in 1954.

Model 6: The Model 6 **204** was made of heavy gauge sheet metal stampings. The barrel and the lower part of the body, consisting of the trigger housing and rear pistol grip, were formed as one unit. The upper part of the body covered the barrel, breech block and return spring like a lid. The breech block was ⌐ shaped; the long arm lay completely over the barrel; the lower arm which carried a fixed firing pin, extractor and feed lug, carried out the usual functions of a breech block. It can be seen that this design served the two purposes of raising the centre of gravity of the entire weapon and keeping the centre of gravity of the bolt well forward. The return spring entered the bolt and had a guide rod which fitted into a recess in the rear of the upper part of the body.

The cocking handle was situated on top of the body and the sights were extremely simple, consisting of a foresight and a fixed aperture backsight set for 100m. The rod stock folded forward on the right of the weapon.

A series of variants were produced **204**. These included different angles of the pistol grip, smooth, ribbed and grooved body covers, a perforated sleeve around the lower half of the barrel, a pistol foregrip and a foregrip integral with the trigger housing. These developments were numbered 7, 8, 9 and 11 and appeared in 1954 and 1955.

Model 10: The Model 10 **204** appeared in 1957 and was the forerunner of the Model 12 (qv). It differed from the Model 12 in having a wire stock like the American M3 which slid forward to the pistol grip, smaller side plates on the pistol grip, a slightly longer magazine opening and a shaped foregrip instead of a pistol grip.

Model 12: This model **205** was produced as a final prototype in 1958 and went into series production in 1959. It was adopted by the Italian Army in 1961 as the M12 SMG. Heavy sheet metal stampings are spot welded or rivetted together. The body is cylindrical and has deep grooves extending the full length. This ensures reliable functioning even if sand, dust, or mud gets in. The body, forward pistol grip, magazine housing, trigger housing and pistol grip are all one unit. The cylindrical breech block slides forward to envelope the breech inside a deep drilling. The fixed firing pin is situated well back. The barrel is 200mm (7.9in) long and of this length 150mm (5.9in) lie inside the breech block at the moment of firing. This design – similar in principle to the Israeli Uzi – keeps the gun very steady at automatic fire and there is virtually no tendency for the muzzle to rise. It can in fact be fired with a reasonable consistency using only one hand.

The weapon has two independent safety systems. There is a grip safety in the front of the pistol grip below the trigger. This locks the bolt, when released, in

201 The Beretta Model 3, 1955, had a grip safety, a forward grip on the magazine housing, and an awkward grip for the right hand since the shoulder piece of the butt stopped two inches from the pistol grip, when retracted.

202 The Beretta Model 4 had a re-shaped butt closing up over the grip safety, and a folding bayonet. This was Marengoni's last design for Beretta.

203 The Beretta Model 5, 1957, was Domenico Salza's first design for Beretta. It was a 1938/49 with a squeeze safety on the fore-end operated by the fingers of the firer's left hand.

153

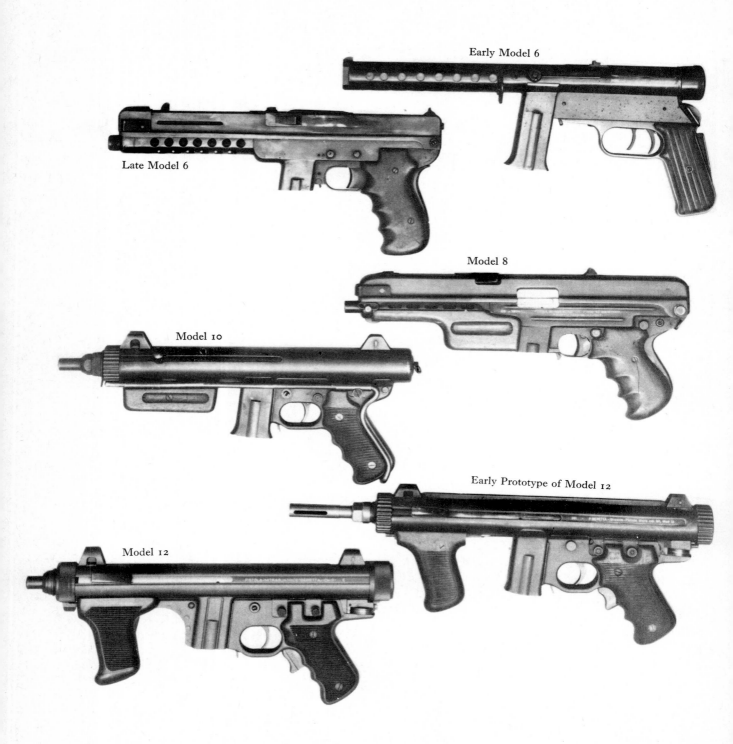

Early Model 6

Late Model 6

Model 8

Model 10

Early Prototype of Model 12

Model 12

154

204

PISTOLA-MITRAGLIATRICE "BERETTA.,-Cal.9   1021

either the forward or cocked position, and so it must be held in to cock the action. There is also a push button safety just above the pistol grip. Until this is pushed from left to right the grip safety is locked and the bolt cannot move. The fire selecter is located in front of the thumb operated safety catch. When pressed to the right it provides semi-automatic fire; when pushed to the left full automatic fire results. The weapon normally has a metal stock which folds laterally to the right; it can be fitted with a quickly detachable wooden butt.

The Model 12 is still in service with the Italian Army. It is an excellent SMG and reflects great credit on its designer Dominico Salza who became Head of the Research Department at Beretta.

OTHER ITALIAN SMGs

FNA-B SMG's: The firm of Fabrica Nazionale d'Armie at Brescia developed several SMG's between 1942 and 1955. They all had interesting and unusual features. The designer of these guns is not known.

Model 43: The M43 **206** was designed, developed and produced at Brescia. Some 7,000 guns were produced and they equipped both Italian and German units. The action was of the delayed blow back system but unlike the very great majority of such SMG's it fired from the closed breech position. To achieve this a two part bolt was used with a lever – similar to the Hungarian M39 – to provide a mechanical disadvantage to accelerate the rear part of the block and by engaging in the body, holding up the bolt head. After a round was chambered the bolt head came to rest. The bolt body closed up and rotated the lever into the body. The closing of the two parts together cleared the firing pin lock and operation of the trigger allowed the spring loaded pin to go forward. The bolt was small and compact and the hammerless firing action must have been unique.

The magazine housing could be swung forward when not in use – again like the Hungarian M39 – and the magazine, usually containing 20 rounds, lay under the barrel. The barrel had a perforated casing and a combined muzzle brake and compensator of the type and shape employed in the Russian PPSh–41 (qv).

204 A series of Salza prototypes, 1952–57, leading to the Model 12. Models 6 and 8 had ⌐ shaped bolts. Models 10 and 12 had wrap round bolts.

205 The Beretta Model 12 was developed in 1958, produced in 1959 and adopted by the Italian Armed Forces in 1961. It is still current.

The gun body and magazine housing were machined from the solid which made it an expensive weapon. The stock was a single rod with a pivotting shoulder plate. It rotated down through 180deg to lock along the right of the body with the butt plate lying along the underside of the barrel jacket.

Model X4: The X4 **207** was produced in 1954. It was made from heavy gauge sheet stampings. The bolt was cylindrical with a fixed firing pin on the front face and a lug on the left which ran in a groove on the inside of the body. Cocking was achieved by a sleeve over the body which engaged this lug and when pulled back, retracted the bolt. The telescoping wire shoulder stock closed up to the rear of the pistol grip. The gun fired only at full automatic. An unusual feature of the weapon was the very deep magazine housing which made loading very quick and simple.

It was claimed that with a production run of 100,000 guns it could be produced at a cost of £5 ($15). It was tested in 1955 but although functioning well there were no buyers.

In 1955 a shorter Model, the X5, was produced without a stock. The barrel length was reduced from 7.5in to 4.6in. The overall length was only 12¼in. This made it a very handy weapon but it too did not sell. With the exception of the Australian SR11 (qv) designed by Russel S. Robinson and the Ingram Models 10 and 11 it was probably the shortest SMG ever designed **208**.

BERNADELLI MODEL VB

This gun **209** was produced by the Vincenzo Bernadelli factory, also located at Brescia, in 1948–49. Only 500 were made and only 300 sold. The remainder are still waiting a customer. In appearance it was similar to the Beretta 38/49 but had a single trigger and a five slot compensator.

FRANCHI MODEL LF-57

This gun **211** was produced by the firm of Luigi Franchi of Brescia. The earliest experimental work was done in the 1950's and a prototype known as the LF-56 appeared in 1956. The production version the LF-57 was produced in the next year. It seems apparent that this weapon was like the Beretta Model 6 **204** designed by Domenico Salza in 1953. The bolt is ⌐ shaped with the long arm above the barrel and the firing pin and extractor together with the feed horn on the lower arm, thus raising the centre of gravity of the gun up to the thrust line of the barrel and preventing muzzle rise at full auto. The grip safety was located at the front of the pistol grip. No other applied safety was fitted. The entire gun – except barrel and bolt – was produced from stampings of heavy sheet steel. The LF-57 was the first gun manufactured in every respect by the Luigi Franchi Company and several thousands were taken by the Italian Navy in 1962.

206 The FNA–B M43. This had a delayed blow back action firing from a closed breech using a two part bolt, a lever delay and – uniquely – an internal spring operated firing pin.

207 The FNA–B X4 produced in 1954. Note ribbed cocking sleeve and also the wide magazine housing designed to facilitate loading.

208 The FNA–B X5 produced in 1955. This had no stock and at 12¼ inches it was one of the shortest SMGs designed.

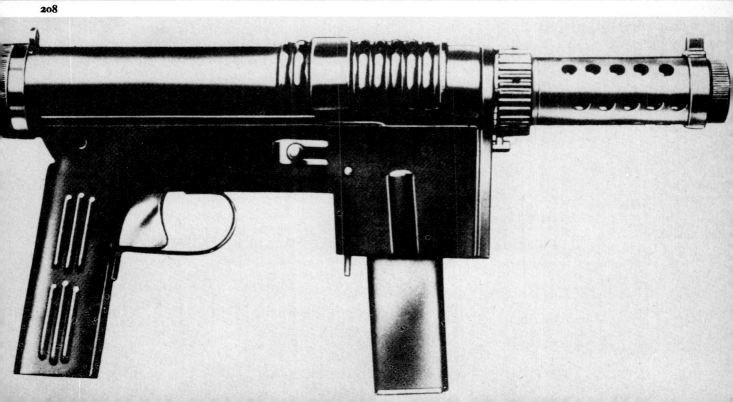

209

210

The LF-57 had a barrel 8.1in long. In 1962 a semi-automatic version with a 16in barrel was made and exported to the United States as the Police Model 1962.

GIANDOSO SMGs

The TZ-45: The two brothers Toni and Zorzoli Giandoso designed several SMGs starting with the TZ-45 **212** designed in 1944 and produced in 1945. This was a blow back operated weapon firing 9mm Parabellum cartridges at either full auto or single shot. The selecter lever located on the right of the trigger housing forward of the trigger, also acted as a safety; when pushed fully forward it locked the bolt. In addition a grip safety was used, placed behind the magazine housing. An original feature was the arrangement of the return spring which was in two parts with a telescoping guide rod. The forward section slid over the rear part as the bolt retracted.

The TZ-45 production in 1945 was limited to 6,000 and these were taken by second line units of the Italian Army engaged in operations against guerrillas. After the war the TZ-45 was manufactured in Burma as the BA-52. It is stated by Nelson and Lochoven that one of the Giandoso brothers went to Burma to set up the factory.

PM 410: The Pistola Mitragliatrice was produced by the Genar Company of Rome in 1954. The number '410' was its length in mm. It was a blow back operated weapon firing at full auto or single shot using a Beretta magazine holding 20, 30 or 40 9mm Parabellum cartridges. It was of conventional design, readily identified by a thickened barrel section at the muzzle which at first sight looked like a conical flash hider. It had no stock but was controlled by a sling slung over the firer's shoulder and gripped near the muzzle by the firer's left

209 The Bernadelli Model VB was produced in 1948–49. Only 500 were made and 300 sold.

210 The Variara SMG was manufactured at Biella in Northern Italy, between 1943–5 and used by partisans. It was a composite weapon with features from the Mk II Sten, the MP 38 and FNA–B Model 43.

211

211 Luigi Franchi Model 57. This weapon has the ⌐ shaped bolt similar to that used by Domenico Salza in the Beretta Model 6 in 1953. The gun was in service with the Italian Navy in 1962.

212 The Tz–45 was designed by Toni and Zorzoli Giandoso, and sometimes called the Mitra Tz–45. It was later produced in Burma as the BA–52.

213 The Genar Pistola Mitra-gliatrice 720. This was designed by the Giandoso brothers and existed in two versions. As the 720 it measured 720mm with a long butt and as the 440 it had a rear, wooden, pistol grip.

214 Genar experimental SMG by Giandoso. This gun is very similar to the PM 470 but had left hand cocking and a 3 slot compensator. The unusual wire wrapping around the barrel is the same.

212

213

214

hand whilst his right hand grasped a conventional pistol grip which incorporated a grip safety at the rear.

PM 470: The Genar Co offered what was basically the same gun with a folding single strut stock. The barrel was ¾in longer and had a two slot compensator. The plain barrel had a heavy coil spring surrounding its exterior to act as a hand guard: the action was that of the TZ-45.

A version with a wooden stock was called the Moschetto Mitragliatrice 735. As the grip safety could no longer be used a safety catch was incorporated behind the magazine housing, beneath the stock.

PM 720 and PM 440

This gun **213** was marketed by the Genar Co and manufactured under contract at Castelfranco Veneto by Simmel-Werke. It was the PM 470 with the choice of two wooden stocks. The long stock produced an overall length of 720mm and the short stock was simply a pistol grip giving a length of 440mm. One or two small modifications to the body to simplify manufacture and re-location of the back sight further forward are the only differences from the PM 470.

THE VARIARA SMG

This gun **210** was mass produced in a clandestine factory near Biella in Northern Italy between 1943 and 1945 and was used by partisans against the German occupying forces.

It was designed to make use of features well proved in other guns. The Sten Mk II formed the basis of the weapon and the bolt and barrel securing system were taken directly from it. The magazine held 30 9mm cartridges.

The FNA–B Model 43 **206** was used as the source of the folding stock and the collapsible magazine housing; the sear and two triggers came from the Beretta Model 38A **190** and the pistol grip and the safety were derived from the German MP 38 **153**. Few of these weapons have survived the passage of time.

THE ARMAGUERRA OG 44

The designer of this weapon **216, 217** was Giovanni Oliani and his initials were used in the name. He worked in the Armaguerra (Military Weapons) factory at Cremona which was created for the production of a self loading rifle. The first prototype was the OG 42. Domenico Salza of Beretta has described this gun in the Italian magazine 'Diana Armi', as the very first gun with the ⌐ shaped bolt and the direct predecessor of the Beretta models 6, 7, 8, 9 and 11. The OG 42 had the magazine fitting into the pistol grip and a folding, forward pistol grip. The OG 44 had the magazine as the forward grip and a grip safety on the rear, pistol grip. It existed with either a metal stock which folded up under the barrel or with a wooden butt as shown in figure **216**. Only 14 specimens were made. Only two are known to have survived. One – with a folding butt – was shown by Salza in the article already mentioned. The other, shown here, is at the Pattern Room at the Royal Small Arms Factory at Enfield.

The entire body of the gun, including the rear pistol grip was made from a single plate of 1.5mm steel. The trigger mechanism was made from steel pressings. The magazine held 25 rounds but the Beretta 30 and 40 round magazines could also be used.

The feature of main interest is, of course, the bolt. The part over the barrel had a cylindrical, grooved cross section with the sides flattened. The lower part containing the firing pin was integral with this.

Firing at 500–550rpm with a muzzle velocity of 1,400ft/s control at this rate was exceptionally good. Its small size and advanced design make it one of the most interesting SMGs of World War II.

215 The FDA SMG. This Italian SMG fired a 9mm short cartridge. It has no butt, is blow back operated, but no details of designer, or who the manufacturer was, are known.

216 The Armaguerra OG 44 was made in prototype only at Cremona. The designer was Giovanni Oliani.

217 The OG 44 was probably the first SMG with the ⌐ shaped bolt with its mass over the barrel.

215

216
217

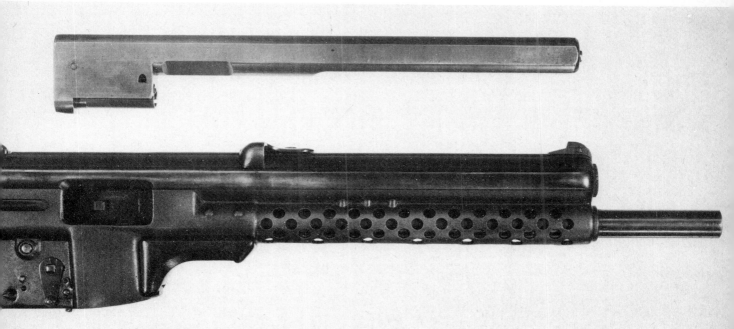

Russian Sub-Machine Guns

The Russians made greater use of the sub-machine gun than any other army during World War II. In part this was forced upon them by the loss of a great deal of their manufacturing capacity as the Germans moved eastwards during the summer and autumn of 1941. Operation 'Barbarossa' was initially so successful that the machine tools were simply no longer available to the Russians to manufacture small arms in the quantities required. Simple designs utilising pressings and stampings and not needing extensive machining operations were adopted from 1942 onwards. Once however these weapons were available, the Russians made tremendous use of them, and even went to the extreme length of equipping entire Battalions of tank riders who were armed with no other weapon. The troops, as their name implies, gave the closest possible support to armoured units and provided the intimate co-operation between infantry and tanks without which the latter cannot operate successfully – particularly in close country where enemy infantry are able to use short range anti-tank weapons with relative impunity. The SMG was also employed extensively in the Infantry Battalion where commanders and 2 or 3 others of the 8 man section were equipped with this type of weapon. It was used by armoured units, gun detachments, drivers and supply troops.

The total number of SMGs made by the Soviet Union is not known but there is no doubt that it exceeded 10 million.

THE FEDEROV AVTOMAT
The first Russian weapon to resemble the modern accepted shape of the SMG was designed by Vladimir Grigorevitch Federov. He was born in St Petersburg in 1874 and always intended to adopt a military career. He entered the Artillery Academy in 1897 and graduated in 1900. In 1905 he produced a conversion of the Mosin-Nagant 7.62mm bolt action rifle to a self loading action. This was never accepted in spite of trials carried out as late as 1926. During his work on the Mosin he concluded that using a cartridge of reduced impulse would permit the design of a light weight rapid firing weapon. He chose to use the Japanese 6.5mm rimless round for 2 reasons. Firstly it produced the reduced impulse – compared with the 7.62mm × 54R cartridge – and secondly its short case made automatic action and a short bodied weapon easier. The lack of the rim made

magazine feeding much more dependable. To enable the weapon to maintain accuracy when firing at its cyclic rate of 600 rounds/min he introduced a pistol grip forward of the magazine on which the firer could pull down to keep the muzzle from rising **218**.

Federov used a system of short recoil operation for his weapon in which the barrel came back about ⅜in locked to the barrel. Attached to the side of the barrel was a lever which struck a projection in the body and was pivotted to throw the breech block rearwards with increased velocity after unlocking occurred. The locking system consisted of a dumb-bell shaped piece mounted on the outer surface of each side of the chamber. The upper projections of the dumb-bell were the pivot at the front and the locking surface at the rear. The lower humps provided the pivotting surface at the front and the barrel latch at the rear. When the gun was ready to fire, the upper projection was located behind a lateral extension from the side of the bolt which formed a locking stud. Thus when the bolt was blown backwards the barrel came back with it. After ⅜in of free travel to allow the pressure to drop to a safe low level, the lower front projection came into contact with a raised boss on the floor of the body and this rotated the locking piece down at its rear end and the bottom of the pivotting member entered a cut away in the floor of the body and stayed there. Thus whilst the accelerator increased the bolt velocity, the barrel remained latched to the rear. When the bolt came forward under the drive of the return spring it picked up the top round from the 25 round magazine and chambered it. The contact with the accelerator freed the locking piece from the bottom of the body and as the barrel ran out the lock was carried up behind the bolt locking stud and the gun was ready to fire again.

The muzzle velocity of this weapon was 2,200ft/s and with a weight of 9.6lb it could well be claimed – as some authorities do – that this is the first assault rifle and not a true SMG. However there is no doubt that in the fighting that went on in 1919 between the White Russians assisted by their Western Allies and the Red Armies, the 3,000 Avtomats produced at Sestorets were used in a role which was that of a SMG. All subsequent Soviet sub-machine guns were blow back operated. In this method the barrel is fixed securely to the body of the gun and cannot therefore move relative to it. The gun fires from an unlocked breech and so the cost and complication of making a breech locking system is avoided.

Throughout the period 1934–45 all Soviet SMGs used the 7.62mm cartridge which had a case length of 25mm. This is generally known as the 'P' cartridge and it is basically a pistol cartridge with all the limitations that implies. The case is semi-bottle-necked and has a long near parallel sided case from the neck to the extractor groove which provides obturation during the blow back operation.

In 1926 a SMG was designed by Fedor Vasilevitch Tokarev. Tokarev was born in 1871 at Egorlikskaya. His parents were Cossacks and he became an apprentice to his village blacksmith when he was eleven. When he was fourteen he worked for a gun maker and in 1888 he became a trade student at the Novocherkassk Military Trade School, emerging after four years as a NCO craftsmen. He was posted to the 12th Don Cossack Regiment. Four years later he returned to the Trade School as an Instructor in gun making. In 1907 he studied at the Officers' School at Oranienbaum. After graduation he served at the Sestorets Factory and in 1921 he went to the Tula Arsenal. His fame lies principally with his modification to the Maxim gun, his SL rifle of 1939, and his pistol which was in service until comparatively recently. The Tokarev SMG fired the

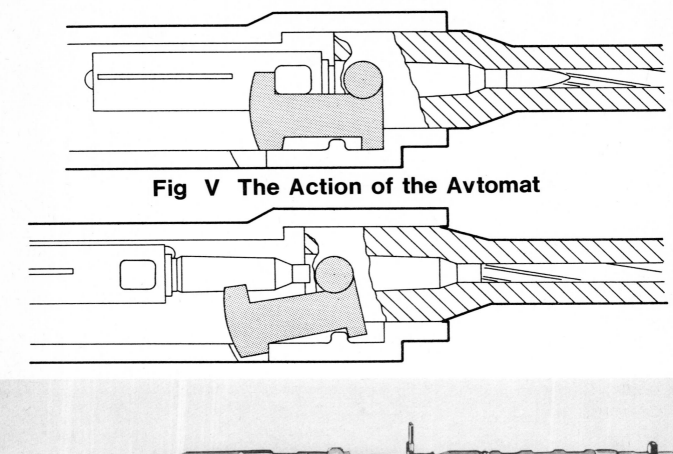

Fig V The Action of the Avtomat

7.62mm Nagent revolver cartridge at a rate of 1,100–1,200 rounds/min. The rimmed round was not satisfactory and only experimental models were made. The arm can be recognised by its two triggers – one for single shot, one for full auto and the unusual shape of the magazine housing. A sketch of this weapon is shown at **220**.

THE PPD 1934/38

The next SMG was the Degtyarev model of 1934. This was the PPD-1934/38. The designation PP – Pistolet Pulemet – meaning 'machine pistol' appears on all subsequent Soviet SMGs. All use the Russian 7.62mm × 25mm type P pistol cartridge.

218 The Federov Avtomat. This was a short recoil operated gun of unusual action (see page 163). It fired the Japanese 6.5mm rimless cartridge. It is claimed by some experts to be the first assault rifle.

Vasily Degtyarev was born in Tula in 1890. He left school at eleven and was employed in Tula Arsenal operating a machine testing springs for the new Mosin rifle. He was drafted into the army and served at Sestorets Small Arms Factory where he worked under Federov. He later went to Oranienbaum where weapon testing was carried out. In 1916 he designed an automatic carbine. Little is known of this weapon except that it was not accepted during the Czarist regime. His chief claim to fame was the Degtyarev light machine gun which was produced in several versions and prodigious numbers for the Russian armies during World War II. He produced an anti-tank rifle and after the war came his RP46 and the RPD LMGs. He became a Major General of Engineers, Doctor of Technical Sciences, won four State Prizes, was a Deputy of the USSR Supreme Soviet and died in 1959 at the age of sixty-nine.

The PPD 1934/38 was a weapon based partly on an early Suomi design and partly on the Schmeisser MP-28. The magazine generally found on the gun is a 71 round drum magazine clearly copied from the Suomi. It is readily identified by the extension projecting above the drum, which fits into the receiver. It is said that some of the earlier magazines were of 73 round capacity and had a smaller number of feed followers. There is also a curved box magazine which held 25 rounds but this is rarely seen. The gun fires from an open breech and is of typical blow back design. One feature of interest is that both barrel and chamber are chrome plated. The barrel jacket was machined from the solid and, in fact, there were neither pressings nor stampings employed in the construction of the gun.

There were several variations of the PPD 34/38 and it seems that they fitted

219

into 3 main categories:

220

219 Vladimir Grigorevitch Federov – Head of the Small Arms Design Office at Kovrov in 1924. Designer of the Avtomat in 1916.

220 The Tokarev 1926 SMG fired the rimmed Nagent revolver cartridge at 1,100–1,200 rounds a minute. It fired single shot from the front trigger and full auto from the rear. Only experimental guns were made.

1. The earliest version took the 73 round magazine and the change lever, fitted in front of the trigger, was a 'flag' which could be rotated to show either '1' or '73'. The firing pin had an external cocking arrangement similar to the Schmeisser, the bolt was polished and the safety finger plate on the cocking handle was rounded. The trigger guard was of one piece construction. The ejection slot in front of the back sight was very narrow.
2. The standard gun took a 71 round drum and the change lever was so marked. There was a fixed firing pin and the bolt was blued. The safety plate was rectangular and the trigger guard was in two parts rivetted together. The ejection slot was much wider.
3. The late model differs from both the other models in having a barrel

jacket with only three sets of slots as opposed to eight. Otherwise it is similar to the standard gun.

The PPD 34/38 was easy to fire and simply stripped. The milled cap at the rear of the receiver was unscrewed and the return spring and bolt were withdrawn.

THE PPD 1940

The PPD – like its predecessor – was designed by Degtyarev and produced at Tula and Sestorets. It was used in the Finnish campaign and replaced the 34/38. The barrel housing is similar to that of the 34/38 but they are not interchangeable. It can be distinguished from the earlier gun by the wooden fore end in front of the magazine 223. The early model 1940 had a tangent rear sight like the 1934/38 but later versions had a simple V notch rear sight. The drum magazine does not have a vertical extension to fit into the gun but has a single lip fitting directly into the magazine holder in the receiver. There is also only one follower.

Although the receiver and cap, return spring, trigger mechanism and sling fittings are interchangeable with those of the 34/38, the bolt is not. This has a moveable firing pin controlled by a lever on the bolt head which ensures that the bolt is fully closed before the round is fired.

THE PPSh-41

The next sub-machine gun was designed by George S. Shpagin, Hero of Socialist Labour, and later Lieutenant General in the Red Army. He collaborated with Degtyarev in producing a 12.7mm heavy machine gun which was used throughout World War II. The PPSh-41 224 did not come into service until mid-1942 but the gun used stampings for the receiver and barrel jacket, the bolt was simple to construct and by the end of the war over 5 million guns had been made. It is now obsolete in the Soviet Army but has been manufactured in Hungary as the 48M, in North Korea as the Type 49 SMG and in China as the Type 59 SMG. The origin and date of manufacture of the weapon can be determined by the markings on top of the receiver. The back sight also helps in identification. Soviet and Iranian PPSh-41 have V back sights, North Korean Type 49 and Chinese Type 50 have aperture rear sights. All these weapons are basically the same except the North Vietnamese K50 which will be covered later. Some PPSh-41s were converted to 9mm during the war and some by Iran after the war. These are rare.

The PPSh-41 is a blow back operated, selective fire weapon with a wooden butt. The barrel is chromium plated and the weapon is extremely reliable and sturdy. The earliest Russian models had a tangent leaf rear sight but in late 1942 a simple flip over back sight, giving 100 or 200m, was introduced.

The magazine is either the 71 round drum of the PPD 40 or a 35 round slightly curved box magazine. The PPSh-41 is identified readily by the shape of the front end of the barrel jacket which extends beyond the muzzle and is sloped back from top to bottom. There is a gas exit port on the top so the extention acts as a compensator to reduce muzzle climb at full auto. The change lever is no longer a 'flag' but a sliding catch enclosed within the trigger guard. Pressing forward gives full automatic fire; the rearward position operates the disconnector to give single shots. The cocking handle can be locked either forward or to the rear. The weapon can be stripped easily. After ensuring safety, press forward on the receiver catch at the rear of the body and swing the barrel down. Pull the

166

221   The PPD 1934/38. All Russian SMGs have 'PP' meaning Pistolet Pulemet – or machine pistol. This was designed by Degtyarev – a great machine gun inventor. It took a 71 round drum magazine which had an extension piece fitting inside the gun.

222   Vasily Degtyarev, Major-General of Engineers, Doctor of Technical Sciences, Winner of four State Prizes, Deputy of the USSR Supreme Soviet – designer of the LMG and SMG.

223   The PPD 1940, also designed by Degtyarev, was used against the Finns in the Battles of the Lakes in 1940. It can be distinguished from the 1934/38 by the magazine well. The drum has no extension neck.

224   PPSh-41 was designed by George Shpagin. It can readily be distinguished by the backward sloping combined muzzle brake and compensator. This is an early model.

221

223

224

226

225 George S. Shpagin, Hero of Socialist Labour and Lt General of the Red Army. His SMG was made in vast numbers.

226 Later version of the PPSh–41 taking the drum magazine. Sights were simplified.

cocking handle rearward, rotate the bolt return spring and buffer up and out of the receiver.

The drum magazines on the PPD and PPSh series are not interchangeable on the gun but the procedure for filling them is the same and is now described in outline. Press the control button in the rear of the drum and swing down the latch on the front cover of the drum, lift off the cover and latch. Grasp the cruciform rotor in the centre of the drum and wind the spring two complete turns anti-clockwise. During the first four clicks, which correspond to one revolution, the cartridge conveyor must be held stationary. The spiral track insert should now be rotated as far as possible in an anti-clockwise direction. Seventy-one rounds can now be placed in the grooves of the spiral, bullet nose upwards. When all the cartridges have been loaded grasp the rotor and turn it slightly anti-clockwise against its own spring; at the same time press in the central button to release the spring, easing the rotor clockwise until it stops. Replace the cover on the magazine and place the latch back in the locked position. It should be noted that the serial numbers on the magazine and on the gun should coincide. If they do not then it is best, if possible, to fire a few rounds to ensure functioning.

The SMG is loaded by inserting the drum or box magazine into the magazine opening and sliding it up into place until the magazine catch engages. The safety catch on the cocking handle is slipped out and after the cocking handle has been drawn to the rear the gun is ready to fire. The selector lever goes forward for automatic fire and rearward for semi-automatic. The cocked bolt can be held to the rear – if so required – by pushing in the safety catch on the cocking lever.

The sights can be set by flipping the leaf to '10' or '20' which represents 100 or 200m. The bolt remains in the forward position when the ammunition is exhausted.

The K-50m SMG, 228: used by the Viet Cong in South Vietnam is a modified Chinese Type 50 SMG which itself is derived directly from the PPSh-41. Firstly it fires either the Russian 7.62mm × 25mm Type P pistol cartridge or the 7.62mm × 25mm Type 50 Chinese pistol cartridge. The barrel jacket has been shortened and the muzzle compensator and fore grip have been eliminated. The lower part of the receiver has been changed in shape and a French pattern sliding metal butt stock has replaced the original wooden stock.

THE PPS-42

In 1942 the German troops had surrounded Leningrad. The PPS-42 was designed and produced by A. I. Sudarev – a Soviet engineer – for use against the encircling enemy. In fact the troop trials could hardly have been carried out under more demanding circumstances.

The gun is made of sheet steel of heavy gauge stamped into shape, rivetted and spot welded. The butt stock is of folding, metal design (except the Polish copy, the 43/52) and when it is folded this provides the easiest means of distinguishing it from the PPS-43. In the 42 the shoulder piece folds over and around the ejection port on top of the receiver. The stock of the PPS-43 has been shortened and lies behind the slot, when folded.

The gun was designed for quick production and simplicity. It uses only a simple 35 round box magazine which will NOT fit earlier guns. It fires only at full automatic but as the cyclic rate is reduced to 650rpm – from the PPSh-41 rate of 900 – a skilled firer can manage single shots by dexterous trigger operation. A sheet metal muzzle brake cum compensator of distinctive shape is attached to the front of the barrel jacket. The rear of it supports the muzzle. It is welded – NOT integral with the jacket as the PPSh-41 – at the bottom of the jacket and rivetted at the top.

THE PPS-43

This is a Sudarev improved version of the PPS-42. It can easily be distinguished from the 42 by retracting the bolt. The return spring guide rod will be seen to project through the bolt face to act as an ejector **229**. Other differences from the PPS-42 are:

227 Hungarian 48m. This was a copy of the PPSh–41.

228 North Viet Nam Model K50. Barrel jacket has been shortened and compensator-muzzle brake removed. Pistol grip and French MAT type sliding butt fitted.

229 The PPS–43. Designed by Sudarev in Leningrad as the PPS–42, the folding stock was shortened to lie behind the ejection port and the return spring rod passed through the bolt to act as an ejector.

230 Mikhail Kalashnikov – was called up for Military Service at 19. When 20 he was a sergeant, tank commander, and won the Order of the Red Star for gallantry. He designed the AK–47 which has now superseded the SMG in the Soviet Army. Became Hero of Socialist Labour, winner of Stalin and Lenin State Prizes and Deputy of the USSR Supreme Soviet.

231 The AK–47 7.62mm assault rifle. It was modernised in 1959 as the AK–M and is now the standard Russian personal weapon.

228

168

1. Safety is located forward of the trigger guard.
2. Magazine slopes forward at a steeper angle.
3. Folding stock is shorter.
4. Pistol grips are of rubber rather than wood.
5. Muzzle brake is not welded to the bottom of the jacket but to an extra strap which gives support to the muzzle.

Stripping the 42 and 43 is straightforward. The receiver lock is above and behind the pistol grip which can be swung down when the lock is operated. Pull the cocking handle slightly back and then swing the bolt downward out of the receiver. Pull the return spring out of the bolt.

The PPS-43 is now obsolete in USSR but is still used in Poland as the Model 43/52 which differs in having a lengthened receiver and a rigid wooden butt. In China the PPS-43 is known as the Type 43 Copy – NOT as sometimes believed the Type 54 SMG.

The Soviet SMGs have been sturdy, well made, cheap, reliable and above all unsophisticated. They served the Union well and although they are no longer in service with the Red Army they are still in use with many Asian countries and have produced the greater part of the guerrilla armament in that continent.

The SMG is no longer used in Russian or satellite countries in Europe. The AK-47 7.62mm designed by Mikhail Kalashnikov has been adopted by Russia. All the Eastern bloc except Czecho-Slovakia have assault rifles firing out to 300–400m based on this design. Czecho-Slovakia has its own assault rifle – the Vz58.

230

227

229

231

Other Sub-Machine Guns

AUSTRALIAN SMGs

The inability of the British to furnish large quantities of Sten guns and the Americans so far away, having nothing to offer except the Thompson, led the Australian Government to produce its own weapons and considering the limited population and its considerable war effort in other fields, a remarkable number of good designs were produced.

THE OWEN SMG

The most famous was the Owen gun. This saw service wherever the Australian Army was engaged and even as late as the Malaysian anti-Communist campaign in 1950s it was frequently preferred by British troops to their own Mk V Stens and early Sterling SMGs, in the jungle operations.

The designer of the Owen was Lt Evelyn Owen. He produced prototypes in late 1940. A pre-production order of 100 was placed. Of these, 50 were for 9mm, 10 were made for .32 ACP, 20 were designed for .38 and 20 for the .45 ACP cartridge. The tests were largely troop trials and the 9mm Parabellum cartridge proved the most popular. The Mk 1/42 Owen **232** was adopted on 20 November 1941 and the first order for 2000 guns was placed with Lysaght at the Newcastle Works, Port Kemble, New South Wales. The design had previously been patented on 22 July 1941. Production rose to 2800 a month in April 1942 and ended in September 1944; by then some 45,000 models in various marks had been produced.

The Owen is easily recognised by its vertically mounted, forward sloping, box magazine which worked very well. The gun suffered none of the Sten's stoppages and in close country, jungle etc the magazine did not catch in undergrowth as side mounted magazines tend to do. At short ranges the offset sights were no disadvantage. The increased silhouette was accepted and was slightly less prominent since the gun was usually painted in jungle camouflage. The Mk 1/42 had a skeleton butt, similar to that of the Mk 1 Sten, which was readily detachable. The barrel had cooling rings over the pistol fore grip and a four slot compensator. The barrel had a quick release, operated by a plunger above the top of the body, designed not to provide a change system as in a light machine

232 The Owen Mk 1/42 9mm SMG had a very enviable reputation with Australian troops who praised its lack of stoppages, simple maintenance and ease of control. Later versions had holes cut in the frame to lighten the gun.

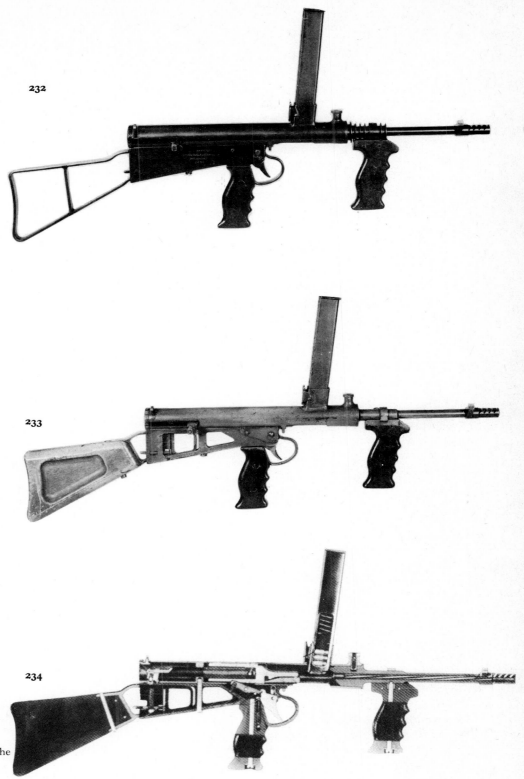

232

233

234

233 The Owen Mk 1/43 had the holes in the frame of the later 1/42. Early versions had the 1/42 cooling rings on the barrel; later verions had a plain stepped barrel as shown.

234 Sectioned drawing of later version of Mk 1/43 Owen.

gun, but to facilitate cleaning. A lot of machining was used and at 10.7lb, with a loaded magazine, it was unnecessarily heavy.

The Owen fired from the open bolt position. Great care was taken in design to keep dirt out of the action. The cocking handle was on the right at the rear of the body and engaged the reduced diameter spring guide at the rear of the bolt. A fibre disc around the guide prevented any dust which entered the cocking slot from getting forward to the bolt. As a result the gun was very reliable under adverse conditions.

Later models of the Mk 1/42 were lightened by cutting holes in the side frame. The Mk 1/43 **233** had this lightened frame but early production models retained the cooling rings on the barrel. Later models had a plain barrel with a step about 1½in from the breech and the front pistol grip was secured directly to the barrel.

The Mk 1/44 was similar in appearance to the Mk 1/43. Later production embodied a bayonet lug on the barrel.

In 1952 a large number of Owens were re-furbished and fitted with wooden butts; a bayonet boss for a long 12in bayonet **236** and a further safety were added. This safety was a sheet metal cover at the rear of the body which when laid down, came in front of the cocking handle.

In February 1943 the Newcastle works produced a small number (given by Nelson and Lockhoven as 202) of guns designated the Owen Mk 11/43 **235**. These had a wooden butt and an unusual bayonet with a tube mounting which slipped over the compensator. The new butt projected forward under the body and the trigger housing was consequently modified. The Mk 11/43 was tested in England in September/October 1943 (see page 92). It did not do very well and was not considered to have sufficient advantages over the Mk 1 to warrant the disruption of production that its adoption would have caused and it was never adopted.

THE AUSTEN

This gun was designed by Uarre Riddell in 1941. It was produced by Diecasters Ltd and W. T. Carmichael at Melbourne from June 1942 to March 1945 when manufacture ceased. Some 20,000 were produced. The gun was not liked by Australian troops who preferred the Owen.

The name, of course, is an abbreviation of 'Australian Sten'.

The designer used features from the Stens and the German MP 40. In the Mk 1 gun **237** the bolt which he used with the telescoping return spring was taken, together with the folding stock, from the MP 40 and the stamped out body, the barrel, trigger housing and trigger mechanism from the Mk II Sten. A back sloping pistol foregrip, an improved butt stock lock and a fixed cocking handle, were original features. With a fixed cocking handle the cocking slot had to be continued to the rear of the body to permit stripping. The magazine took 28 rounds of 9mm Parabellum ammunition, was a single position feed and identical to that of the Sten except that it had a collar to act as the magazine stop. It should be noted that the firing pin was incorporated in the return spring housing and unlike the Sten was not a simple 'pip' on the front face of the bolt.

The Mk II Austen **239** although originally described as a modification to the Mk I differed radically in many respects. The tubular body of the gun was enclosed in a two piece aluminium frame. The trigger housing and rear pistol grip were part of the rear aluminium assembly, which in enclosing the rear part of the body, acted as the rear location for the telescoping return spring. The finned forward aluminium casting fitted over the barrel and contained the magazine

235 The Owen Mk II/43 was produced in February 1943. Only 200 were made. It took a bayonet with a tube slipping over the compensator.

236 The Owen refurbished in 1952. Note 12in bayonet and sheet metal safety over the breech. When dropped, as shown, it blocked the cocking lever.

237 The Austen Mk I 9mm SMG was designed in 1941. It was a combination of the features of the British Sten and the German MP40. The stock and separate firing pin were German in conception. The rest came from the Mk II Sten.

238 Silenced Austen Mk 1. Few of these were made. Note single strut butt.

237

235

236

238

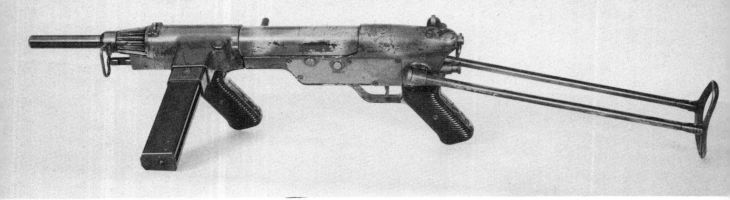

239

240

241

242

housing and forward pistol grip. The firing pin was fixed to the front face of the bolt and this led to a simpler return spring housing. The stock folded as in the Mk I but the catch was located centrally at the rear of the body. Some of the Mk II guns had a spigot extended forward from the front aluminium frame to take a bayonet of the knife type. Prototype No 2 was sent to England and was subjected to comparative trials against the Welgun, the Patchett SMG, Mk IVB Sten, the Andrews and the Owen. It performed sufficiently well to warrant production. During 1944 and 1945 it was manufactured by Diecasters Ltd and W. T. Carmichael.

POST-WAR SMGs

On 6 May 1943 the Australian Army sent out a questionnaire to a very large sample of soldiers with battle experience. This covered all the points of user requirements such as magazine position, position of cocking handle, type of butt, need for a bayonet, sight graduation, magazine capacity, ease of stripping, need for single shot fire and many other similar aspects. The results were studied and a design team under Major S. E. M. Hall incorporated as many as possible in a weapon called the Kokoda **240**. This gun was largely based on the Owen concept but had the magazine inserted in the grip and had a US M3 type sliding butt. The weapon was tested and certain improvements were found necessary. The balance needed adjusting and the gun got very hot. The modified weapon was called the Military Carbine Experimental Model 1 MCEM1 **241**. It was taken to England by Major Hall and tested at Pendine on 8–16 September 1947 against the Sten Mk V, Patchett Mk 2, the new British MCEM3 (see page 103) and the BSA SMG. The Australian MCEM1 got excessively hot and the welds holding the trigger housing to the body, fractured. The MCEM1 was sent back to Australia. Major Hall remained in England and headed a design team working on one version of the British Experimental 7mm rifle. The MCEM1 was further developed as the MCEM2.

The MCEM2 **242** had an unusual cocking handle on top but still retained the Owen characteristics together with some features from the American M3. The barrel was expanded in section at the muzzle to serve as a flash eliminator and fitting for the No 5 rifle bayonet. It was sighted for 100, 150 and 200yd. It was not considered to be suitable for production and further development went on.

THE F1

In 1959 and 1960 two further experimental models were produced. These were known as the X1 and X2 and the final version, the X3 **244** went into production as the F1 at the end of 1962. The F1 has a cylindrical body extended forward and perforated for cooling over the barrel. The magazine is a curved box taking 34 9mm Parabellum cartridges with a two position feed. It is very similar to the Sterling magazine and is interchangeable with that of the Canadian C1 SMG – itself differing only slightly from the Sterling. The F1 is designed with the butt coincident with the line of the barrel, to prevent the muzzle rising and this leads to a high, stamped sheet, offset backsight which folds flat when not required. The cooking handle is on the left of the body and has an attached cover to prevent the ingress of dirt through the cocking slot. The cocking handle can be latched to the bolt to provide bolt closure if the return spring force is inadequate.

Although very different from the Kokoda in appearance all the features of that weapon – derived from users' requirements – are incorporated, including the bayonet and a reduction in weight over the Owen SMG; the overhead feed of the Owen has been restored.

239 The Austen Mk II used a two piece aluminium frame surrounding the body. The firing pin was fixed. Note the spigot under the muzzle for a bayonet.

240 The Kokoda 9mm SMG was the result of a 24 part questionnaire sent out on 6 May 1943 to get users' preferences. Over 1500 replies were received. Surprisingly 1293 wanted the magazine below and only 163 on top.

241 The Australian 9mm Military Carbine Experimental Model No 1 was developed from the Kokoda. Note the cocking handle on the left.

242 The MCEM2 was an improvement on the No 1. Note cocking sleeve on top, change of fore-grip, re-designed trigger, new closing cap, sights and bayonet.

SR MODEL 11

This SMG was designed by Russel S. Robinson at the Shepherd Robinson Arms Development Company in Woolwich near Sydney in 1943. The designer has since achieved considerable success and developed a machine gun which was tested at Enfield in the UK and later became the T 200 in the US machine gun programme. He is currently the designer of Colt's CR-26, a 26mm automatic cannon, which is a contender for the Bushmaster weapon programme.

The SR Model 11 was originally called a constant reaction machine pistol. It fired the 9mm Parabellum cartridge at 600rpm. The idea that Russel Robinson worked on was to endeavour to eliminate the high impulse peaks which occurred every time the gun fired and to make a smooth, averaged, rearward push sustained throughout the duration of the burst. He pointed out that firing at 600rpm the smoothed out force would not amount to more than 8lb. The SR 11 came near enough to this to be fired with control using only one hand. A further concept was to eliminate the twist imparted to the weapon by the bullet which spins at 1500 revolutions a second as it goes through the rifling. The photograph 243 shows the thread on the outside of the barrel which produced barrel rotation as the bolt was blown back. By this means the series of twisting effects – torque – was smoothed out during the burst to produce a constant torque reaction of low level. The two smoothing processes reduced the linear and rotational effects of the bullet's passage to such an extent that the weapon weighing only 2.9lb could be readily controlled. Other unusual features were incorporated in the gun. The 16 round semi-expendable magazine was automatically ejected when empty and the bolt held to the rear. When a new magazine was inserted, the holding open device was released and the bolt took the top round into the chamber ready for firing – either auto or semi automatic fire being available. The canvas holster also carried the removable telescopic stock which when attached and pulled out, allowed the weapon to be fired from the shoulder. The SR 11 was tested by the Ordnance Board in England in 1944. It was found to be extremely accurate at full auto but when fired as a pistol, using one hand, it was equally erratic. Design changes to produce accurate single shot fire resulted in the SR Model 16 for which, so far, there has been no official requirement.

CANADIAN SMGs

Throughout World War I the Canadian Long Branch Arsenal produced Sten guns for the British, Commonwealth and other Allied forces.

When the British Army adopted the Patchett designed SMG manufactured by the Sterling Armament Co, the Canadian Forces took a slightly modified version of the L2A3 which they called the C1 130 and this has been manufactured at Canadian Arsenals Ltd. The C1 magazine differs from that of the L2A3 in taking 30 rounds instead of 34 and having a conventional follower to feed the rounds forward instead of rollers. There is also a 10 round magazine. It takes the FAL bayonet, from the Canadian version of the FN rifle, instead of the No 5 bayonet.

FRENCH SMGs

Unlike the Italian and German Armies, the French did not develop a SMG in World War I. Equally, unlike the British Army, they did do something about obtaining a SMG in the years before World War II.

There were three principal French design and production centres. The largest and most active in SMG design was that at Chatellerault whose weapons

243 Russel S. Robinson's 9mm SR 11. The butt was detachable and it could be fired at 600rpm with one hand. Note the screw thread on the barrel which caused it to rotate to neutralise the effect of the twist of the bullet on the weapon.

244 The F1 9mm SMG. Note magazine on top. Offset sheet metal rear sight is shown folded flat. The straight through butt gives good control.

245 The Vigneron M2 9mm SMG was designed by Col Vigneron when he retired from the Belgian army. It was made by Precision Liegoise at Herstal and used by all Belgian forces.

246 The FN 9mm SMG was designed by M. Saive – a very well known designer of Fabrique Nationale d'Armes de Guerre at Herstal. Only a limited number were produced in the early 1950s.

243

244

BELGIAN SMGs

245

246

177

247 Another FN SMG designed by Saive. It was a compact weapon, firing 9mm Parabellum ammunition but again numbers were limited.

248 A very interesting toggle joint SMG in 7.63mm and 9mm produced by FN in 1935. Produced under licence from the Heinemann Model 1932 **144**. The front trigger gave full automatic, the rear gave single shot. Note the very heavy barrel. Magazines took 20 or 40 cartridges.

249 The M.I.53 9mm SMG was manufactured from Sten components by Imperia, Nessonvaux in Liege. It was submitted for tests in 1953 after the Vigneron M2 had been adopted.

249

250 The RAN 9mm SMG was designed by Withold Porebski at Repousmetal, Brussels in 1953. It also fired the Energa anti tank grenade. Few were sold.

bore the prefix MAC – Manufacture d'armes de Chatellerault – but which has now been closed down. Weapons designated MAT were produced at Tulle and those at Saint Etienne had the letters MAS in front of the year in which the pattern was sealed.

In 1935 MAS produced an experimental SMG, the MAS 35, which fired the French 7.65mm Long cartridge. The gun had a single tube butt stock with a flat plate welded below it for the shoulder piece. It was decided not to go into production of this gun but to carry out development work and then produce a more finished weapon. This was done and the subsequent production weapon was the MAS 38.

MAS MODEL 38

It will be seen from the photograph **259** that the MAS 38 had a distinctive 'broken back' appearance. This was produced because the bolt travelled a long way back into the butt stock, and the barrel was angled to the body to avoid a high sight line. As the breech block was travelling at an angle to the line of the bore, the front face was sloped backwards and downwards to fit flush against the chamber face as the round was fully chambered. The long backward travel of the bolt – well past the sear – meant that by the time it reached the sear on its forward travel it had built up a considerable velocity and therefore kinetic energy, which had to be dissipated on impact between the bent of the block and the sear. To prevent damage the sear was spring buffered – probably a unique feature in a SMG.

The gun fired an unusual cartridge for SMGs – the 7.65mm Long – which is a low powered, accurate cartridge with limited penetration. The magazine well had a plate which was spring loaded to close as the magazine was withdrawn, to exclude dirt and dust. The provision for the applied safety was also possibly unique. To lock the bolt in either the forward or rear position, the trigger was pushed *forward* inside the trigger guard. The gun operated by blow back and the cocking handle was disconnected from the bolt when it was pulled fully to the rear. This served two purposes. Firstly it prevented the cocking handle from reciprocating with the bolt and, secondly, it ensured the ejection port was held open when the gun was firing. When the cocking handle was pushed

251

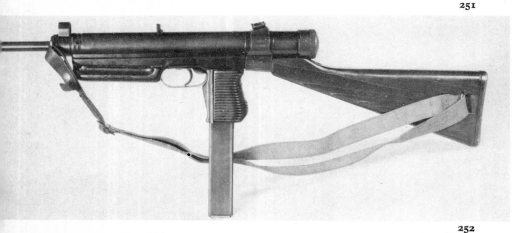

252

253

254

CZECH SMGs

251 The Czech ZK 383 9mm SMG was designed by Josef and Frantisek Koucky in 1933 at Brno. It was produced until 1948. The gun has alternative rates of fire of 500 and 700. The higher rate is achieved by removing a 6oz weight from the bolt. It had a quick change barrel. It was the standard Bulgarian army gun until 1960 and was used also by the German SS in World War II. Some World War II weapons were marked Vz (Model) 9.

252 The Czech Model 23 9mm SMG was designed by Vacklav Holek (designer of the Bren LMG prototype) in 1948. Production ceased in 1950 after 100,000 had been made. This was the first production 'wrap round' bolt. 6¼ inches of the 11 inch barrel fitted inside the bolt. The Model 23 was used by Czecho-slovakia, Syria and Cuba.

253 The Czech Model 25 9mm SMG had a forward folding stock and the shoulder piece formed a forward pistol grip. Otherwise it was similar to the Model 23.

254 The Czech Vz61. The Skorpion. With butt folded forward it can be used as a conventional pistol firing .32 ACP cartridges.

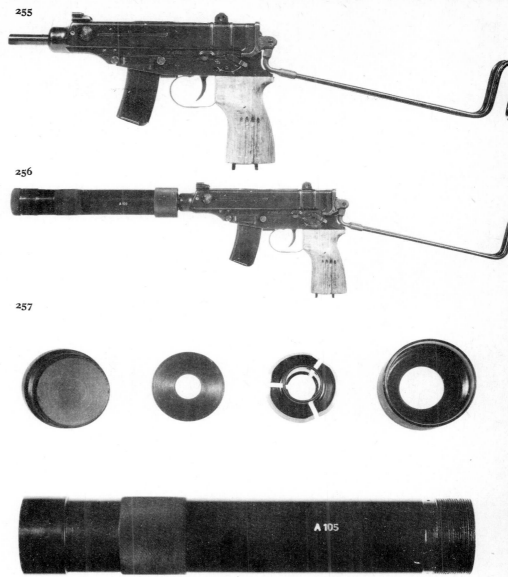

255 The Skorpion with butt extended. It is issued to tank crews for immediate covering fire out to 200m until the main armament or coaxial MG can be swung round. There is an inertia pellet in the butt to reduce the rate of fire to 840 rpm.

256 The Vz61 with silencer. It has been sold widely in Africa and the Palace Guard of President Nkruma of Ghana was armed with it.

257 The Vz61 silencer stripped showing (*left to right*) rubber muzzle plug, one of a series of discs, cone and end cap. Below is the body of the silencer.

forward, a cover moved over the ejection opening to keep dirt out.

When the 'phoney war' ended in the spring of 1940 the French Army had 3,750 Thompson M1928 .45 SMGs obtained from the USA by their purchasing commission and a number of Vollmer 9mm SMGs purchased from Germany in the mid 1930s. The MAS 38 was produced in 1939 and first deliveries went to the Garde Mobile – security police – but none went to the army. The Corps Francs (Commandos) were the first military units to get the weapon and this was at the end of the winter of 1940 – after Marshal Pétain had signed the Armistice with Hitler. Production of the MAS 38 continued throughout the occupation and provided the main French assault weapons at the beginning of the Indo-China campaign.

When World War II ended the French Army had:

The Thompson 1928 A1, M1 and M1A1 taking .45 ACP
The MAS 38 firing the 7.65mm Long cartridge
The Sten Mk II, Mk III and Mk V firing the 9mm Parabellum
The USA M3 SMG firing the .45 ACP cartridge
There were also a number of MP40's 'liberated' from the German Wehrmacht, and a quantity of 9mm Parabellum of German manufacture.

259

260

261

262

259 The MAS 38 – produced at St Etienne – fired the low powered 7.65mm Long cartridge. It was produced throughout World War II for the French forces and used in Indo-China.

260 The MAC 47–2 9mm SMG followed the 47–1 and differed in having a skeleton butt and a barrel jacket. The gun could not be fired with the butt closed.

261 The MAC 48–2.9mm SMG produced very inaccurate fire due to the displacement of the shoulder stock from the line of the barrel.

262 The MAS 48C4 9mm SMG used a two part bolt and a lever delay device which was found to be unnecessary with a low powered cartridge.

263

264

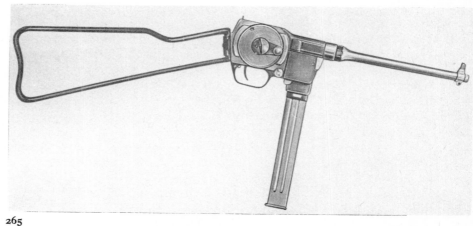

265

266

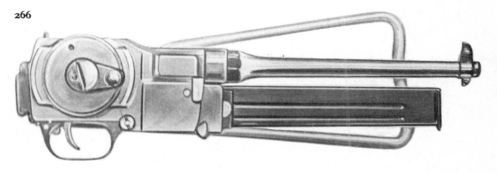

263 The MAS 1949 fired the USA .30 carbine cartridge. The trigger gave single shots halfway back and full auto, at 700rpm, when fully depressed.

264 The MAT 9mm Model 49, is the current SMG of the French Armed Forces. It is neat, compact and reliable.

265 The PM9 (MGD) 9mm SMG, 1954, had a flywheel device which allowed a short bolt travel and also a variable rate of fire. It was also produced by Erma (See page 127.)

266 The PM9, marketed by the Société Pour l'Exploration des Brevets at Grenoble, could be folded into a very small space. It was too expensive to sell widely.

267

267 The Gevarm D4 9mm SMG was produced in prototype only, by the ammunition firm of Gevelot. It followed the D3 which had a wooden butt. Both were simple blow back weapons.

A programme for future weapons was set up in 1946 by the Section Technique de l'Armée (STA). Experience showed the 7.65mm Long cartridge to be accurate but lacking penetration; the .45 ACP was powerful but led to a heavy weapon; the 9mm Parabellum gave adequate accuracy, range and penetration and since this was the round used by nearly all European countries, it was decided to employ this cartridge.

STA allocated the design of the future SMG to two national arms production centres – Chatellerault and Saint Etienne.

MAC SMGs

The MAC 47-1: This was a novel weapon. The barrel (which had no jacket) and the chamber were made as two separate parts with a screw thread connection. The MP40 magazine housing swung forward under the barrel so that the magazine lay parallel to the bore when not in use and a shutter sealed the weapon against dust. There was no applied safety. The return spring was under the body with the trigger mechanism and was very unusual. It was a short powerful coil spring *across* the body and acted in torsion. A lever set in a recess under the bolt was attached to the end of the spring and as the bolt came back the spring was tightened. Cocking was achieved by an external cocking lever under the trigger lying forward parallel to the trigger housing. This was rotated downwards. The breech assembly was of the delayed blow back type using a lever to obtain a differential movement of the bolt body relative to the bolt head. The butt was of stamped sheet. It could be folded forward to lay along the right of the body of the gun but the weapon could NOT be fired in this position since the ejection slot was completely covered.

The MAC 47-1 was light and handy but the return spring system – although ingenious – was not successful because after prolonged use the spring lost its tension and the forward action became very sluggish. The butt was criticised because it was considered too large and would not permit firing when closed.

The MAC 47-2: This differed from the 47-1 in the following details: There was a tubular barrel jacket with oval perforations. The butt was a skeletal design – based on the Mk II Sten, with a cross bracing. It pivotted to lie along the gun and the cross brace very neatly masked the ejection opening. It therefore prevented firing from the folded position **260**.

The MAC 48-1: The barrel of this gun was pressed into the front of the body and held by turning over a lip in the body onto the barrel, over the chamber. A perforated jacket extended halfway along the barrel. The body of the gun was cylindrical and made of a single welded pressing. The bolt in configuration and action was based on that of the Sten gun, with a single large diameter return spring. The cocking handle was on the left and reciprocated with the bolt.

The ammunition feed opening for the MP40 magazine was welded directly onto the underside of the body and was made long enough to act as a forward hand grip and had a shaped wooden covering. The rear pistol grip had a grip safety. The butt really was rather odd. It was attached to the bottom of the pistol grip, was made of wood and fixed. On the right of the butt was a pressed steel plate which could be swung out and was then intended as a rest for the firer's right elbow when firing from the hip. When firing from the shoulder the plate was hinged back and fitted into a groove cut in the wood. The gun fired at automatic only. Since the barrel was nearly 6in above the shoulder plate there was an immense turning moment and the muzzle rose very rapidly and all accuracy was lost.

The MAC 48-2: The 48-2 had the following differences from the 48-1. The barrel jacket had more perforations for improved cooling. There was both automatic and single shot fire. There were two triggers – the forward gave single shot and the rear gave automatic fire **261**.

The MAC 48 LS: The 'LS' stands for lightened and simplified. All the components with the exception of the barrel, butt and breech block were made of pressed steel. The barrel was shorter and a perforated tubular jacket surrounded it almost to the muzzle. The jacket was integral with the body and the pistol grip. It consisted of two semi-cylindrical shells made of a sheet pressing and welded. The cocking lever did not reciprocate with the bolt but was attached to a cover outside the body which closed the cocking slot when the cocking handle was forward. The ejection slot was closed by a spring loaded cover which opened when the bolt was retracted. The feed housing folded forward and with the magazine under the barrel, the feed slot was sealed off. There was a grip safety. The butt was of the US M3 type, sliding into two tubes – one on each side of the body. The official French terminology for this system – the 'tromboning' action – describes it well.

The MAC 48 SL was produced in small quantities for troop trials and was used in Indo-China.

At the same time as the Chatellerault Arsenal was producing the weapons mentioned, the Sainte Etienne establishment was also busy. A number of prototypes were turned out designated types C1-4. The general line followed in all these weapons was much the same and all employed two part blocks. Each was a detail improvement of the others until the final version, the C4, emerged.

THE MAS TYPE C4

This gun was produced at St Etienne in 1947 and 1948. It was the fourth in a series of experimental models and although limited numbers were made it never came into universal use with French troops **262**.

The weapon operated on the delayed blow back system. The general configuration of the two part bolt was somewhat similar to the German Heckler and Koch design used in the G3 rifle and the MP5 SMG (qv). The bolt body was ⌐ shaped with the long arm extending well forward in a tube, over the barrel, with the return spring entering it from the rear. The vertical portion carried the firing pin. The light bolt head lay under the long arm of the bolt body and in front of the vertical arm. The bolt head carried a horizontal lever, one end of which entered a recess in the body of the gun and the other end pressed against the bolt body. Thus as the gas pressure was applied to the bolt head, the lever had to rotate. The lever had a velocity ratio of nearly 2 : 1 so the rotation accelerated the bolt body but the bolt head was held up until the pressure fell to a safe level. This is the system used in the French MAS AA 52 GPMG and although suitable for the high powered 7.5mm machine gun cartridge, was not necessary for the 9mm Parabellum cartridge, for which a simple blow back one 185

piece bolt is adequate. The magazine folded under the barrel; the cocking handle
– again like the Heckler and Koch design – was on the left, well forward, just
behind the foresight. Single shot fire came from partial movement of the trigger,
full auto from sustained pressure.

THE MAT MODEL 1949

This is the current SMG of the French Armed Forces 264. It was produced by
the Tulle Arsenal and is of simple, orthodox blow back design without any
unusual features. The body is rectangular in section, made of heavy sheet metal
stampings, welded, and there is a circular perforated jacket extending forward
around the barrel to some 3in from the foresight. The bolt is of square section
with a small round section projecting at the front. This pushes the cartridge
into the chamber and enters into a recess machined in the breech face. As the
bolt reciprocates during the firing cycle it slides over the return spring guide
rod which passes right through the bolt and is located in a hole in the breech face
above the chamber. The magazine is inserted in a housing which forms the
forward grip when the gun is fired. The housing pivots forward and catches in a
stud under the jacket bringing the magazine under the barrel when not in use.
There is a grip safety behind the pistol grip which holds the bolt in either the
forward or cocked position. The gun fires only at full automatic. The square
section body is well sealed against the entry of foreign matter. The pivotting
housing closes the magazine well and there is a spring loaded ejection cover
which is automatically released as the bolt is cocked. The MAT 49 was used in
Indo-China and Algeria.

THE PM9 (MGD)

This weapon was offered by the Societe Pour l'Exploration des Brevets MGD
in 1954–55. The company – as its title suggests – developed promising patents
and exploited successful developments. The PM9 was a unique weapon 265.
The best analogy to the bolt action is to consider the bolt as a connecting rod
joined to a crank revolving through 180deg first in one direction and then back
again. During the return stroke, and following feed stroke, the rear end of the
bolt, attached to a flywheel, oscillated. The first cocking movement tensioned
a spiral spring which drove the bolt forward again. This reduced the trans-
lational movement of the bolt and produced a short body length. The initial
tension of the spring could be adjusted and this permitted the rate of fire to be
varied at will. The magazine could be folded forward under the barrel, there was
no barrel jacket, and the skeleton butt stock could be folded to lie along the left
side of the gun. The photograph 266 shows how compact this design was and
also shows the circular casing holding the flywheel and spring.

The design was taken up by Erma in Germany – see page 127 – but it met with
no success. The complication produced little obvious advantage, at high cost.

Scandinavia

FINNISH SMGs

The principal weapon designer in Finland was Aimo Johannes Lahti. His
SMGs were known as 'Suomi' which means Finland. The first gun he originated
was the Model 1922 which fired the 7.65mm Parabellum cartridge. This had a
long barrel with annular rings for cooling, inside an open jacket. There was a
large lever under the breech, allowing a quick barrel change. It fired at either
single shot or automatic, with a selector lever located on the right side of the body.

268 The Finnish 7.65mm
Suomi Model 1926 was designed
by Aimo Johannes Lahti. This
had a quick change barrel, a
unique buffer and rate of fire
controller. It was possibly the
first SMG in which the cocking
handle did not reciprocate with
the bolt. It had a long curved
magazine.

269 The Finnish 9mm Para-
bellum Model Suomi Model
1931 was designed by Aimo
Lahti and introduced the 50
round double compartment
magazine, partitioned down the
centre, and with separate follower
and springs. This gun was sold
widely in Scandinavia, Switzerland and South America.

270 The Finnish Model 1931
fitted with a long muzzle brake.

268

No effort was made to market this gun, and it was followed by another experimental type which had alternative feed from the left or from below. This had a shorter barrel and a jacket with four long cooling slots on the top half. It was fitted with a bipod. It had selective fire using the 7.65mm Parabellum cartridge.

The Model 1926: This gun was adopted by Finland, but only limited numbers were made. The 7.65mm Parabellum cartridge was the official choice but some models were made using the 9mm Mauser. These can be recognised by the rearward extension of the body to accommodate the larger buffer required by the more powerful cartridge. The barrel could easily be removed from the slotted jacket, using a small rotating release forward of the magazine housing. The buffer was of unusual design. It acted in part by compressing air as the bolt came back, and there were four alternative sized holes for escape of the air which could be aligned by rotating the end cap. This, to some degree, allowed for ammunition variation and gave some measure of control of the rate of fire.

This was one of the first guns in which the cocking handle did not reciprocate with the bolt. It was attached to a rod running under the body and engaging the

269

270

under side of the bolt. It was spring loaded and when released, after the gun was cocked, moved forward. The bolt had a separate firing pin controlled by a lever pivotted in the top of the bolt head. This lever was rotated by the return spring guide as it moved forward. The magazine holding 36 cartridges was curved sharply forward under the gun and this feature allows recognition of the Model 1926 **268**. The wooden butt had an unusually high comb which rose almost to the line of the axis of the bore. The gun was superceded in 1931.

The Model 1931: This gun is stamped '1932', the date patent rights were granted, and is sometimes called the Model 32. However it was adopted in Finland in 1931 and was called by the Fins the Model 1931 **269**. It was also taken by Madsen in Denmark, Husqvarna in Sweden and later (see page 204) by Hispano-Suiza in Switzerland. It became the standard weapon in Norway.

The bolt and firing system were changed from those used in Model 1926. The bolt was of the reduced section type – ie about twice the cartridge diameter at the front and much larger at the rear end. This was hollowed out to take the return spring. The separate firing pin and pivotting lever of the Model 1926 were replaced by a fixed firing pin on the bolt face. The gun was machined from the solid and this resulted in a heavy gun but one producing better than average accuracy. Fifty 9mm Parabellum cartridges were contained in a magazine which has been copied extensively. It had two compartments, side by side, separated by a partition, which extended to about $1\frac{1}{2}$in from the top, with separate followers and springs. The rounds fed to a single position feed. There was also a 71 round drum magazine which was later copied by the Soviets in the PPD 1934/38 SMG. In the late 1950s the Suomi was modified to take the 36 round wedge shaped Swedish Carl Gustav magazine.

The M44: This gun **272** was very similar in appearance to the Russian PPS-43 **229** even to the shape of the one piece, sheet metal, muzzle brake. Its operation and method of construction were also similar. It differed only in using the 9mm Parabellum cartridge in the 50 round Suomi magazine. The 71 round drum could also be used. The gun was made at the Tikkakoski Arsenal. The manager of this arsenal, Willi Daugs, later took the drawings to Spain where the German designer Ludwig Vorgrimmler took up the design and produced the DUX gun (qv).

The M44 – with the Carl Gustav 36 round magazine – is still used in the Finnish Army.

SWEDISH SMGs

The Model 1937: This was produced by the state armament factory Carl Gustav Gevarsfaktori at Eskilstuna, for the Swedish Army. It was a copy of the Finnish Suomi Model 1931, with a shortened barrel, and fired the Model '07 9mm Browning Long cartridge from a lengthy 56 round magazine. These guns were later modified into the Model 37-39.

The Model 37-39: This was manufactured under license from Finland by Husqvarna Vapenfabriks AB, a commercial firm, in 1939 and 1940. It was a copy of the Finnish Suomi Model 1931 (above) modified as follows. The barrel, and its open jacket, were shortened by $4\frac{1}{4}$in. A larger, arctic type, trigger guard was fitted and the shape of the cocking handle was changed from a knob to a smaller curved hook. The sights were simplified since shortening the barrel reduced the effective range. The stock shape was changed by raising the butt to give a semi-straight through design and strengthening the small of the butt. Apart from the foregoing the details are the same as those of the Suomi M 1931.

271 The Finnish 9mm Suomi Model 1932 was developed from the Model 1931 for close quarter firing. Note it has no butt and a modified barrel casing.

272 The Finnish Model 44 was produced at the Tikkakoski Arsenal and the design is based on the Soviet PPS-43. It formed the basis of the Dux SMG in 1951–9.

273 The Finnish 9mm Model 46 was developed from the Model 1944.

274 The Swedish M/37-39 was the Swedish version of the Finnish Suomi Model 31 with the barrel shortened by $4\frac{1}{4}$ inches and the butt raised.

271

272

273

274

The gun was sold widely abroad **274**. The standard barrel length Finnish Suomi model 1931 was also manufactured and marked 'HV' with the Swedish crown. This gun was known as the M37-39F **275**.

The Model 45: This gun was produced by the state arsenal, Carl Gustav, and is the standard weapon in the Swedish armed forces. It is made from stampings, using heavy gauge steel sheet, and rivetted. It is a blow back operated gun and its action inside the cylindrical body is almost identical to that of the Sten gun. When it first appeared it used the Suomi 50 round magazine already in service in the Model 37-39 **274**. About 1948 the magazine was changed for a two position feed, 36 round type. This magazine has been recognised as the best yet developed and has been copied – or similar types developed – in Czecho-Slovakia, other Scandinavian countries and used by the German firm of Walther in the MPL SMG **172** (qv). The magazine, viewed from above, tapers to the front giving a wedge shape, which ensures that the round, when fed, is pointing inwards towards the chamber. To enable both the 50 round double compartment Suomi magazine, and the new 36 round type to be used in the gun, the magazine housing was modified so that it could be detached from the gun and changed at will. The model incorporating this pinned-on magazine housing was known as the M45B **277** and was introduced in 1949–50. In 1951 the 36 round magazine was available in quantity and the Suomi magazine was discontinued. The magazine housing for the gun was then made a permanent fixture, taking only the Carl Gustav magazine **278**. Thus there are three types of M1945. The first taking only the Suomi magazine, the second or 45B with a detachable housing to take either magazine and lastly the current type taking only the Carl Gustav magazine.

A special heavily loaded 9mm Parabellum cartridge is used with the M1945 known as the M39B. The bullet has a thicker jacket and is heavier. Thus although the muzzle velocity is not much greater – due to the heavier bullet – the chamber pressure is higher and the round cannot safely be used in pistols and some older SMGs. The penetration of this bullet is greater than the standard 9mm Parabellum.

The 'Hovea' SMG: This was developed by Husqvana Vapenfabrik AB and the name comes from the initials of the maker. It was developed for trials to determine the future weapon for the Swedish Armed Forces, held in 1945. It did well in the tests but not unnaturally the Government decided to use the

275

275 The M/37–39F had the standard length barrel of the Suomi Model 31 and the 50 round magazine.

bolt was blown back in the usual way. The gun was quite neat with a forward-rotating wire butt stock lying under the body when so required. It was an expensive weapon and the firing system was more complicated than that of most guns of the period.

The Model 1946: This was made by Madsen and called the P16. It was designed for ease of production and the body was made of two pressed steel frames which lie together, hinged at the rear, held together at the front by the barrel locking nut. This produces the narrow, flat sided appearance which distinguishes the Madsen weapon. In practice this makes stripping in the field difficult because the gun opens like a suitcase and there is a distinct possibility of losing the springs.

The gun can readily be distinguished from subsequent models by the cocking handle. This is a flat plate, lying on top of the body, with milled flanges extending down on either side. Subsequent models have a conventional knob on top. The stock is typical of Madsen design being of tube bent into a rectangle with hinges mounted on the rear of the body and at the heel of the pistol grip, to allow the assembly to swing to the right of the body. There is an unusual grip safety which is located not in the pistol grip but behind the magazine housing. This has to be pressed forward by the left hand, which is holding the magazine, to lower a separate sear which engages in the bent of the bolt and holds the bolt partly open if the trigger is pressed. There is also a conventional safety catch, holding up the trigger sear, above the trigger on the left of the body.

The Model 50: This was generally similar to the Model 1946 but had a simplified cocking lever consisting of a small knob on top of the body, integral with the bolt **281**. This gun was demonstrated extensively in 1950. Among the spectators from India, Canada and the USA was a delegation from the United Kingdom. The British party was so impressed that the gun was tested in England against the BSA and Patchett SMGs (see page 193) and was recommended for adoption with an improved magazine for all 'non-tooth' units ie support troops, signals, engineers etc if the British EM2 rifle was taken into service for fighting units. In the event the EM2 did not come into service and the Patchett was adopted for all troops. The improved magazine mentioned was used in subsequent Madsen models replacing the single position feed, straight, flat sided, 32 round magazine of the Model 50.

The Model 53: The differences of this model from its predecessor are few. The two position feed 32 round box magazine is curved and fullered to allow dirt to drop to the bottom of the magazine. The barrel locking nut now engages a thread on the barrel and pulls the barrel forward until a flange on the breech end comes up against the inside of the body to hold it firmly in position. Previous models had a thread on the body and the barrel locking nut engaged this and pulled the two halves of the body together around the barrel **282**.

Hovea Model 49: This is a copy, produced under licence, of the Swedish Husqvarna Hovea SMG which has been dealt with in the previous section. The Model 49 is now the standard SMG for all Danish Armed Forces. It has been made at the state factory Vabenarsenalet since 1949 and has given good service.

SWISS SMGs
SIG SMGs

The Schweizerische Industrie Gesellschaft (SIG) is located at Neuhausen am Rhine Falls in Northern Switzerland separated from Germany by the great River Rhine. As the name indicates there is a large waterfall in the river which provides the area with ample electrical power. The firm of SIG has established a world-wide reputation for small arms, railway rolling stock, machine tools and food packaging machinery. It was involved in small arms production well before World War I and manufactured the first self-loading rifle to go into large-scale production, designed by Mondragon for the Mexican Army.

Model 20: After World War I the Germans were not permitted to produce weapons in quantity and the firm of Theodore Bergmann, Suhl, offered the Hugo Schmeisser designed MP 18.1 **141** to SIG to manufacture under licence. The weapon was modified by SIG to take a left side magazine mounted at right angles to the barrel instead of sloping back as in the original MP 18.1. This leads one to suppose that the Schmeisser modification in about 1925 to the MP 18.1 at Haenel was based on SIG practice. The Swiss weapon can always be distinguished from the German since it has 'Brevat (patent) Bergmann' on the top of the magazine housing whereas the modified Schmeisser has 'System Schmeisser' over the body on the magazine housing strap. The gun was made in 7.65mm Parabellum, and 7.63mm Mauser. The 7.65mm version was sold to Finland and the 7.63mm was taken by the Japanese navy who added a bayonet fitting. Production lasted from 1920 to 1927. In 1930 a modified version was offered. This had a front pistol grip just behind the magazine which was located on the right side. It did not sell.

Model MKMO: In 1933 the MKMO **283** appeared. It had some very unusual features and was an advanced design. It had a locked breech blow back operated system, firing at full automatic only from an open breech position.

A two part bolt was used with the bolt head lighter than the rear part in the bolt body. Trigger operation released the sear from the bent under the bolt body and the compressed return spring drove the two parts forward with a displacement between them. The rear part of the bolt, impelled forward by the return spring, pushed behind the bolt head and the inclined plane at the front attempted to lift the bolt head throughout its forward travel. Since the bolt head was in contact with the top of the body, no lift was possible until the bolt head reached the open ejection port. The inclined plane on the bolt body then lifted the rear of the bolt head, pivotting it up into the opening. The bolt body then closed up to the bolt head, and the firing pin, moving forward with it, fired the cap whilst the bolt was still moving forward – ie floating firing. When the forward momentum was overcome the bolt head came back about $\frac{1}{8}$in and as it came into contact with the lip of the ejection port it came to a halt and was locked.

The bolt body continued back and cammed down the bolt head using an inclined plane exactly as the Bren piston cams the bolt out of locking. Before the bolt head was freed the bullet had left the muzzle and the residual pressure was sufficient to blow the bolt head and body to the rear – still displaced from each other. The system worked quite well with truly parallel sided cases such as the 9mm Mauser (see page 26) but not so well with bottle-necked cases such as the 7.65mm Luger (see page 26). It was unique in SMGs because it incorporated a true 'locking' of the bolt head as opposed to the 'delay' imposed in the roller system of the German Heckler and Koch MP 5 **178** and the lever used in the Hungarian M39 **177**. The locked breech allowed the use of the powerful Mauser 9mm cartridge which gave accurate shooting out to 275m but the cost of the machining of bolt and body made it excessively expensive and no large orders were received.

The designers were Gaetzi and End, and Pal de Kiraly, the Hungarian

283 The MKMO was designed and produced in 1933 for SIG by Gaetzi and End with Kiraly as consultant. The MKMO was operated by blow back but had a locked breech. It was the first SMG to have a magazine pivotting under the barrel.

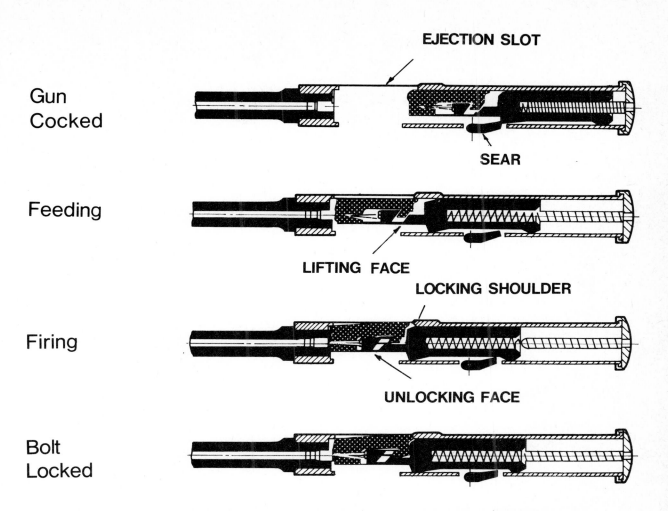

EJECTION SLOT

Gun
Cocked

SEAR

Feeding

LIFTING FACE

LOCKING SHOULDER

Firing

UNLOCKING FACE

Bolt
Locked

Fig VI Locked Breech Action of SIG MKMO

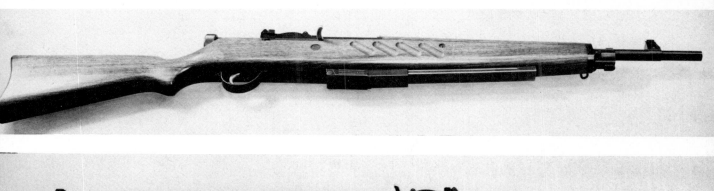

engineer, was employed as a consultant. Kiraly was responsible for the design of the magazine housing which could be rotated forward to allow the 40 round magazine to fit in a long recess under the wooden forestock. It could readily be positioned for firing by pulling the hinged retaining flap. Thus when the gun was carried with the loaded magazine so located it was completely safe whether the bolt was cocked or forward. Dropping the gun with the bolt forward allowed bolt recoil but there was no round positioned in the feedway to be chambered and fired. Kiraly took this magazine fitting back to Danuvia where it was incorporated in his design of the M39 SMG. The MKMO was made in 9mm Mauser, 9mm Parabellum, 7.65mm Parabellum and 7.63mm Mauser until 1937 when production ceased. It was very cleverly designed, beautifully made but unfortunately these features cost too much and were not appreciated by buyers who opted for simple cheap models produced in quantity elsewhere.

A shorter version for police work, known as the MKPO, was produced in 1935. This was mechanically identical to the MKMO but had a smaller magazine capacity and a shorter barrel and fore end with no bayonet boss.

The MKMS: This was produced in 1937 and was a simplified version of the MKMO. The two part breech block, with the locked bolt head, was replaced by an orthodox single piece bolt operated as a straight blow back system with a separate firing pin. The external contours remained largely unchanged. The ejection port was removed from the top and located on the left side. The cocking handle had a substantial knob mounted on the end of the handle like a rifle **284**. The gun was made in 9mm Parabellum and 7.65mm Parabellum – both cartridges of much lower power than the 9mm Mauser and more suitable for a simple blow back operated weapon.

A police version, the MKPS **285**, was produced at the same time. Again this had a shorter barrel than the military model and no bayonet fitting.

The MP41: In early 1940 the Swiss General Staff realised that their neutrality might have to be fought for and a quick survey, concluded in May, found that there were less than 500 SMGs serviceable in the country. The ammunition situation was even worse because that in stock was 9mm Parabellum and 7.65mm Parabellum and of the SMGs available only 2 per cent took this type. It was necessary to take some quick decisions and these were delegated to the KTA which can best be rendered as the 'Defence Technical Branch'. The KTA was advised by the Government Ordnance Factory – Waffen Fabrik (WF) – and also had established relations with SIG. These two factories represented the main source of supply in Switzerland. KTA ordered 100 SMGs from WF and 50 from SIG. The WF guns were designed by Colonel Adolf Furrer and will be described later in this chapter. The SIG gun was a new model known as the MP41 **286**.

The MP41 had a basic mechanism similar to the MKMS. It was a blow back gun with a one piece bolt and a separate firing pin. It retained the folding magazine housing which allowed the magazine, holding 40 9mm Parabellum cartridges, to pivot forward into a groove under the wooden fore end. The release catch was located behind and below the foresight. It was operated by the firer's left hand and the magazine fell back under its own weight and latched into position for firing. The cocking lever remained on the right and the large knob, which gave a very good grip when the firer's hand was wet or oily, was retained. The safety lever was moved to the right of the gun and could be operated whilst the firer retained his hold on the pistol grip – a new feature which was introduced for the first time on an SIG SMG. The rear sight was placed further forward

284 The MKMS in 1937 was a simplified gun with a conventional one piece breech block and a separate firing pin.

285 The MKPS was a police version of the MKMS with a short barrel and no bayonet fitting. It is shown with the magazine folded under the gun.

286 The SIG MP41 had the action of the MKMS and the pivotting magazine. This gun was rejected in favour of the Furrer SMG – an inexplicable choice.

287 A modified version of the MP41 without the folding magazine. Note the annular cooling rings concealed by the wooden fore-end of the standard gun.

284

285

286

287

and was of a more simple design than that used on the MKMS. SIG were well satisfied with this gun which they had tested very extensively and were convinced it would be relatively inexpensive to produce in quantity. However they were treated very shabbily and without holding comparative tests the KTA decided to adopt the Furrer SMG for the Swiss Army. As we shall see, this measure – possibly prompted by a sense of near panic – produced little but trouble and expense. The MP41 was not selected and with world markets denied by Swiss neutrality laws and the practical impossibility of export to neutral countries, SIG had to drop this design after making no more than 200 pre-production models. The MP41 was a good gun and given a reasonable chance would have sold well.

A modified version **287** was produced in prototype without the folding magazine and without the wooden fore-end of the standard model. A conventional 30 round magazine was used fitting below the gun.

The MP44: This gun was designed primarily to utilise manufacturing methods which would cut production costs. The bolt was almost unchanged from that of the MKMS with its separate firing pin. The annular cooling rings on the barrel of the MP41 were removed. Instead of a wooden fore-end, recessed below to hold the magazine, a sheet metal stamping was employed. The barrel jacket and housing for the magazine were also stamped from sheet. One feature new to the SIG guns was the introduction of selective fire with partial trigger pressure giving single shot, and sustained pressure producing full automatic fire **288**.

The MP44 had a short production run since the MP46 **289** came in quite soon. This gun can be distinguished from the MP44 by a series of ribs pressed into the stamped fore-end to give greater rigidity. The bolt assembly was redesigned to cut cost and the firing pin was no longer easily removed.

Neither the MP44 or 46 sold well – both were too heavy and in spite of the changes over previous models – too expensive.

The MP48: The lessons of the MP44 and 46 resulted in the MP48. Instead of machining from the solid or using stampings, the decision was made to utilise precision – or 'lost wax' – castings wherever possible. Such castings demand somewhat heavier initial outlay but this extra cost can easily be recovered with a long production run since considerably faster production can be achieved and labour costs are reduced. The bolt and action remained unchanged from the MP46. The folding magazine arrangement was retained but since the wooden fore-end was removed, the 40 round magazine lay under the barrel in full view and projected slightly beyond the muzzle as the barrel length was reduced from the 11.8in of the MP46 to 7.8in in the MP48. The release catch was located on the left of the magazine housing and when pressed allowed the magazine to fall freely into the firing position. A tubular steel butt stock of the US M3 type was fitted. In early versions of the MP48 **290** this ran in grooves cut in the woodwork around the body. In later production the slots were cut on the inside of the wood and a smooth exterior was preserved.

The MP48 carried further SIGs efforts to reduce the rate of fire. From the table at page 218 it will be seen that the MKMO fired at 900rpm, the MP41 at 850rpm, the MP44 at 800rpm and the MP48 at 700rpm.

Although the MP48 was lighter, more compact and more competitive than its predecessors, it sold only to Chile during the ten years it was offered.

The MP310: In 1957 SIG decided to abolish date designation of their weapons. They had found that offering a weapon which so clearly showed its age was not

288 The SIG MP 44 was designed to cut production costs. It retained the MKMS bolt. The annular cooling rings went. Single shot came from partial trigger pressure and full auto from complete retraction. The folding magazine was restored.

289 The MP 46 quickly replaced the MP 44. It can be distinguished by the grooves strengthening the fore-end.

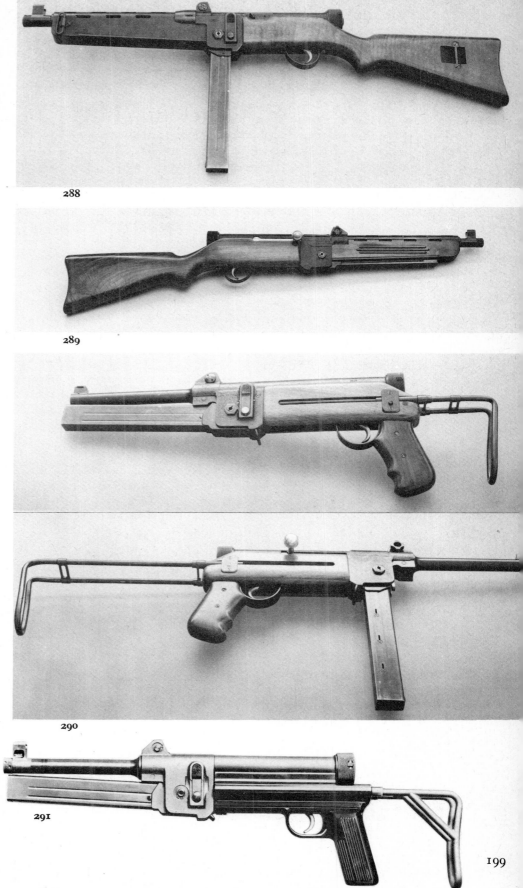

290 The MP 48 used precision castings. Note the folded magazine extends beyond the muzzle. In the version shown the telescoping wire stock runs in grooves in the body. In later versions the slots were inside the wood.

291 The MP 310 came out in 1958. It was the last model offered for sale although a prototype of a successor has been ready for some while.

288

289

290

291

good sales policy since many countries – especially those who had recently achieved independence – wanted something more recently developed than that possessed by their neighbours. This 'upmanship' attitude often resulted in a well tried and established weapon being rejected in favour of a gun with its faults still to be discovered. SIG allocated the prefix '310' for SMGs. Pistols were '210', assault rifles '510' and machine guns '710'. Thus the machine gun '710–3' is the third produced since the nomenclature was adopted.

The MP310 **291** is a cleaned up version of the MP48, produced in 1958. Internally it is unchanged but it incorporates castings and, where possible, plastics. The wooden furniture has now disappeared and the butt stock slides in metal tubes on the sides of the body. The magazine lies under the barrel when not in use but the pivotting point of the housing is slightly further back so the magazine no longer projects beyond the muzzle. Unlike the MP48 the foresight is not set at the end of the barrel but is placed $\frac{1}{2}$in further back.

There is no safety catch on this model and reliance is placed on the magazine being folded forward when the gun is not being used. The manufacturer appreciates that not everyone will agree with this and a separate safety can be fitted 'to order'.

The MP310 is a weapon of the highest order. The materials used are the best obtainable and the standard of workmanship and finish adds to the high reputation SIG possess as makers of the best quality weapons. About 1,000 of these guns have been sold to the police forces of Switzerland, Chile and the Philippines.

FURRER SMGs
Colonel Adolf Furrer was a designer who produced most of his SMGs between 1937 and 1944, for the Swiss Government Factory, Waffen Fabrik, at Berne.

292

293

292 Colonel Adolf Furrer designed for the Swiss Government Factory, Waffen Fabrik, at Berne. In 1939 he produced this experimental gun for a static installation. The toggle lock is like that of a Luger pistol laid on its side.

293 In 1940 this twin barrelled gun for use by an aircraft observer appeared. It used short recoil operation with an action very similar to that of a Luger pistol inverted.

294 Furrer's Model 1941. This was also short recoil operated with a more complex toggle explained on page 203.

295 The Furrer MP 41/44. This was a modified version of the MP 41 and was adopted for the Swiss Army. It was complicated, expensive and laborious to produce.

296 Due to the slow production of the MP 41/44 the Swiss purchased Suomi SMGs of the Model 1931. The bayonet lug and simplified sights were added for this Swiss Model M43.

Early Models: In 1939 there appeared a single barrelled prototype Furrer SMG. It seems from the photograph shown **292** that this was intended for use in a static position since the gun was held in a mounting which had a lever to control elevation, and a forward pintle. The firing arrangement with two grips is typical of medium machine gun practice and was hardly suitable for a SMG in its usual role. The locking system was a toggle and was almost identical to a Luger pistol laid on its side. Feed was from a box magazine inserted from the right of the gun.

Several versions of this gun were made and a picture[1] has appeared showing different firing grips, a barrel with a large, detachable, flash hider and small differences in the toggle.

The next prototype, in 1940, was the 'Fliegerbeobacter-Doppelpistole' or twin barrelled, aircraft observer's, gun **293**. This was a double barrelled gun with a single body casing incorporating two toggle locking systems. Above the body were two curved, 40 round magazines. Centrally mounted behind the body was a single pistol grip and trigger. Located on top of the body was the selector switch marked 'F', 'S'. 'D'. There was also a barrel selection switch on the side of the body which pushed through to select which barrel would be fired. On this gun the action was almost identical with the Luger pistol – assuming the pistol to be upside down ie the toggles broke downwards. A detachable curved wooden butt could be fitted into the square hole shown in the metal casing above the pistol grip. The foresight was a cross wires in a circular mount located between the muzzles; the backsight was a very coarse U cut in a vertical bar projecting from the body in front of the selector switch. The toggles were marked 'Waffenfabrik, Bern'.

Model 1941: This gun **294** incorporated a toggle locking system which differed considerably in detail from that used in the Luger Pistol or the Maxim Medium machine gun. Like both these weapons it was short recoil operated. Since this

294

295

296

method of operation has not been touched upon before a brief explanation is in order.

When the gun fires, the breech is fully locked to the barrel. The gas force drives the bullet forward and an equal force is exerted on the base of the case to push the breech block back. Since the breech block is attached to the barrel via the locking system, and the barrel is free to recoil within the body of the gun, the breech block pulls the barrel rearwards. The breech block remains locked to the barrel for a short while and during this time the pressure in the chamber drops to a safe level. This is known as 'mechanical safety after firing'. After the barrel and bolt have travelled back, locked together, for about $\frac{1}{4}$in, unlocking takes place and the barrel is arrested. The breech block is accelerated backwards to carry out the functions of extraction and ejection. The barrel may remain stationary or in some designs will be driven forward again by its own spring. The return spring then drives the bolt forward to feed and chamber the next round and to lock onto the barrel. The cycle is then repeated as the next round is fired. In all short recoil operated guns there will be found a barrel extension. In guns with rotating bolt locking this will consist only of the length required for the locking recesses and an accelerator device. With a toggle joint locking system the extension will reach back several inches behind the breech, and in the Furrer MP41 it reaches right back to the return spring.

The Furrer MP41 toggle joint is shown in the drawings below. The mechanical arrangement consists of two toggle arms and a link. For convenience the toggle arms are numbered 1 and 2. Arm 1 is attached to the bolt. Arm 2 is joined to arm 1 and can pivot at the joint. Arm 2 is securely attached at its mid point to the barrel extension and can see-saw at this attachment point. The rear end of arm 2 is attached to the link and can swivel at the joint. The other end of the link is secured to the gun body. Although this is a fixed point the link can swing freely around it.

The following description of the toggle action relates to the drawing. At the moment of firing, arm 1 and arm 2 make a straight line behind the chamber in prolongation of the axis of the bore. The bolt is forced backwards by gas pressure and arms 1 and 2 are rigid and move back together. Since arm 2 is fixed to the barrel extension, this must move with arm 2 and pulls the barrel back. The link hangs down and is inclined slightly towards the breech when firing occurs and it is swung about its attachment point to the body as arm 2 moves back. It swings through the vertical line and there is no tendency to lift the rear of arm 2. This gives the required mechanical safety after firing.

As arm 2 continues back, the link continues to revolve and now it lifts the rear of arm 2 causing the junction of arm 2 and arm 1 to drop. This accelerates the bolt rearwards, so extracting the empty cartridge case.

The return spring is compressed by the barrel extension and reasserts itself to drive the barrel extension forward, carrying the central pivot of arm 2 with it. As the link is now parallel to the barrel extension, the other end of arm 2 revolves downwards and forwards, pushing arm 1 and the bolt forwards. The bolt feeds and chambers the next round, which is fired when the two toggle arms form a rigid straight line again. It must be remembered that the drawing is a plan view – looking down on the gun – and so the toggle breaks to the left of the gun and the magazine is on the right. The drawings are virtually self explanatory so long as it is clearly understood that the link is attached to the gun body and so does not move; the central pivot of arm 2 moves backwards and forwards with the barrel extension to which it is attached. Short recoil operation is common in machine

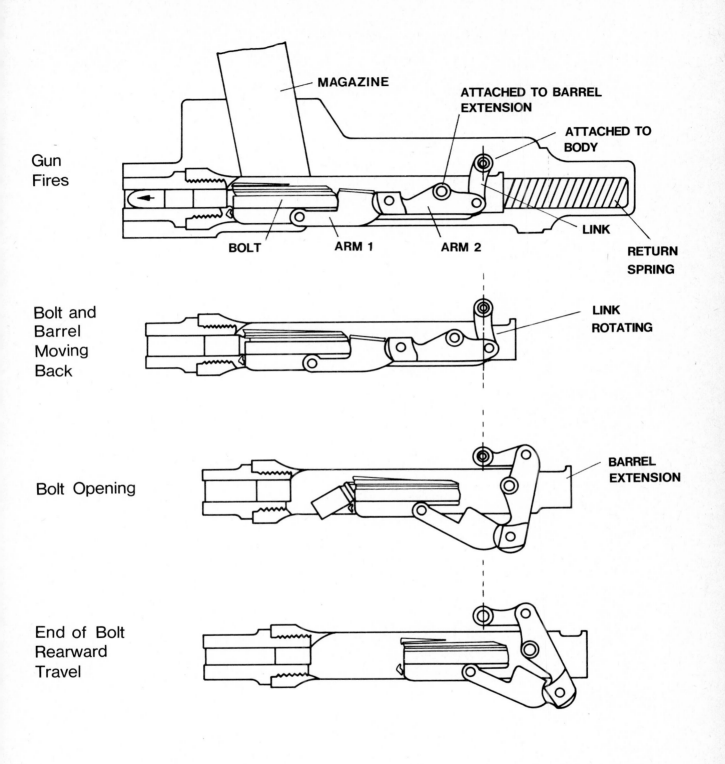

Gun
Fires

MAGAZINE

ATTACHED TO BARREL
EXTENSION

ATTACHED TO
BODY

BOLT

ARM 1

ARM 2

LINK

RETURN
SPRING

Bolt and
Barrel
Moving
Back

LINK
ROTATING

Bolt Opening

BARREL
EXTENSION

End of Bolt
Rearward
Travel

Fig VII Toggle Action Breech of Furrer MP 41

203

guns and very common in pistols but the Furrer MP41 was the first SMG to use this system in a service gun and so it is unique. It can readily be seen that compared to the blow back system the mechanism is complex and is infinitely more expensive and time consuming to produce. It is therefore totally incomprehensible that the MP41 should have been preferred to the SIG Model 41 – without any comparative trials being held.

One hundred MP41s were ordered in December 1940 and delivered in the spring of 1942. A larger order was placed in July 1941 and delivery of the guns started in January 1943. During the year 4,800 were put into the hands of troops.

It would seem not unreasonable to suggest that the precipitate ordering of the MP41 was a panic measure and proved very ill-judged. The guns were difficult to produce, only small quantities were ever in service and it was probably the most expensive sub-machine gun ever to be built. On the other hand the SIG Model 41 was a better gun in every way – simpler and quicker to produce, and of a proved design. It could have been supplied at about one-quarter the price in half the time.

The MP41 was modified slightly during the autumn of 1943 and termed the MP41/44 **295**. The difference were slight but perceptible. The long cocking handle of the MP41 was replaced by a small knob; the shape of the trigger guard was changed; the rear sight was simplified and both back and foresight given protectors; a pivotting forward pistol grip was added; the bayonet lug was removed.

THE HISPANO-SUIZA MP43/44
The Finnish Tikkakoski Arsenal offered the standard 1931 Suomi SMG to Switzerland in 1942. The Swiss Armament programme was not proceeding well and in November 1942 Switzerland ordered 5,000 of these guns. In February 1943 Hispano-Suiza reached an agreement to produce the Finnish gun under licence. The original gun purchased from Finland **296** was called the MP43 and it had a bayonet lug added for the Swiss bayonet, and simplified sights. The gun produced by Hispano-Suiza had a different magazine housing and was known as the MP43/44 **297**. The gun was largely machined but its cost and production time were far less than that of the Furrer MP41. The Finnish Model 1931 – the Swiss Model 43 – was designed by Aimo Johannes Lahti. Production for the Finnish Army and for Switzerland, was carried out at Oy Tikkakoski Ab. The gun fired the 9mm Parabellum cartridge, using a reduced diameter bolt similar to the Thompson SMG but with a fixed firing pin. It fired from an open breech and was operated by blow back. It was a heavy, well proven gun but in comparative tests with the SIG Model 41 it showed no advantages over that gun.

Production continued for a period after World War II and the Model 1943/44 became the standard SMG of the Swiss Army.

THE REXIM SMG
This gun was designed by Colonel Favier and was originally called the 'Favor'. The Swiss firm Rexim of Geneva introduced the weapon as the Rexim FV Mk IV in 1953 and it was manufactured at the Spanish Arms Plant at Corunna. The first lot was of 5000 SMGs produced in 1954 but Rexim were unable to sell these and went bankrupt in 1957. The Spanish manufacturer offered the gun as 'La Corunna' but although the Spanish Government tested it, no takers were found and no nation adopted it. It was seen during the fighting in the Congo and again in Nigeria during the Civil War in 1969 **298**.

297

298

297 The MP 43/44 was produced by Hispano-Suiza for the Swiss Army during and after the war.

298 The Rexim-Favor Mk 4 SMG was designed by Colonel Favier and originally called the 'Favor'. It was made in Spain and called there the 'Corunna'. It fires from a closed breech using an ingenious arrangement of springs and no orthodox delay device.

The gun is unusual in that it fires from the closed breech position without using a delay device. The necessary hold up of the breech block is accomplished by having two strong springs both of which have to be compressed as the bolt comes back. These two springs are placed one within the other. The inner spring is a telescoping type, based on the Erma pattern, and enters the bolt. It acts solely as a return or operating spring. The larger diameter outer spring bears against a hollow cylinder which acts as a hammer. The gun is cocked in the usual way with a handle on the right of the gun; when the cocking handle moves forward a round is fed and chambered by the bolt driven forward by the inner spring. A spring retracted firing pin is located in the bolt head. When the trigger is operated the sear releases the hollow hammer which is driven forward by the large diameter outer spring. The cylinder strikes a connecting piece – or yoke – and this drives the firing pin forward, overcoming the resistance of its spring, to hit the cap and fire the round. The blow back drives back the bolt and the hammer and compresses both springs. If the sear is up – ie the gun is set to single shot or the trigger has been released – the bolt goes forward but the hammer cylinder is held back. If the gun is set to auto, the bolt as before, goes forward, but the inertia of the cylinder as it goes forward again, causes it to reach the yoke slightly after the bolt has closed. This ensures that the bolt does not bounce – and compress the telescoping return spring – and it ensures that the firing pin is not pushed forward whilst the round is being fed and chambered.

The SMG could also be used to project a grenade to a range of 110m using a ballistite cartridge. A spike bayonet and a compensator were also features of the gun. It was made by stamping but had many parts, was expensive to produce, suffered from cook-off and offered no advantages over other models available at the time.

REFERENCE
[1]*The World's Sub-Machine Guns*, page 472.

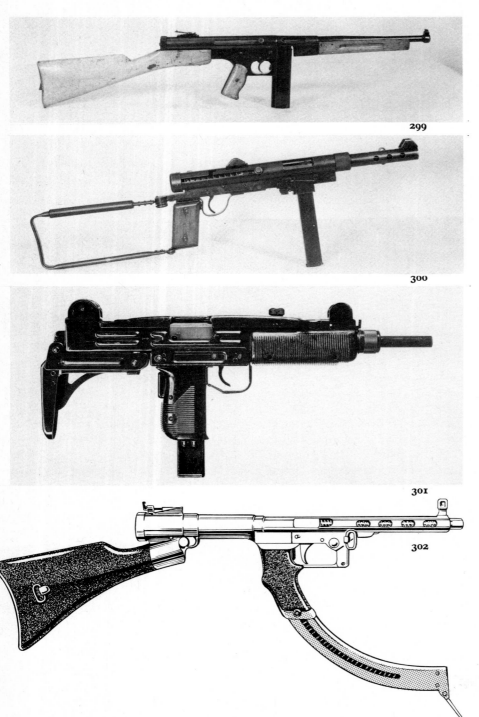

299 Egyptian manufactured Thompson .45 SMG of the early 50s using an American barrel made by Auto Ordnance. The standard of workmanship was poor.

300 The 'Port Said' SMG was manufactured in 1951. This photograph shows one captured by British troops during the invasion of Egypt in 1952. It is a direct copy of the Swedish Carl Gustav M1945 (B) with the detachable magazine housing. See **277**. The Egyptian forces are now fully equipped with Russian AK–47 assault rifles.

301 The Israeli 9mm Uzi SMG. Designed by Capt Uziel Gal it was adopted by West Germany for the Bundeswehr and is currently produced by FN at Herstal. It uses the wrap round bolt, a grip safety and enjoys a high reputation.

302 Japanese Nambu 8mm SMG Model 1 used in limited numbers against Chinese troops in the late 30s. Investigated in England in 1938 as a weapon for tank crews and quickly thrown out. The magazine held 50 rounds and was 10½ inches deep.

303

304

305

303 The Japanese 8mm Model 100 (1940) was extensively employed by the army in SE Asia. The cylinder under the muzzle is to take the Model 30 (1897) bayonet. It fired an 8mm cartridge.

304 Experimental 9mm SMG made by Shin Choo Kogyo KK, successor to the Nambu concern, at Tokyo in 1960. It would appear to be based on the Sten Mk IVA but differs in having the magazine below the gun with a grip safety.

305 Japanese experimental SMG with butt extended.

306 .45 SMG captured in Korea. The barrel jacket recoils with the bolt and the spring is compressed between the front of the barrel jacket and a collar at the rear of the barrel. There is some doubt whether it is Japanese or Chinese – probably the latter.

307 Polish 'Mini' WZ–1963 9mm Parabellum SMG. The trough-like projection beneath the barrel is a form of compensator preventing any gas from expanding downwards. Firing its 25 rounds at 600rpm it is not easy to control. Single shot comes from a limited trigger pull. A single strut butt can be fitted. Designed by Professor Wilniewczye.

308 Spanish copy of the German MP 28II – used in the Civil War chambered for the 9mm Bergmann Bayard cartridge.

309 Spanish Labora, 1938 firing the 9mm Bergmann Bayard cartridge. It was expensive to make and was machined from the solid during the Civil War. It had a very small bolt and light spring. Note the small magazine capacity. The long 36 round magazine is more often seen.

310 Spanish Star. Model Z–45 in 9mm Bergmann Bayard. This picture shows a unique silencer made by partisans in some small local workshop.

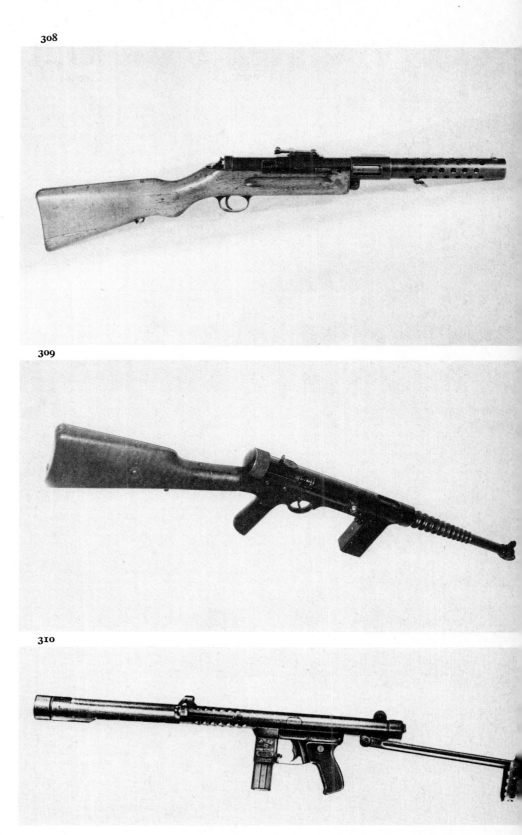

308

309

310

Tabulated SMG Data

	Length with Butt Extended ins	Unloaded Weight lbs	Barrel Length ins	Ammunition	Magazine Capacity Rds	Loaded Magazine Weight lbs
AMERICAN SMGs						
Armalite AR-18S	30.125	6.75	10.125	.223 Remington	30	1.2
					20	0.7
Atchisson Model 57	24.0	4.0	8.0	9mm P	32	1.5
Atlantic	35.4	8.2	10.6	.380 ACP	30	1.2
Atmed	34.5	9.5	11.5	.45 ACP	30	1.6
Colt Commando	31.375	6.0	9.75	.223 Remington	20	0.7
Compact	24.0	5.25	7.75	9mm P	32	1.35
Cook	23.25	7.0	9.5	9mm P	32	1.3
				.45 ACP	30	2.1
Foote MP-61	26.0	6.1	8.0	.45 ACP	30	2.1
Foote MP-970	24.5	6.5	8.0	9mm P	32	1.5
Hyde Model 35	35.0	9.5	11.25	.45 ACP	20	1.0
Hyde-Inland M1 & M2	32.1	9.25	12.1	.45 ACP	20	1.2
					30	1.9
Imp	17.0	3.75	10.0	.221 Fireball	30	1.0
Ingram Model 5	25.0	6.0		.45 ACP	25	
6	28.5	6.5	8.0	.45 ACP	20	1.3
7	28.5	6.5	8.0	.38 Super	20	1.3
8	30.0	7.25	9.0	.45 ACP	30	1.75
9	29.0	7.75	8.0	9mm P	40	1.5
10	21.57	5.75	6.0	9mm P	32	1.35
				.45 ACP	30	2.2
11	18.0	3.25	5.125	9mm short	32	1.125
M3	29.8	8.15	8.0	.45 ACP	30	2.1
M3A1	29.8	8.15	8.0	.45 ACP	30	2.1
Pedersen device	13.4[1]	2.0	24.0	.30 pistol	40	1.0
Reising Model 50	35.75	6.75	11.0	.45 ACP	12	0.9
					20	1.4
Model 55	31.25	6.25	10.5	.45 ACP	12	0.9
					20	1.4
Scamp	11.6	3.25	6.5	.22 CF	27	0.6
Sedgley	35.0	7.5	11.0	9mm P	20	1.0
Smith & Wesson Carbine	31.0	8.25	9.75	9mm P	20	0.8
Model 76	30.375	7.3	7.78	9mm P	36	1.5
Stoner	36.5	7.75	15.5	.223 Remington	30	1.1
Thompson M1921	33.75	10.75	10.5	.45 ACP	30	1.6
M1928	33.75	10.75	10.5	.45 ACP	30	1.6
M1 & M1A1	32.0	10.45	10.5	.45 ACP	20	1.25
Turner	34.5	5.3	15.5	.45 ACP	20	1.3
UD42	32.2	9.12	11.0	9mm P	20	1.0
Woodhull	29.8	7.0	14.5	.45 ACP	10	0.75
AUSTRALIAN SMGs						
Austen Mk I	33.25	8.75	7.8	9mm P	28	1.5
Mk II	33.25	8.5	7.8	9mm P	28	1.5
F1	28.1	7.2	8.0	9mm P	34	1.6

Type of Fire: A = Auto S = Selective	Cyclic Rate of Fire rpm	Muzzle Velocity ft/s	Type of Butt Stock	Illustration	Remarks
S	800	2560	Fibre glass, hinged	50	
S	NK	1200	Wire, sliding	60	
S	700	1040	Wood	—	Copy of Spanish Star TN 35
S	NK	920	,,	22	
S	750	2700	Sliding single tube	49	
S	450	1200	,, ,, ,,	46	
A	550	920	Fixed single tube	47	
S	NK	920	Folding	58	
S	650	1200	NK	57	
S	725	920	Wood	20	Sometimes 2 magazines brazed side by side
S	525	920	,,	23	
S	550	2500	None	53	Also 10 rd magazine
A	500	920	Wood	39	
A	600	920	,,	40	
S	700	1350	,,	41	
S	600	920	Folding frame	—	
S	600	1200	Wire, sliding	—	
S	900	1175 920	,, ,,	43	Stock closed – 11.6in
S	1000	960	,, ,,	43	Stock closed – 9.8in
A	400	920	,, ,,	24–28	Cocking handle
A	400	920	,, ,,	29	Finger cocking
Single shots	—	1300	Nil	7	Also known as 'Automatic Pistol Calibre .30 Model 1918'. [1] = Length of Device.
S	550	920	Wood	30, 31	Finger cocking
S	500	920	Wire, folding	32	
3 rd bursts	1500	2100	Nil	61	Also single shots
S	475	1200	Wood	36	
Single shots		1250	Plastic	54, 55	
S	600	1250	Folding frame	56	
S	660	2900	Folding, plastic	52	Length butt folded = 26.5in Gas operated. Closed breech
S	800	920	Wood	12	Also 18, 20, 50 and 100 rd magazines
S	675	920	,,	14	,, ,, ,, ,,
S	700	920	,,	16, 17	
Single shots	—	920	Skeleton	37	Gas operated
S	700	1200	Wood	35	Sometimes known as High-Standard SMG
S	NK	920	,,	38	
S	500	1200	Wire, folding	237	
S	500	1200	,, ,,	239	
S	600	1200	Wood	244	

	Length with Butt Extended ins	Unloaded Weight lbs	Barrel Length ins	Ammunition	Magazine Capacity Rds	Loaded Magazine Weight lbs
Kokoda	27.0	8.0	8.0	9mm P	30	1.4
MCEM 1	27.0	8.4	8.0	9mm P	30	1.4
MCEM 2	30.0	8.4	8.0	9mm P	30	1.4
Owen Mk 1/42	32.0	9.35	9.85	9mm P	33	1.4
Mk I/43	32.0	8.8	9.85	9mm P	33	1.4
Mk II/43	32.0	7.65	9.85	9mm P	33	1.4
SR 11	10.5	2.9	5.25	9mm P	16	0.85
BRITISH SMGs						
Andrews	25.5	6.2	6.8	9mm P	30	1.3
Biwarip	26.0	5.1	NK	9mm P	30	1.4
Brondby	34.5	5.3	15.75	Mauser 7.63mm	20	0.9
BSA	27.5	56.	8.0	9mm P	32	1.4
BSA – Kiraly	38.75	8.5	16.125	9mm Mauser	40	1.75
Dineley	27.5	8.2	9.25	Mauser 7.63mm	20	0.9
Howard-Francis S/L Carbine	32	8.1	12.75	Mauser 7.63mm	12	0.7
Jurek M1	21	5.4	7.8	9mm P	20	1.0
M2	17	5.5	7.8	9mm P	20	1.0
L2A1 L2A2 L2A3 L2A4	28	6	7.8	9mm P	34	1.7
L34A1	33.25	7.7	7.8	9mm P	34	1.7
Lanchester Mk I	33.5	9.6	7.9	9mm P	50	2.3
Mk I*	33.5	9.6	7.9	9mm P	50	2.3
X1	20.75	6.75	7.9	9mm P	32	1.4
X2	31.0	6.5	7.9	9mm P	32	1.4
MCEM 1	25.0	6.4	2.75	9mm P	40	2.0
MCEM 2	14.25	5.0	8.5	9mm P	18	0.8
MCEM 3	28.75	7.5	7.0	9mm P	20	0.9
MCEM 6	26.0	6.7	9.5	9mm P	18	0.8
Mitchell		4.75	5	9mm P	34	1.7
Norm	29.0	8.8	8.0	9mm P	32	1.6
Patchett Mk I	28.0	6.2	8.25	9mm P	34	1.7
Mk II	28.0	6.0	7.8	9mm P	34	1.7
Carbinette (Machine Pistol)	25.25	6.5	6.5	9mm P	34	1.7
Patchett Pioneer	28.0	6.0	7.8	9mm P	34	1.7
ROFSten	31.0	8.2	8.25	9mm P	22	1.2
Sten Mk I	33.25	7.2	7.8	9mm P	32	1.4
Mk I*	31.25	7.0	7.8	9mm P	32	1.4
Mk II	30.0	6.65	7.75	9mm P	32	1.4
Mk IIS	33.75	7.7	3.6	9mm P	32	1.4
Mk III	30.0	7.0	7.75	9mm P	32	1.4
Mk IVA	27.5	7.5	3.85	9mm P	32	1.4
Mk IVB	24.5	7.5	3.85	9mm P	32	1.4
Mk V	30.0	8.6	7.8	9mm P	32	1.4
Mk VI	33.75	9.5	3.75	9mm P	32	1.4
T42	28.0	7.4	5.25	9mm P	15	0.9
Sterling Mk 3	28.0	6.0	7.8	9mm P	34	1.7
Mk 4	28.0	6.0	7.8	9mm P	34	1.7
Sterling/Patchett Mk 5	33.25	7.7	7.8	9mm P	34	1.7
Prototype	26.75	8.0	7.8	9mm P	34	1.7
Veseley V42	33.0	7.1	10.0	9mm P	60	2.5

Type of Fire: A=Auto S=Selective	Cyclic Rate of Fire rpm	Muzzle Velocity ft/s	Type of Butt Stock	Illustration	Remarks
S	500	1200	Wire, sliding	240	
A	430	1200	,, ,,	241	
A	450	1200	,, ,,	242	
S	700	1375	Skeleton	232	
S	680	1375	Wood	233	
S	600	1375	,,	235	
S	600	1100	Telescoping tube	243	Length without butt. Butt 8.5in–14in
S	660	1180	Spare magazine	101	
S	600	1200	Detachable rod	63	
S	NK	1410	Detachable wire	62	Gas operated
S	600	1200	Folding	114–117	
S	730	1480	Wood	64, 65	
S	700	1410	,,	66	
Single shots	—	1410	,,	97	
S	1000	1200	Holster	112	Holster – canvas over steel frame
S	350	1200	,,	110, 111, 113	,, ,, ,, ,, ,,
S	600	1200	Folding	124–128	L2A4 – experimental only. See 127
S	475	1000	,,	135–137	
S	600	1200	Wood	68, 70	
A	600	1200	,,	69	
S	NK	1200	None	71	
S	NK	1200	Steel tube	72	
S	700	1100	Steel tube with wood	105	Double side-by-side magazine
S	1000	1200	Holster, steel and canvas	107	Length without holster. Holster 12½in long
S	690	1200	Steel tube with wood	106	
S	600	1220	Holster, steel and canvas	108	
S	700	1000	Folding	99	Only 2½in of rifled barrel
S	NK	1200	Folding frame	102, 103	
S	600	1200	Folding	121	
S	600	1200	,,	123	
S	600	1200	,,	119	Body telescoped. Spring loaded bayonet
S	600	1200	,,	122	
S	600	1200	Wood	104	
S	550	1200	Skeleton	73	
S	550	1200	,,	74	
S	550	1200	Rod	75–81	
S	450	1000	Skeleton	82–85	
S	550	1200	Rod	86–88	
S	575	1200	Folding	89, 91	
S	575	1200	,,	90	
S	600	1200	Wood	92–95	
S	475	1000	,,	96	Silenced Mk V
S	500	1200	Folding	77	
S	600	1200	,,	124	Identical to Patchett Mk 2 and L2A1 except for firing pin and crackle finish
S	600	1200	,,	126	Identical to L2A3 except for firing pin and crackle finish
S	475	1000	,,	136	Identical to L34A1 except for finish
S	600	1200	,,	138	Takes No 5 Mk I and L1A3 bayonets
S	700	1250	Wood	98	Double compartment magazine

	Length with Butt Extended ins	Unloaded Weight lbs	Barrel Length ins	Ammunition	Magazine Capacity Rds	Loaded Magazine Weight lbs
V43	33.0	6.6	10.0	9mm P	60	2.5
Viper 1	21.25	4.75	4.7	9mm P	32	1.4
2	22.25	4.8	6.0	9mm P	32	1.4
3	24.0	5.0	7.5	9mm P	32	1.4
Welgun	27.5	6.8	7.8	9mm P	30	1.3

CANADIAN SMGs

	Length with Butt Extended ins	Unloaded Weight lbs	Barrel Length ins	Ammunition	Magazine Capacity Rds	Loaded Magazine Weight lbs
C1	27.0	6.5	7.8	9mm P	30	1.16

CZECHO-SLOVAKIAN SMGs

	Length with Butt Extended ins	Unloaded Weight lbs	Barrel Length ins	Ammunition	Magazine Capacity Rds	Loaded Magazine Weight lbs
ZK 383	35.4	9.4	12.8	9mm P	30	1.25
ZK 466	27.0	6.4	7.8	9mm P	30	1.3
ZK 467	25.0	7.5	10.0	9mm P	30	1.28
ZK 476	22.0	7.0	8.0	9mm P	30	1.25
ZK 480	32.0	7.5	14.0	9mm P	36	1.5
CZ 1938	31.0	8.0	8.5	9mm short	24 Box / 94 Drum	1.1 / NK
CZ 247 47 }	30.9	6.4	7.8	9mm P	40	1.8
Model 23 Model 25 }	27.0	6.8	11.2	9mm P	40	1.7
Model 24 Model 26 }	26.6 / 27.0	7.25	11.2	7.62mm Special	32	1.3
Vz 61	20.2	3.4	4.4	.32 ACP	20	0.9

DANISH SMGs

	Length with Butt Extended ins	Unloaded Weight lbs	Barrel Length ins	Ammunition	Magazine Capacity Rds	Loaded Magazine Weight lbs
Model 1945 (P13)	31.5	7.1	12.4	9mm P	50	2.25
Model 1946 (P16)	31.25	7.0	7.8	9mm P	32	1.3
Model 1949 (Hovea)	31.8	7.4	8.5	9mm P	36	1.5
Model 1950	31.25	7.0	7.8	9mm P	32	1.2
Model 1953	31.5	7.0	7.8	9mm P	32	1.4
Model 'Suomi' (P2)	34.25	10.3	12.5	9mm P	50	2.25

FINNISH SMGs

	Length with Butt Extended ins	Unloaded Weight lbs	Barrel Length ins	Ammunition	Magazine Capacity Rds	Loaded Magazine Weight lbs
Model 1926	36.5	9.75	13.75	7.65mm	36	1.5
Model 1931	34.25	10.3	12.5	9mm P	50	2.25
Model 1944	32.7	6.2	9.8	9mm P	36	1.5

FRENCH SMGs

	Length with Butt Extended ins	Unloaded Weight lbs	Barrel Length ins	Ammunition	Magazine Capacity Rds	Loaded Magazine Weight lbs
Gevarm D3	31.2	8.0	12.2	9mm P	32	1.6
MAC 47-1	25.0	4.6	8.25	9mm P	32	1.4
47-2	25.0	4.6	8.25	9mm P	32	1.4
48-1	31.5	7.6	11.0	9mm P	32	1.4
48-2	31.5	7.6	11.0	9mm P	32	1.4
48LS	25.25	6.0	7.9	9mm P	32	1.4
MAS 1938	24.9	6.4	8.8	7.65mm Long	32	1.1
Type C4	25.5	6.6	8.2	9mm P	32	1.4
MAT Model 49	26.0	8.0	9.0	9mm P	32	1.4
PM9 (MGD)	25.5	5.6	8.4	9mm P	32	1.4

GERMAN SMGs

	Length with Butt Extended ins	Unloaded Weight lbs	Barrel Length ins	Ammunition	Magazine Capacity Rds	Loaded Magazine Weight lbs
Dux 51	32.7	6.2	9.8	9mm P	36	1.5
53	32.5	7.7	9.9	9mm P	50	2
59	31.2	6.6	9.9	9mm P	32	1.3
Erma EMP	37.4 / 35.5	9.2	11.8 / 9.9	9mm P	32	1.5
Erma EMP Silenced	46.75	10.45	9.785	9mm P	32	1.5

Type of Fire: A=Auto S=Selective	Cyclic Rate of Fire rpm	Muzzle Velocity ft/s	Type of Butt Stock	Illustration	Remarks
S	700	1250	Folding	—	" " "
S	690	1150	Metal		
S	690	1175	frame with	} 109	
S	690	1200	wood insert		
S	760	1185	Folding rod	100	
S	550	1200	Folding	130	Based on L2A3
S	700	1250	Wood	251	
S	650	1250	Wire, sliding	—	
S	700	1250	Wood	—	
S	600	1250	"	—	
S	650	1310	"	—	Also folding stock
A	600	950	"	—	
S	550	1250	"	—	247 had bayonet
S	600	1250	Wood, folding rod	252, 253	
S	600	1800	Wood, folding rod	—	Cartridge more powerful than Russian 'P'
S	840	1040	Wire, fold over	254–257	10.6in stock folded. Called Skorpion
A	850	1310	Tube, folding	—	Also wood stock
A	480	1250	Folding	—	
A	600	1250	Rectangular tube	—	
A	550	1250	" "	281	
A	550	1250	" "	282	
S	900	1310	Wood	—	
S	750	1250	"	268	
S	900	1310	"	269, 270	Also 71 rd drum
A	650	1310	Folding	272	Also 71 rd drum. Also 50 rd Suomi
S	600	1200	Wood	267	D4 has folding butt
A	640	1200	Sheet metal	—	
A	640	1200	Skeleton, folding	260	
A	475	1200	Wood	—	
S	475	1200	"	261	
A	600	1200	Sliding	—	
A	600	1150	Wood	259	
S	500	1200	"	262	
A	600	1200	Sliding	264	
S	750	1200	Skeleton, folding	265, 266	Also wooden butt
A	650	1210	Folding	272	Identical to Finnish M44
A	500	1200	"	174	
A	550	1200	"	175	
S	500	1250	Wood	151	Length of standard model
S	350	1000	"	152	Not drilled barrel

215

	Length with Butt Extended ins	Unloaded Weight lbs	Barrel Length ins	Ammunition	Magazine Capacity Rds	Loaded Magazine Weight lbs
MP 38	32.8	9.0	9.9	9mm P	32	1.5
MP 40	32.8	8.9	9.9	9mm P	32	1.5
MP 38/40	32.8	9.0	9.9	9mm P	32	1.5
MP 41	34.0	8.2	9.9	9mm P	32	1.5
MP 44	28.4	8.0	9.9	9mm P	32	1.5
MP 56	27.0	7.0	10.3	9mm P	32	1.4
MP 58	27.6	6.6	6.5	9mm P	32	1.5
MP 59	28.8	7.0	8.3	9mm P	30	1.5
MP 60	31.1	7.3	9.5	9mm P	36	1.5
MP 64	30.0	6.8	9.5	9mm P	36	1.5
Vollmer	37.4	8.8	12.6	9mm P	32	1.5
Heckler & Koch HK 53	30.1	7.4	8.85	5.56mm	40	1.25
MP 5	26.0	5.6	8.85	9mm P	30	1.1
M39 (Hungarian)	41.25	8.2	19.65	9mm Mauser	40	1.8
Mauser M57	24.0	7.0	10.3	9mm P	32	1.1
M60	30.3	5.5	9.9	9mm P	36	1.3
MP 3008	31.3	6.5	7.8	9mm P	32	1.5
MK 36.II	44.5	10.5	19.8	9mm P	32	1.5
MP 18.1	32.1	9.2	7.9	9mm P	32	2.35
MP 28.11	32.0	8.8	7.8	9mm P	32	1.5
MP 34.1	37.6	8.9	12.6	9mm P	32	1.5
MPi 69 (Austrian)	26.4	6.9	10.2	9mm P	25	1.0
Walther MPL	29.4	6.6	10.25	9mm P	32	1.4
MPK	26.0	6.3	6.75	9mm P	32	1.4

ITALIAN SMGs

	Length with Butt Extended ins	Unloaded Weight lbs	Barrel Length ins	Ammunition	Magazine Capacity Rds	Loaded Magazine Weight lbs
Armaguerra OG44	30.3	6.8	11.6	9mm P	25	1.0
Beretta Model 1918	33.5	7.2	12.5	9mm P	25	1.0
1918/1930	33.5	7.2	12.5	9mm P	25	1.0
1935	37.0	7.5	16.0	9mm P	25	1.0
1938A	37.25	9.25	12.4	9mm M 38	40	1.7
1	28.0	8.0	7.8	9mm P	40	1.7
1938/42	31.5	7.2	8.4	9mm P	40	1.7
1938/44	31.5	7.2	8.4	9mm P	40	1.7
1938/49 (4)	31.5	7.2	8.4	9mm P	40	1.7
2	31.5	7.2	8.4	9mm P	40	1.7
3	28.0	7.6	7.8	9mm P	40	1.7
4	28.0	7.6	7.8	9mm P	40	1.7
5	31.5	7.2	8.4	9mm P	40	1.7
6 (1953)	24.8	5.75	7.8	9mm P	40	1.7
7-11						
12	25.4	6.6	7.9	9mm P	40	1.7
		7.5				
Bernadelli Model VB	32.7	7.4	11.8	9mm P	40	1.7
FNA–B Model 1943	31.1	7.0	7.8	9mm P	40	1.7
X4	26.0	6.6	7.8	9mm P	40	1.7
X5	12.25	6.3	4.6	9mm P	40	1.7
Franchi Model LF57	26.75	7.1	8.1	9mm P	40	1.7
Giandoso Model MM 735	29.7	7.2	8.2	9mm P	40	1.7
PM 410	16.1	4.3	7.4	9mm P	40	1.7
PM 440	17.4	5.1	7.5	9mm P	40	1.7
PM 470	29.7	5.5	8.2	9mm P	40	1.7
PM 720	28.4	5.1	7.5	9mm P	40	1.7
TZ–45	33.5	7.2	9.0	9mm P	40	1.7
OVP	35.5	8.0	11.0	9mm P	25	1.0
Variara	32.3	6.2	11.8	9mm P	30	1.5
Villar Perosa	21.0	14.3	12.6	9mm P	25 (each)	1.0 (each)

Type of Fire: A=Auto S=Selective	Cyclic Rate of Fire rpm	Muzzle Velocity ft/s	Type of Butt Stock	Illustration	Remarks
A	500	1250	Folding	153	
A	500	1250	,,	154, 156	MP 40/II had double magazine
A	500	1250	,,	155	
S	500	1250	Wood	157	
A	500	1250	Rigid tube	158	
S	N/K	1250	Folding	163	
A	670	1250	,,	165	
A	620	1250	Sliding	166	
A	500	1250	Folding	167	
S	NK	1250	,,	169	
S	600	1250	Wood	—	Also 7.65 and 7.63mm
S	600	2460	Sliding	179	
S	650	1310	,,	178	Also a rigid butt stock
S	750	1475	Wood	177	M43 had folding stock and both had folding magazines
S	800	1250	Folding	170	
S	750	1250	,,	171	
S	500	1250	Fixed skeleton	159	
S	500	1270	Wood	145, 146	MP 28.II magazine
A	400	1250	,,	141	Snail magazine
S	500	1250	,,	142, 143	Also 9mm, 7.65, 7.63
S	650	1250	,,	147	,, ,, ,,
S	550	1300	Wire sliding	176	
A	550	1250	Folding	172	
A	550	1250	,,	172	
S	525	1400	Folding or wood	216, 217	
A	900	1250	Wood	183	
Single shot	—	1250	,,	184	
Single shot	—	1250	,,	—	
S	600	1375	,,	185–190	Also 10, 20 & 30 rd mags
S	550	1250	Folding	191	
S	550	1250	Wood	192–194	
S	550	1250	,,	195, 196	Also 20 rd mag
S	550	1250	,,	197–199	
S	550	1250	Folding	200	Prototype
S	550	1250	Wire sliding	201	
S	550	1250	,, ,,	202	Prototype
S	550	1250	Wood	203	
S	550	1250	Folding	204	Prototype
				204	Prototypes of Model 12
S	550	1250	Folding Wood	205	
S	600	1250	Wood	209	
S	400	1250	Folding	206	Delayed blow back
A	600	1250	Wire sliding	207	
A	700	1200	None	208	
A	500	1200	Folding	211	
S	600	1250	Wood	—	
S	600	1250	None	—	
S	600	1250	Short, wood	—	
S	600	1250	Folding	—	
S	600	1250	Wood	213	
A	500	1200	Wire sliding	212	
S	900	1250	Wood	182	
S	550	1350	Folding strut	210	
A	1200 (each)	1300	None	180, 181	2 barrels. Delayed blow back

	Length with Butt Extended ins	Unloaded Weight lbs	Barrel Length ins	Ammunition	Magazine Capacity Rds	Loaded Magazine Weight lbs
RUSSIAN SMGs						
Degtyarev PPD 1934/38	30.6	8.25	10.75	7.62mm 'P'	25	1
					71	4.25
PPD 1940	31.0	8.0	10.5	7.62mm 'P'	71	4
Federov Avtomat	37.0	9.7	NK	6.5mm Japanese	25	1.5
Shpagin, PPSh-41	33.1	8.0	10.6	7.62mm 'P'	35	1.5
					71	4.0
Sudarev PPS–42	35.7	6.5	10.75	7.62mm 'P'	35	1.5
PPS–43	32.25	7.4	10.0	7.62mm 'P'	35	1.25
SWEDISH SMGs						
Model 37–39	30.25	8.75	8.25	9mm P	50	2.25
Model 37–39F	34.25	10.3	12.5	9mm P	50	2.25
Models 45 and 45B	31.8	7.6	8.0	9mm P	50	2.25
Model 49 (Hovea)	31.8	7.4	8.5	9mm P	36	1.5
SWISS SMGs						
Furrer MP 41 ⎫ MP 41/44 ⎬	30.5	11.5	9.8	9mm P	40	1.9
Hispano-Suiza MP 43 ⎫ MP 43/44 ⎬	33.9	10.4	12.4	9mm P	50	2.25
Rexim-Favor Mk 4.	34.3	8.4	13.4	9mm P	32	1.5
SIG Model 1920	32	9.0	8.0	7.65mm P	50	2.2
MKMO	40.25	9.8	19.25	9mm Mauser	40	1.7
MKPO	32.7	8.9	11.8	9mm Mauser	30	1.25
MKMS	40.25	9.8	19.25	9mm P	40	1.7
MKPS	32.7	8.9	11.8	9mm P	30	1.25
MP 41	31.4	9.6	12.1	9mm P	40	1.7
MP 44 ⎫ MP 46 ⎬	32.8	8.7	11.8	9mm P	40	1.7
MP 48	28.2	6.4	7.8	9mm P	40	1.7
MP 310	29.0	7.0	7.8	9mm P	40	1.7
Solothurn S17–100	24.0	8.0	7.8	9mm Mauser	30	1.25
Steyr-Solothurn S1–100	33.5	8.6	7.8	9mm Steyr	32	1.25

Type of Fire: A=Auto S=Selective	Cyclic Rate of Fire rpm	Muzzle Velocity ft/s	Type of Butt Stock	Illustration	Remarks
S	800	1600	Wood	221	Box magazine Drum magazine
S	800	1600	,,	223	
S	600	2150	Wood	218	Short recoil operated
S	900	1600	Wood	224, 226	Box magazine Drum magazine
A	700	1600	Folding	—	
A	700	1600	,,	229	
S	900	1250	Wood	274	
S	900	1310	Wood	275	
S	600	1210	Folding, rectangular tube	276–280	'B' takes either 50 or 36 rd mag Last model takes 36 rd mag
A	600	1250	,, ,, ,,	—	
S	900	1310	Wood	294, 295	Short recoil with toggle action
S	800	1310	Folding	296, 297	Copy of Suomi 31 (269)
S	600	1310	Folding	297	
A	600	1200	Wood	—	Copy of MP 18.1 (141)
A	900	1600	,,	283	⎫ Locked breech blow back. Also in
A	900	1310	,,	—	⎬ 9mm P., 7.65mm P
A	900	1250	,,	284	
A	900	1200	,,	285	
A	850	1310	,,	286, 287	
S	800	1375	,,	288, 289	
S	700	1200	Sliding	290	
S	900	1200	,,	291	
S	500	1375	None	—	
S	500	1375	Wood	149, 150	

Photo Credits

Armalite Inc., 50
Vincenzo Bernadelli SpA, 209
Pietro Beretta, 183, 185, 186, 190, 191, 192, 197, 198, 199, 200, 201, 202, 203, 204, 205
Colt's Patent Firearms Corp., 53, 61
A Cormack, 298
Crown Copyright, 20, 30, 63, 96, 98, 101, 110, 111, 134, 136, 234, 235, 240, 269, 277, 298, 307
M Dinely, 238, 309
Erma-Werke, 163, 164, 165, 166, 167, 168, 169, 265, 266
Fabrique Nationale, 245, 246, 247, 248, 249, 250
Finnish Army HQ, 268, 270, 271, 272, 273
Carl Gustav, 274, 275, 276, 278, 279
Heckler & Koch GbMH, 179
Imperial War Museum, Frontispiece
Mauser-Werke, 170, 171, 172, 173, 174, 175
Military Armament Corporation, 39, 40, 41, 42, 44, 45, 48, 51, 57, 58, 59, 60
T. Nelson, 22, 34, 36, 46, 112, 113, 158, 207, 208, 213, 260, 261, 262, 263
Novosti, 218, 219, 221, 222, 225, 230
Pattern Room RSAF Enfield, 1, 2, 3, 4, 5, 6, 12, 14, 15, 16, 17, 18, 21, 25, 27, 28, 29, 31, 32, 33, 35, 55, 56, 62, 66, 76, 77, 78, 79, 81, 84, 87, 88, 89, 90, 91, 92, 94, 95, 96, 97, 99, 100, 102, 103, 104, 105, 106, 108, 109, 117, 118, 119, 120, 121, 122, 123, 124, 125, 126, 127, 128, 129, 130, 132, 133, 135, 145, 147, 148, 151, 153, 154, 157, 159, 160, 161, 162, 177, 178, 181, 182, 184, 187, 188, 193, 194, 195, 196, 206, 210, 212, 214, 215, 223, 224, 226, 227, 228, 232, 233, 236, 237, 239, 241, 242, 251, 252, 253, 280, 282, 299, 300, 308
RMCS Shrivenham, 26, 43, 47, 49, 52, 54, 64, 65, 67, 68, 69, 70, 71, 72, 73, 74, 75, 82, 83, 85, 86, 93, 107, 114, 115, 116, 138, 139, 140, 141, 150, 152, 155, 156, 180, 189, 229, 231, 244, 254, 255, 256, 259, 264, 301
Shin Chuo Kogyo, 304, 305
SIG, 283, 284, 285, 286, 287, 288, 289, 290, 291
Steyr-Daimler-Puch A. G., 176
W. E. Smith, 80, 144
Swiss Arsenal, Berne, 292, 293, 294, 295, 296, 297
D. Truby, 310
US Army, 7, 23, 24, 37, 38, 299, 303, 306
Carl Walther, 172
West Point Collection, 8, 9, 10, 11, 13, 19

In-Text Illustrations
Figs I-VII drawn by J. Parker.

Index

*References in **bold** type are to photograph numbers.*
References in ordinary type are to page numbers.

223